I0868079

Sacred and Secular Transactions in the Age of Shakespeare

RETHINKING THE EARLY MODERN

Series Editors
Marcus Keller, University of Illinois, Urbana-Champaign
Ellen McClure, University of Illinois, Chicago
Feisal Mohamed, CUNY Graduate Center

Sacred and Secular Transactions in the Age of Shakespeare

Edited by
Katherine Steele Brokaw
and Jay Zysk

Northwestern University Press
Evanston, Illinois

Northwestern University Press
www.nupress.northwestern.edu

Copyright © 2019 by Northwestern University Press.
Published 2019. All rights reserved.

Printed in the United States of America

10 9 8 7 6 5 4 3 2 1

Library of Congress Cataloging-in-Publication Data

Names: Brokaw, Katherine Steele, 1980– editor. | Zysk, Jay, 1983– editor.
Title: Sacred and secular transactions in the age of Shakespeare / edited by Katherine Steele Brokaw and Jay Zysk.
Other titles: Rethinking the Early Modern.
Description: Evanston, Illinois : Northwestern University Press, 2019. | Series: Rethinking the early modern
Identifiers: LCCN 2019008931 | ISBN 9780810140493 (cloth text : alk. paper) | ISBN 9780810140509 (e-book) | ISBN 9780810140516 (paper text : alk. paper)
Subjects: LCSH: Shakespeare, William, 1564–1616—Criticism and interpretation. | Secularism in literature.
Classification: LCC PR3069.S38 S23 2019 | DDC 822.3/3—dc23
LC record available at https://lccn.loc.gov/2019008931

CONTENTS

FOREWORD

Sarah Beckwith

The editors of this timely and illuminating volume of essays have shrewdly titled their collection *Sacred and Secular Transactions in the Age of Shakespeare*. In this way they make the distinction between the social and historical process of *secularization*, a complex and uneven set of transformations, whose myths and narratives have been indispensable to the very idea of a social science; and secularism as an attitude, a stance, a position, even an ideology taken with regard to religion. "The Secular" is, despite the definite article, not one thing, or one story. But both the largely refuted, in any case contested, historical process of secularization and the ideology of secularism have been bound up with other components of grand narrative: laicization, deism, disenchantment, scientism, the very (modern) idea of religion that was spawned by the doctrine of secularism.

Shakespeareans have sometimes been held captive by pictures of religion born of secularism. The result can be forms of nostalgia or derision, melancholy or scorn, obverse faces of the picture holding them captive. And though the criticism of both the secularization thesis and the ideology of secularism is well under way in other quarters (as the work of Stanley Hauerwas, Rowan Williams, Charles Taylor, Talal Asad, Akeel Bilgrami, Louis Dupré, Hans Blumenberg, Michael Buckley, John Milbank, John Sommerville, José Casanova, Marcel Gauchet, Brad Gregory, among others, has shown), Shakespeareans have continued to argue for the religiosity or the secularity of Shakespeare's theater while making some fairly large and sometimes ill-advised assumptions about the terminology in play.

Secularism, a concept under attack as early as 1965, by the British sociologist of religion David Martin, is best described as an ideology that promotes the privatization of religion and banishes it from the public sphere. The fact that it masked itself as history and as sociology has made it harder to disentangle the shared grammar of religion and politics over an extended period in a unified social world. The work of David Martin and William Cavanaugh has been particularly important for unknotting the narratives at work here, in particular "the secular" from secularism.

This refreshing set of essays examines wooing, wonder, theatrical space, structures of government, ideologies of race, and liturgies as ways of considering various transactions between sacred and secular in Shakespeare's plays, and as a way of conceptualizing the space of theater in Shakespeare's time. Indeed one of the most fruitful perspectives the collection offers is a new sense of the centrality of performance to narratives of the secular. For if secular modernity is bound up with the homogeneous space and time of the nation-state, then the theater offers alternative ways of thinking through the performance of space and time on stage, with Shakespeare one of the most fluid and profound practitioners of those vital dimensions of embodied practice.

Readers will find significant food for thought and provocation to further reflection in these fascinating essays.

ACKNOWLEDGMENTS

The editors are grateful to the many people who have shaped *Sacred and Secular Transactions in the Age of Shakespeare*. First and foremost, we wish to thank Margreta de Grazia and Brian Cummings, who led a rich, provocative, and quite timely seminar on the topic of Shakespeare and secularity at the Fortieth Annual Meeting of the Shakespeare Association of America in Boston in 2012. The thinking in that seminar, along with Margreta's and Brian's work on the topic, has influenced many of the essays gathered here. We are grateful to Margreta and Brian for their support of this book, for their warm guidance offered to us across the many stages of this project, and for contributing an afterword. Our thanks are likewise due to Sarah Beckwith for generously offering a foreword to the volume.

The editorial staff at Northwestern University Press has been supportive and encouraging. Our deepest thanks go to the press's editor in chief, Gianna Francesca Mosser, who has patiently answered many questions large and small across every phase of the book's development. We are also very pleased that the volume has found a home in the Rethinking the Early Modern series at Northwestern University Press and owe our thanks to series editors Marcus Keller, Ellen McClure, and Feisal Mohamed. The anonymous external reviewers offered helpful suggestions for revising the introduction and various portions of the manuscript; for the time and detail they offered this project, we are most grateful.

Our contributors have dazzled us not only with their capacious insight and creative readings but also with their generosity of time and intellectual energy (not to mention an unflappable commitment to undertaking several rounds of revision and making multiple deadlines!). We are particularly grateful to Kent Cartwright, Jennifer Rust, and Will West for reading and commenting on various drafts of the introduction and prospectus materials.

We also extend gratitude to the Shakespeare Association of America for nurturing much of the work in this volume over the years and bringing many of the contributors into one another's orbits. The association and academic organizations like it are truly the lifeblood of collaborative humanistic research.

Katie Brokaw would like to thank Jay Zysk for being, as ever, the ideal sounding board and collaborator and an absolute model of academic friendship. She's also grateful for the research support provided by the University of California, Merced, and for the inspiring students and colleagues she's privileged to learn from there. Finally, many thanks are owed to her remorselessly positive partner, Paul.

Jay Zysk owes a profound debt of gratitude to Katie Brokaw, who matched her abundant energy for this project with a lasting dose of optimism. She is an ideal collaborator and coeditor. He would also like to thank his colleagues and students at UMass Dartmouth, who together create a warm, invigorating environment for intellectual discovery and collaboration. Most importantly, Jay would like to thank his wife, Courtney, for her continual patience, support, and love, and he dedicates his share of this project to his daughter, Hailey.

Sacred and Secular Transactions in the Age of Shakespeare

Introduction

A Hermeneutics of Sacred and Secular

Katherine Steele Brokaw and Jay Zysk

With 2016 marking the four hundredth anniversary of Shakespeare's death and 2017 marking the five hundredth anniversary of Martin Luther's Ninety-Five Theses, we may well consider how narratives about both religious reformation and the process of secularization continue to shape the study of Shakespeare today. One of these stories—told with many variants—is that for all their obvious religious investments, both the Protestant Reformation and the plays of Shakespeare contributed to the process of secularizing the Western world, moving it from a medieval, superstitious, and thoroughly religious society to a secular modernity. *Sacred and Secular Transactions in the Age of Shakespeare* complicates such a narrative. The essays collected here demonstrate the reasoned, sophisticated, and secularizing forces at work in pre-Reformation England even as they join with scholarship informed by the "religious turn" in early modern studies to demonstrate how "habits of thought," in Debora Shuger's phrase, shaped by traditional and reformed theologies persisted in Shakespeare's age and beyond.[1] This volume resists the tendency to reinforce the periodic borders and categorical oppositions that have long been used to frame Shakespeare's plays as motivating "a drastic swerve from the sacred to the secular" or acting as a "substitute for the metaphysical aid of the medieval church."[2] Instead, we insist that representations of and transactions between sacred and secular in Shakespeare's plays create theatrical meanings as joint forces acting upon and with one another. The Shakespeare discussed in this book is a playwright who writes, acts, and thinks across the conceptual border between religion and secularity, who eschews fixed historical periods and polarizing worldviews.

The notion that theatrical activity can be interpreted with particular attention to the transaction of the religious and worldly—what we would like to call a hermeneutics of sacred and secular—unifies the essays in this volume. While Shakespeare's continued influence makes his work unique among early modern playwrights, the interpretive density of sacred and secular transaction in his plays is representative rather than unique. It also reflects literary and dramaturgical traditions that precede the rise of London's commercial playhouse. From the bumbling soldiers of the York *Crucifixion* play to the Robin Hood plays staged in English parishes to the anti-Catholic polemical plays of John Bale, both performative and hermeneutic practices in early English drama long relied on transactions between sacred and secular. Playing spaces, including city streets, pageant wagons, churchyards, and public theaters, were a particularly fertile place to represent the interplay of divine matters with things of the world.[3] As Brian Cummings argues, "Both in the past and in our own society, the secular and religious, far from being incommensurate, intersect in creative and profound ways."[4] This volume takes the creative potential of these intersections seriously by building upon, nuancing, and challenging definitions of the very categories of "sacred" and "secular" as laid out by the scholarship of the religious turn, as well as various master narratives of secularization from Max Weber's theses of the rise of the Protestant work ethic and accompanying "disenchantment" of the world to Charles Taylor's propositions about the roots of our "secular age."[5]

The dynamic interplay between sacred and secular is, for our contributors, not a point to be observed but an interpretive framework to be employed. What emerges throughout this book is the idea that "secularization" is less a historical event than a hermeneutic practice. *Sacred and Secular Transactions in the Age of Shakespeare* ultimately pursues the different and sometimes conflicting ways that secularization can be understood as an interpretive act, which then raises questions about the cultural protocols of representation within both Shakespeare's plays and the critical domains in which they are studied and taught. Commenting on the religious turn in early modern studies, Julia Reinhard Lupton astutely contends that "religion is a form of thought . . . The 'religious turn' encounters religion as a turn, a speculative turning-away from both nature and culture in their infinite variety, to thought in its singular capacity to cut through the local habitations of lived experience."[6] In complementary fashion, the contributors to this volume pursue the idea of secularization, which itself has been cast as a "turn" (a turn away from deism to nondeism, supernatural to empirical, premodern to modern, the thrall of the church to the liberty of individualism), as a "form of thought." To call a text, object, ritual, or playwright secular is to impart particular interpretive pressures invested with particular institutional and ideological motivations. It has been more than a decade since Margreta de Grazia pointed out that periodization works "less as a historical marker than a massive value judgment," yet the presumption that a distinctly "secular" and "early modern" Shakespeare is superior to the literature, culture, and very people that preceded him no less persists.[7] By tracing the pressures and motivations that catalyze secularization and its various narratives, this volume's hermeneutics of sacred and secular enacts different readings of Shakespearean drama that shift our focus from literal religion to a wider examination of the transactions of sacred and secular in diverse aspects of early modern life and culture. While spiritual interests by no means fall away, our contributors address topics such as race, geography, government, architecture, music, and the visual arts—topics that find a home as readily in early modern studies as they do in cultural studies writ large.

Sacred and Secular Transactions in the Age of Shakespeare advances the notion that so-called secularization was not a fixed event or epistemic rupture but a fluid process, one that was in motion long before Shakespeare's birth and one that continues long after his death. By nuancing sweeping "secularization theses" the volume reflects on how we in the twenty-first century position ourselves against an early modern culture in which secularization was not defined in terms of a linear historical movement from superstition to reason but rather in terms of a dynamic hermeneutic model in which sacred and secular interact. Thinking about secularity involves thinking at a metacritical level about how to interpret history, religion, drama, and temporality in the context of the medieval past, the reformations of the sixteenth century, and the critical dispositions that define Shakespeare studies as a scholarly field today.

The contributors to the volume demonstrate that older interpretations of Shakespeare's plays that assert either primarily secular or primarily religious stances oversimplify the complex dynamic of sacred and secular at the heart of a play's meanings. Such a dynamic is at play, for example, in Jennifer Rust's piece on the ecclesiastical underpinnings of governmental power represented in *Measure for Measure* as well as in Emma Maggie Solberg's essay on medieval mechanical statues, doubt, and *The Winter's Tale*. Both essays focus on excavating the medieval nature of sacred and secular transaction and its influence on Shakespearean dramaturgy. Furthermore, William West analyzes *Titus Andronicus*, a play that crosses the pagan and the Christian as well as the sacred and the secular, by showing how the tension between Tamora's insistence of control when she presents herself as Revenge and Titus's feigned superstition about the allegorical figure creates a model for defining how the "secular" operates in dramatic terms. Other essays reveal how Shakespeare's plays themselves examine transactions of church and world, as in Helga Duncan's analysis of sacred and secular space in *The Tempest* and Rachael Deagman's complementary exploration of the sacred and secular inflections of the Blackfriars Theatre in the context of Shakespeare and Fletcher's *All Is True*.

Even as these essays reconsider ideas about secularization in Shakespeare's plays, they also rethink Shakespeare in the age of the secular (assuming we can even call our modern age secular). Shakespeare becomes a unifying element for these conversations because of his central role in modern secularization narratives as well as the ubiquity of his work around the contemporary globe. Shakespeare's copious use of medieval and Tudor source material and dramaturgy as well as the continuous and ever-expanding proliferation of his work in the centuries since his death makes these texts particularly apt for meditations on the limits and uses of the term "secular," a term initially coined to describe a particular age, a finite number of years. Keeping in mind both what preceded and came after the age of Shakespeare, this volume examines dramatic meanings as being implicated in the medieval past and the modern present, extending beyond the age, or *saeculum*, of the early modern.

It's also crucial to this volume that Shakespeare wrote for the theater. The early modern theater draws together a number of discourses—social, political, aesthetic, theological—by embodying and voicing contradictory points of view. And this collection contains diverse disciplinary perspectives, theoretical angles, and arguments regarding Shakespeare and secularity, a diversity befitting its polyvalent subject matter. Employing literary language, music, actors' bodies, material goods, and representing historical events, contemporary life, racial biases, and otherworldly abstractions, the theater itself is a particularly apt cultural form on which to test permutations of secular and sacred transaction. Another way to put it is that theater operates in a particular space and within an immanent time frame while representing different spaces and times and thus transcending itself. It is therefore important to understand secularity as a concept that first emerges as a way to define space and time.

In what follows, we first examine some key early modern meanings of the word "secular" as such a temporal and spatial category. We then consider how "secularity" and "secularization" have been reconceived in modern and postmodern secularization narratives, which have been particularly influential on the way we read, teach, and perform Shakespeare today. We conclude with a brief account of a hermeneutics of sacred and secular and its implications for both the essays gathered here and wider conversations in the field of Shakespeare studies.

Grammars of the Secular

The term "secular," along with "secularity" and "secularization," is most often understood to mean "nonreligious" and therefore seen as part of "a hermetically sealed concept of opposition" with the sacred.[8] Yet as Talal Asad writes, "the 'religious' and the 'secular' are not essentially fixed categories," for "there were breaks between Christian and secular life in which words and practices were rearranged, and new discursive grammars replaced previous ones."[9] Asad's formulation is useful, for it reminds us that the reduction of "secular" to "nonreligious" skews the term's etymological history.

"Secular," which derives from Latin *saeculum* and *saecularis*, originally denoted a measure of time or long span of years, such as a "generation" or "age."[10] But when compounded as *saecula saeculorum* ("through all ages of ages," or, more idiomatically, "forever and ever"), the phrase refers to infinite time. These original usages are not necessarily hostile toward or dismissive of religion. In fact, they are employed in both the Vulgate and the Latin liturgy to suggest the endurance of God's eternal power over the finite epochs of earthly time. For example, the liturgical trope *per omnia saecula saeculorum* distinguishes eternal time, which is boundless, from earthly time, which is fleeting.[11] The phrase is also used in many liturgical hymns. The fourth-century *Te Deum laudamus* (which Angela Heetderks examines in her essay on *All Is True*) includes the line *Et laudamus nomen tuum in saeculum, et in saeculum saeculi* ("And we praise your name forever, forever and ever"). The phrase *in saecula saeculorum* also appears in scripture, occurring frequently in the book of Revelation as well as in several of the Pauline letters.[12] Indeed, when Ben Jonson refers to Shakespeare as "not for an age but for all time," he preserves something of these original Latin meanings, perhaps even adapting the liturgical and biblical uses of *saecula saeculorum* to refer to Shakespeare's capacity to outreach the limits of his own *saeculum*. Jonson's use of the term implies not an unfolding trajectory of progress but rather a transcendent *longue durée*. The use of "secular" to signify temporal and eternal continuity—both worldly age upon age and God's power to transcend such measures of time—runs counter to contemporary uses of "secular" that define periodic ruptures between a dominantly religious Middle Ages and a dominantly secular modernity.

In addition to its associations with time, a second early modern meaning of "secular" points to spatial and institutional differentiations between church and world. Beginning in the late thirteenth century, "secular" was applied to clergy such as Shakespeare's Friar Laurence who intervened in worldly affairs rather than leading a cloistered life.[13] "Secular" was also used well into the sixteenth century to designate ecclesiastical authority over worldly matters such as land, the most notable example being Henry VIII's dissolution of the monasteries over a period of years starting in 1536. The transfer of places such as the Blackfriars Monastery to secular use is relevant for our interests given that, as Rachael Deagman explains in her essay, this monastic space was used for the divorce trials between Henry VIII and Catherine of Aragon before being converted into an indoor playhouse. The redistribution of church property and land for worldly use does not suggest that ecclesiastical structures or spiritual affairs ceased to matter but posits instead a different and more dynamic relation between religious and secular. In this instance, "secular" is often related to the term "profane," which etymologically means "outside the temple." The sacred spaces of church and sanctuary, where, for example, many Eucharistic miracles were said to occur, is thus distinguished from the profane spaces of street and field and home.[14] The "secular" therefore attempts to describe that which is bound by time and enclosed in a nonsacred earthly space. But religion, a human practice, is also time bound and sublunary even as it seeks to comprehend and worship the transcendent and heavenly. This fact perhaps starts to explain why conceptions of the sacred are always bound up in conceptions of the world. The practice of labeling spaces as sacred or profane, and the ways that practice is complicated by the exigencies of such human usage, inform both the theatrical stages on which Shakespeare's plays were performed and the narrative spaces they create.

Only well after the death of Shakespeare did the term "secular" become associated with a grand narrative of progress toward modernity, indicated by the term "secularization." As Jan Bremmer points out, "*Secularization*, as a term to denote a number of developments connected with modernity, was accepted much more slowly than we would perhaps think today."[15] The word "secularization" did not enter the lexicon until the start of the eighteenth century; then, influenced by an Enlightenment concept of reason, the term's significations expanded in the nineteenth century to the "giving of a secular or non-sacred character or direction to art, study, etc."[16] This points in the direction of a modern secular humanism (different from sixteenth-century humanist thought) that rejected religious belief as a principle for morality and ethics and instead supported "the disillusioning of man from either subjection to divine agency or incorporation in the world of spirits and demons."[17]

Such antagonism between the divine and human drives modern understandings of secularization not only in the domains of sociology, theology, and anthropology but also in the field of early modern literary studies. As Tobias Döring points out in his essay, the definition of the secular is determined by hermeneutic acts that continually redefine the term, its implications, and its ideological and polemical investments. Modern understandings of "secular" sometimes privilege a grand narrative of progress that splits the disenchanted, godless world of secular modernity from the superstitious, deistic ceremonies of the premodern world; there are many such versions of these "emancipatory narratives, telling of the release from various forms of past bondage."[18]

This narrative also skews both the Protestant Reformation and the literary production of the sixteenth and seventeenth centuries toward the development of modernity and the creation of an autonomous human subject. The aforementioned uses and meanings of "secular" indigenous to early modern culture, however, suggest much more dynamism between church and world, sacred and secular than post-Enlightenment understandings permit. To understand the impact of modern assumptions about secularization on the field of Shakespeare studies, let us consider two influential and related critical movements that often distinguish between categories of sacred and secular: religious turns and secularization narratives.

Religious Turns and Secularization Narratives

Secularization is, at its core, a narrative—a way of framing and interpreting the world. The dominant narratives of secularization that have emerged over the past century or so have advanced related arguments for literary and historical periodization, with some mourning the loss of a Christian past in which the numinous pervaded the world and others upholding the triumph of rationality over superstition.[19] The conversations around "secularization" in early modern studies have for some time been part of the field's turn to religion, a movement motivated by New Historicism's interest in the cultural poetics of literary texts. Such a "turn" has drawn extended attention to biblical interpretation, translation, and citation; the changing doctrines, liturgical practices, and ecclesiastical structures of the Church of England; the lived experience of the sacred in the context of devotional practices like meditation and pilgrimage; and the place of Roman Catholicism—as an element of inescapable influence, fond nostalgia, or abhorrent residue—in a post-Reformation world. Several key studies have argued that early modern literature advances reformed ways of thinking in opposition to the "old religion."[20] Adopting (directly or indirectly) Michel Foucault's concept of epistemological shift, these studies tend to plot the relationship between early modern literature and religion along a linear axis of historical difference that moves progressively toward modernity—to the autonomous individual guided by reason and empiricism, freed from the Church's thrall. The Protestant Reformation, these studies suggest, acts as a catalyst for such a shift toward modernity. Such claims run counter to the formulations of nineteenth-century secularists like Friedrich Nietzsche, who, as Margreta de Grazia writes, saw the Reformation as "reinstating and redoubling religion," and thus "not the beginning of the secular course of history, but its dead end."[21] This volume doesn't see the Reformation as either catalyzing or ending secularization. Instead, it emphasizes that no part of the sixteenth century's reform movements wished to remove religion from public life but rather that religious debates had worldly investments. These worldly investments account for the interplay between sacred and secular that our contributors not only locate in Shakespeare's plays but also see as already vibrant and alive in late medieval and early Tudor dramatic performances. Thus the exploration of sacred and secular transaction can be understood as one of Shakespeare's many appropriations of earlier dramatic histories.

Some secularization narratives mourn the loss of a medieval Christian past in which the numinous pervaded the world, while others uphold secularization as the triumph of reason over superstition. Although difficult to define uniformly, "secularization" is often described in terms of two kinds of change. The first concerns changes in belief; the second concerns changes in institutions and institutional authority. A pervasive oversimplification of the term "secular" in the first sense results in labeling individuals as secular when they are agnostic or atheist. Yet the rise in nondeists, especially as tied to issues of doctrine and the lived practice of one's faith, is only part of the story of the secularization of individual subjects. The second kind of change used to think about secularization involves the distinction between public and private as a means to trace the way institutions—governments, charities, and so forth—have divorced themselves entirely or nominally from religious affiliation or control. Thomas Jefferson's notion of the "separation of church and state" is but one manifestation of such institutional secularization.[22]

One of the twentieth century's most enduring narratives of secularization comes from Max Weber, who, borrowing a term from Friedrich Schiller, argues that the world has been secularized through a process of "disenchantment," whereby a religious society imbued with a shared and public sense of the sacred is transformed into a group of isolated individuals who make private, personal decisions on matters of faith. For Weber, the term "disenchantment" is a relatively neutral description of a perceived historical phenomenon, but it has been used by more contemporary theorists of secularity to pursue various ideological arguments in which "disenchantment" connotes either a positive change (shaking off the delusions of angels and devils and the subjection to divine authority) or a negative one (the loss of collective beliefs and morality).[23] For Weber and many others, disenchantment is the result of the rise in scientific bureaucratic rationality, by which natural phenomena are explained by science and institutions are no longer governed by the church, thus moving religion from an inescapable epistemology and public reality to a more personal and optional way of understanding the world.

Charles Taylor adapts and revises Weber's arguments in *A Secular Age*, where he mourns the trajectory outlined by Weber as making life "devoid of deep resonance and meaning" and "a victory for darkness."[24] Taylor's book, one of the most widely read on the topic of secularization, focuses on the shift of conditions regarding religion and secularity. Taylor's "Reform Master Narrative" argues that various attempts to reform Christianity were driving forces of secularization, more so than any scientific or economic developments. For Taylor, the desire to purge Christianity of superstitions, starting in the Middle Ages, began an "erosion of certainty" that changed the way humankind perceived themselves as beings in time. Perceived increasingly in secular terms, time became a resource to be managed and measured, and life was therefore lived in a self-sufficient "immanent frame" rather than—and Taylor laments this—being lived in "a transcendent realm" or according to a concept of the life cycle marked by the liturgical calendar and the administration of the sacraments.[25]

While he doesn't exactly praise it as such, Taylor suggests that the modern secular age is marked by an ability to choose among multiple (non)faith options and to peaceably coexist among mixed faith communities.[26] Other scholars have treated secularization as far more divisive. The early modern historian Keith Thomas, for example, points out that Protestant clergy encouraged something like rational, scientific thinking in their parishioners because it combated the occult superstitions of Catholicism.[27] In a similar fashion, John Sommerville's *The Secularization of Early Modern England: From Religious Culture to Religious Faith* argues (as its title implies) that as daily life was divorced from ecclesiastical control and supplanted by a more personalized faith, state institutions were differentiated from religious ones, thereby secularizing English society.[28] Eamon Duffy, by contrast, is more sympathetic toward religion in his account of England's transformation from late medieval Catholicism to the establishment of the Church of England, seeing religious reformation as a time of more losses than gains.[29]

Duffy's story of the long sixteenth century as a time of irrevocable changes to collective religious culture is of a piece with various theories, including Weber's and Taylor's, that maintain that the Protestant Reformation was a catalyst for the eventual secularization of the modern West. Weber famously argues that the Calvinist "Protestant work ethic"—characterized by privileging self-discipline and deinstitutionalizing ecclesiastical authority in favor of individual faith—created a more powerful engagement with the secular world and gave rise to a mind-set conducive to capitalism. Whereas Weber sees religious authority and ideology as retreating from the public sphere and bringing about a detheologization of the world, Carl Schmitt argues that the concepts underwriting modern politics are secularized versions of theological concepts; for Schmitt, religious thought doesn't retreat but rather is transformed.[30] In a similar vein, Brad Gregory maintains that the Protestant Reformation did not announce itself as a secularizing movement but nonetheless exerted an unintended influence in shaping a pluralistic world defined by the rejection of sacramentality and the decentralization of ecclesiastical authority.[31]

This brief survey of secularization narratives suggests that the recurrent tendency to view the Protestant Reformation as the impetus for secularization not only skews the importance of religious and theological debate to the age of Shakespeare but also reinforces the periodic divisions between medieval and early modern that have long informed our critical practice. Such commitments to periodization frequently see the Protestant Reformation as a critical axis on which secularization turns. Even the term "early modern" sediments a secularization narrative that views the literary and cultural productions of Shakespeare's world as things to be interpreted in terms of secular modernity in its nascent form.[32] The assumptions held by such narratives of progress *from* the medieval *to* the modern have been called into question by many recent studies that insist on the need to approach questions about Shakespeare and religion across the medieval–early modern divide.[33] This volume advances such critiques of periodization by inviting continued reconsideration of oppositions between religious and secular ideas and representations, especially in the works of Shakespeare, who has long been regarded as heralding modernity, if not also credited with the "invention of the human."[34]

Responses to these critical discussions in Shakespeare studies have been at times overly invested in labeling Shakespeare according to distinct sacred or secular categories. For example, the more extreme versions of the "religious Shakespeare" argument insist on either a "Catholic Shakespeare" (forged from much biographical speculation regarding Shakespeare's lost years and his father's spiritual testament) or an essentially Protestant (if not also Protestantizing) Shakespeare whose plays step in time with the Reformation's every claim.[35] Other critics put forward an exclusively "secular" Shakespeare who embraces a world without miracles where faith in an itinerary of devotional practice no longer gets in the way of reason and liberal humanism.[36] And, inspired by Michel Foucault's interest in state power and Edward Said's privileging of the material world over the (often stereotyped) mysticism of religion, much new historicist criticism has tended to underplay the lasting emotional, social, and cultural influence of religion on early modern literature even as it saw religious discourse as one of the shaping forces of Shakespeare's age.[37] Thus while the turn to religion in early modern studies was in many ways an outgrowth of New Historicism's emphasis on historical context and cultural poetics, this critical movement was also a reaction against it. Major critical positions pertaining to Shakespeare and religion tend, therefore, to reproduce oppositional arguments: in some, we have a religious Shakespeare who invests in God and the Church (be it Catholic or Protestant) above all else; in others, a "godless Shakespeare" who rejects religious superstition to promote the interests of secular modernity.

Such polarizing characterizations come under scrutiny in this volume, especially as late medieval drama and culture emerges as a pivotal way to further nuance secularization narratives. Indeed, the volume's emphasis on the interplay between medieval and early modern marks one of its major contributions to discussions of secularization.[38] It is misleading, many of our contributors suggest, to equate "medieval" with "spiritual" or "religious." In fact, several medievalists have already gone a long way to dismantle the oppositional logic that governs thinking about both sacred and secular issues, pointing out that the Middles Ages gave rise to much of what is prized by the modern-day secularist, such as universities and social services. Steven Justice, for example, combats the notion that the medieval religious subject was naive or unthinking by showing how doubt and questioning were constitutive of medieval Catholic faith.[39] Though Shakespearean drama negotiates the secular and religious differently, perhaps, than earlier dramatic traditions, it is worth noting that much religious drama itself crossed the borders of sacred and secular interests: while it took religious subject matter as a topical focus, it was very often presented in secular spaces and tied to issues of economics, politics, and civic identity.[40] As Paul Whitfield White reminds us, writing in the context of early Tudor parish drama, "In so-called 'secular' plays, assumptions, practices, and experiences that we typically think of as religious could be integral to the development of a play's narrative or characters, and could consequently reaffirm—or question—the truth or appropriateness of those assumptions, practices, and experiences."[41]

What is more, *Sacred and Secular Transactions in the Age of Shakespeare* explores how the tendency to divorce Shakespeare from religion is often of a piece with the desire, even in the most historicist of scholarly approaches, to see Shakespeare as "our contemporary," in Jan Kott's famous formulation, or to see him "in our time," a phrase used in the title of a recent volume of essays collected by the Shakespeare Association of America to commemorate the quadricentennial anniversary of Shakespeare's death.[42] Such formulations implicitly advance an argument for Shakespeare as a secularizing dramatist who charts a move away from religion toward its opposite, from an earlier time to our own time. The phrase "in our time" is particularly instructive, for it denotes a *saeculum* in the sense that it is a particular temporal measure—an age or span of years differentiated from others in the past. But "our time" is secular in a second sense, too, insofar as Shakespeare "in our time" is often a Shakespeare who is our progressive, modern, and worldly contemporary, one who easily shuffles off the coil of retrograde spirituality. This is a Shakespeare who embraces modernity's enthusiasm for what Taylor calls a "self-sufficing or exclusive humanism"—and a Shakespeare who, in Brian Cummings's words, emerges as "both an agent of change—heralded as the first truly modern author, in his charismatic self-presence; and its observer in action."[43]

This volume's emphasis on the transactions between sacred and secular in Shakespeare's plays allows us to see how a historicized Shakespeare and a contemporized Shakespeare are not mutually exclusive, and neither is necessarily more or less religious (or modern, for that matter). To take just one brief example, as this volume was being written TNT's television series *Will* began broadcasts. The series depicts a Shakespeare whose rock-star rebel status comes in part from his being an underground Catholic; the series thus suggests a Shakespeare who is our contemporary and who is also religious, a Shakespeare who synthesizes (and simplifies) the sacred and secular in perhaps inadvertently apt ways. By foregrounding the multiplicity of Shakespeare's positions relative to the religious and the secular, our contributors reflect on a Shakespeare whose works engage our time as well as a Shakespeare who lived and wrote in a different *saeculum*, an age that carried with it different understandings of the transactions between the religious and the secular than do we. Such a Shakespeare synthesizes and nuances critical trends that overemphasize

Shakespeare's religiosity or secularity, instead focusing on why and how transactions between these problematic categories produce meaning. After all, as David Scott Kastan suggests, Shakespeare is not required to endorse a confessional platform in order to engage with religion, and his engagement with religion by no means discounts an interest in the secular world.[44] Accounts of religion as a social, emotional, and intellectual force and of Shakespeare as religiously tolerant revise earlier accounts that saw the playwright and his contemporaries as either mouthpieces for a specific credal identity or harbingers of modern-day secular humanism. Our contributors see the long sixteenth century as continually producing different cultural artifacts—relics and images, hymns, playing spaces, ritual scripts and languages, modes of government, and the theater itself—marked by transactions of sacred and secular meaning. These transactions, and the meanings they produce, suggest to us the relationship between secularization processes and interpretive acts.

Toward a Hermeneutics of Sacred and Secular

In emphasizing the interpretive conditions of sacred and secular transaction, this volume demonstrates that debates about Shakespeare, secularization, and religion raise pivotal questions about hermeneutics, questions about reading and interpretation as conditioned by both intellectual debates on religious controversies and the secularization narratives that have inflected the study of Shakespeare in the modern era.[45] For Shakespeare and his contemporaries, heated arguments over the literal sense of scripture, ecclesiastical structures, and the theological status of the sacraments—controversies that originated long before Shakespeare and endured well after—were all fundamentally debates about how texts were to be read and interpreted. These debates were hot-button issues of the highest consequence; their terms were widely recognized and their consequences (political, religious, subjective) were deeply, and often violently, felt. Just as religion in Shakespeare's England was inextricably linked to interpretive matters, questions about hermeneutics also constituted a discourse in which religious and secular ideas acted upon one another, and these transactions were in turn enacted on the stage.

The volume's interpretive framework, a hermeneutics of sacred and secular, is inspired by Barbara Newman, who frames her provocative study *Medieval Crossover: Reading the Secular against the Sacred* according to a "hermeneutics of both/and," by which she suggests that "when sacred and secular meanings both present themselves in a text yet can't be harmoniously reconciled, it is not always necessary to choose between them."[46] Much scholarship of the past quarter century focusing on Shakespeare and religion applies an understanding of biblical hermeneutics, liturgy and sacrament, and theological controversy to a framework for interpreting both his plays and the wider culture in which they were written and performed. Building upon that work, many essays in this collection argue that these religious matters have worldly investments, which is to say that any interpretive lens focused on religion needs to simultaneously account for the way religious matters were proposed, constituted, and consumed by earthbound people living in particular times. A hermeneutics of sacred and secular thus reveals how spiritual dimensions were defined through human constructions like language and ceremony while also discussing the ways in which worldly matters were often understood according to biblical conventions. The dominance of Christianity in early modern England—a religion in which the word is made flesh, the eternal made present in particular space and time—perhaps underwrites the rich valences of sacred and secular transactions in the language and dramaturgy of Shakespeare.

Recent work has begun to suggest the importance of a hermeneutics that emphasizes such transactions rather than distinct binaries. David Loewenstein and Michael Witmore suggest that Shakespeare's plays "challenge the ways we think about the categories of the secular and the religious in the early modern period and the boundary critics have sometimes constructed between them."[47] Anthony Dawson's related work on sacred and secular interplay maintains that theatrical performance transposes religious ceremonies, texts, and idioms from a literally theological or liturgical register to a metaphorical one without diminishing the sacred context.[48] Ken Jackson and Arthur Marotti suggest that the blurring "between secular and sacred, transcendent and immanent" is such "that we begin to doubt our own vocabulary and historical paradigms in our attempts to describe the strange otherness of Shakespeare's religion."[49] Continuing to think about implications for the modern critic, moreover, Brian Cummings goes so far as to propose that "everything we describe in historical writing via the assumption of a dialectic between the religious and the secular has to be removed and rethought. The realm of the religious includes many things that we think of in secular terms."[50] This volume applies the logic of all these recent formulations to readings of individual plays, showing how an inclusive tension of categories challenges the sequential logic of many secularity narratives.

In focusing the conversation around secularization on the concepts of hermeneutics, transaction, and contact, *Sacred and Secular Transactions in the Age of Shakespeare* also highlights drama's role in troubling familiar understandings of Shakespeare's engagement with sacred and secular materials by creating ambiguity within both these interpretive planes. Indeed, some of the most theatrically captivating scenes discussed in the present volume—Hermione's descent at the end of *The Winter's Tale*, the near-tragic misreading of Hero's chastity in *Much Ado About Nothing*, the Duke's troubling relation to pastoral and political government in *Measure for Measure*, the trial of Katharine of Aragon at Blackfriars in *All Is True*—hinge on the contact rather than the choice between sacred and secular.

When Shakespeare and his contemporaries stage theatrical versions of religious rituals in the secular space of the playhouse, they transform the secular space of the stage into a hybrid platform on which the very separation between secular and religious becomes harder to imagine. Theater can do this, of course, because it is a fictional domain in terms of both its representational action and its audience reception. If the theater as a cultural site is marked off as secular territory, the stage as both a physical and a hermeneutic space marks the boundary between sacred and secular as far more porous. The stage becomes a worldly site in which the sacred is presented not as a set of doctrines or liturgical rubrics but as itself a hermeneutically fluid concept, one shaped, but not replaced, by the signifying patterns of a secular world. The theater is not ultimately a "secular and secularizing institution" as Dawson understands it, in the sense that it translates the sacred into the nonsacred, but rather in the sense, as we have been arguing, that it provides a space in which the contact between sacred and secular ideas can play out, where they can transact.[51]

This volume is divided into four sections, which together demonstrate various permutations of a hermeneutics of sacred and secular at work in Shakespearean drama. The first section, "Defining a Secular Hermeneutics," contains three essays that use and revise various theories of secularization from the past hundred or so years to suggest how the theoretical intersections between the sacred and the secular allow us to reread Shakespeare's plays. William West seeks to define secularity on its own terms rather than seeing it as merely the lack of the sacred, and he does so by reinterpreting the moment in *Titus Andronicus* when Tamora dresses as Revenge to argue that Tamora's attempt at allegorical, otherworldly representation is thwarted by Titus's insistently worldly interpretation. For Kent Cartwright, the treatment of Helen's wondrousness in *All's Well That Ends Well* encapsulates the tense interplay between investments in a religious worldview and a worldly occupation with rationality. In his reading of verbal exchanges involving friars in *Much Ado About Nothing* and *Romeo and Juliet*, moreover, Tobias Döring argues that there is a necessary connection between hermeneutics and secularization, one that theatrical representation of religious speech acts is particularly adept at revealing. The essays in this section suggest how secularity might be defined even as they demonstrate that the boundaries between religious and secular overlap.

The next section, "Political and Social Secularities," illustrates how a secular hermeneutics matters to the worldly, institutional concerns of Shakespearean drama. Jennifer Rust argues that the power the Duke wields in *Measure for Measure* is a form of pastoral governmentality, a reading that challenges New Historicist readings of the Duke's power as absolute and secular. Robert Hornback's essay argues forcefully for the ways in which a protoracism developed in the age of Shakespeare relied on a toxic mixture of pre-Christian classical, metaphysical ideas and biblical hermeneutics. This pair of essays thus demonstrates that the transactions of sacred and secular had profound effects on the way early moderns constructed political and social ideas that continue to matter in the twenty-first century.

The third section turns its attention to "Spaces of the Secular," with three essays that examine how conceptions of sacred and secular space matter to the places imaged by drama as well as to theatrical space itself. Jeanne McCarthy reads the dramaturgy of *Hamlet* through the lens of Tudor children's troupes that performed both in chapels and at court, arguing that Shakespeare inherited ideas about theatricality and spatial meaning from these companies. Rachael Deagman uses the emblematic representation of space in the fifteenth-century morality play *The Castle of Perseverance* to analyze the way conscience is spatially conceived in *All Is True* (*Henry VIII*), a play that pivots—spatially, theologically, and dramaturgically—on Blackfriars, the religious-turned-secular place in which the play was at times performed. Finally, Helga Duncan interprets the space of Prospero's magical cell in *The Tempest* as representing the interplay between church and world, a concept that is central to all the essays in this section.

This volume's final section, "Secular Aesthetics," brings artistic forms across late medieval, early modern, and postmodern contexts to bear on interpretations of the sights and sounds of Shakespearean drama, thus complicating the historical trajectories of various secularity narratives. Angela Heetderks draws attention to acoustic matters when she demonstrates how the *Te Deum*s sung in *Henry V* and *All Is True* invoke the instability of ecclesiastical power, a power that is at once sacred and worldly. Emma Maggie Solberg's reading of the statue scene in *The*

Winter's Tale turns to matters of visual culture, drawing on accounts of medieval movable statues—namely, the Rood of Boxley—to argue that a sophisticated skepticism is at play for the audience when they behold the conflation of life and art in the actor playing Hermione. This set of essays thinks particularly about the unique combinations of images and sounds that make the theater and the way that drama's hermeneutically open qualities are particularly suited to representing a complex braid of sacred and secular meaning. The book concludes with an afterword by Brian Cummings and Margreta de Grazia, whose influential work on Shakespeare, secularization, and periodization not only has deeply informed this volume but also, as their commentary here suggests, continues to remind us of the "creative juxtaposition" of sacred and secular forces at work in the age of Shakespeare—a juxtaposition that emphasizes "less the supersession of one term by the other than their vexed and variable coexistence."

In teasing out the implications of a hermeneutics of sacred and secular for both studying Shakespeare's plays and reflecting on the critical practice of Shakespeare studies as a scholarly field, our contributors explore how the religious reformations of the past—and the debates over language and interpretation they galvanized—continue to inform our critical present in ways that extend beyond religious concerns to include issues like race and identity, language, music, government, the visual arts, and the spatial imagination. Together we show how Shakespeare mobilizes contact between sacred and secular meanings on a stage that itself troubles the boundaries between past and present, immanent and transcendent.

Notes

1. Debora Kuller Shuger, *Habits of Thought in the English Renaissance: Religion, Politics, and the Dominant Culture* (Toronto: University of Toronto Press, 1997). For general assessments of the "turn to religion" in the early modern period, see Ken Jackson and Arthur Marotti, "The Turn to Religion in Early Modern Studies," *Criticism* 46, no. 1 (2004): 167–90, and James D. Mardock, "'Reformation in a Flood': The Religious Turn's Second Wave," in *Stages of Engagement: Drama and Religion in Post-Reformation England*, ed. James D. Mardock and Kathryn R. McPherson (Pittsburgh: Duquesne University Press, 2014), 1–18.

2. Stephen Greenblatt, *Shakespearean Negotiations* (Berkeley: University of California Press, 1988), 126; Louis Adrian Montrose, *The Purpose of Playing: Shakespeare and the Cultural Politics of the Elizabethan Theatre* (Chicago: University of Chicago Press, 1996), 31. Margreta de Grazia has consistently criticized the ways in which modern scholarship has followed the lead of nineteenth-century scholars in reinforcing the singularity of "the Renaissance" and the notion that figures like Shakespeare ushered in the modern era. See, for example, "The Modern Divide: From Either Side," *Journal of Medieval and Early Modern Studies* 37,

no. 3 (2007): 453–67, and "Anachronism," in *Cultural Reformations: Medieval and Renaissance in Literary History*, ed. Brian Cummings and James Simpson (Oxford: Oxford University Press, 2010), 13–34.

3. Paul Whitfield White, *Drama and Religion in English Provincial Society, 1485–1660* (Cambridge: Cambridge University Press, 2008), argues, "It is anachronistic to disentangle too rigorously secular from religious interest" in such plays (4–5). Parish feast days, he notes, provide but one example of "the intermingling of the sacred and the profane in parish culture," for these "holy days" also occasioned dramatic entertainments, church ales, and other forms of festivity (16–17). White goes on to say that the guilds that sponsored much early religious drama were not predominantly religious but rather trade guilds, which "were not exclusively 'secular' organizations; many had their own chaplains, worshiped together on major feast days, and indeed fostered a dynamic religious life for their members" (66).

4. Brian Cummings, *Mortal Thoughts: Religion, Secularity and Identity in Shakespeare and Early Modern Culture* (Oxford: Oxford University Press, 2013), 4–5.

5. Max Weber, *The Protestant Ethic and the Spirit of Capitalism*, trans. Talcott Parsons (New York: Routledge, 2001); Charles Taylor, *A Secular Age* (Cambridge, Mass.: Harvard University Press, 2007).

6. Julia Reinhard Lupton, "The Religious Turn (to Theory) in Shakespeare Studies," *English Language Notes* 44, no. 1 (Spring 2006): 147.

7. De Grazia, "The Modern Divide," 453.

8. Brian Cummings, "Afterword," in *Shakespeare and Early Modern Religion*, ed. David Loewenstein and Michael Witmore (Cambridge: Cambridge University Press, 2014), 303.

9. Talal Asad, *Foundations of the Secular: Christianity, Islam, Modernity* (Stanford, Calif.: Stanford University Press, 2003), 25–26. See also Peter Berger, *The Sacred Canopy: Elements of a Sociological Theory of Religion* (New York: Doubleday, 1967).

10. "Secular," *Oxford English Dictionary Online*, def. 1. For discussion of the evolution of "secularization" in semantic, religious, and philosophical contexts from Augustine to the late twentieth century, see Jan N. Bremmer, "Secularization: Notes Toward a Genealogy," in *Religion: Beyond a Concept*, ed. Hent de Vries (New York: Fordham University Press, 2008), 432–37.

11. The words *per omnia saecula saeculorum* recur at several points during the Mass, especially during the Canon, the highest point of the liturgy, at which transubstantiation occurs. The English translation of *per omnia saecula saeculorum* is also retained in the *Book of Common Prayer*, as at the end of a prayer during the Order of the Lord's Supper in which the priest prays for the monarch.

12. There are at least ten references in the book of Revelation (see 4:9 and 7:12); other New Testament references include 1 Timothy 1:17, Hebrews 13:21, and Ephesians 3:21. Geneva Bible of 1560.

13. "Secular," *OED*, defs. 1 and 2. On Friar Laurence's worldly investments, see David Scott Kastan, *A Will to Believe: Shakespeare and Religion* (New York: Oxford University Press, 2014), 49–57.

14. In the mid-twentieth century, religious historian and philosopher Mircea Eliade interpreted the distinction between sacred and profane to develop the

concept of "hierophany," or the manifestation of the sacred. For Eliade, hierophany explains that only a conception of the sacred can establish structured, hierarchical order to the world, whereas there is no inherent qualitative difference in profane things; Mircea Eliade, *The Sacred and the Profane: The Nature of Religion*, trans. Willard R. Trask (New York: Harcourt, 1987).

15. Bremmer, "Secularization," 437.

16. "Secular," *OED*, def. 7.

17. Cummings, *Mortal Thoughts*, 2.

18. Margreta de Grazia, "*The Swerve*'s Secular Modern," *Exemplaria* 25, no. 4 (Winter 2013): 341.

19. We focus on narratives that put changes in Christian practice at their center, but there are also many scholars accounting for the effects of and changes in Islam, Judaism, and other global religions—as well as globalization itself—in their stories of secularization. On Saidian Orientalism as a critique of Christianity and the centrality of Christianity to many narratives of secularity, see Gil Anidjar, "Secularism," *Critical Inquiry* 33, no. 1 (Autumn 2006): 52–77, and Gauri Viswanathan, "Secularism in the Framework of Heterodoxy," *PMLA: Publications of the Modern Language Association* 133, no. 2 (March 2008): 466–76.

20. These studies include Barbara Lewalski, *Protestant Poetics and the Seventeenth-Century Religious Lyric* (Princeton, N.J.: Princeton University Press, 1979); Huston Diehl, *Staging Reform, Reforming the Stage: Protestantism and Popular Theater in Early Modern England* (Chicago: University of Chicago Press, 1997); Stephen Greenblatt, *Hamlet in Purgatory* (Princeton, N.J.: Princeton University Press, 2001); and Regina Schwartz, *Sacramental Poetics at the Dawn of Secularism: When God Left the World* (Palo Alto, Calif.: Stanford University Press, 2007).

21. De Grazia, "The *Swerve*'s Secular Modern," 343. See also de Grazia, "The Modern Divide" and "Anachronism."

22. In *A Secular Age*, Charles Taylor defines these two ways of thinking about secularization as "Secularity 1" and "Secularity 2." He then focuses on a third option, "Secularity 3," which is "the change . . . which takes us from a society in which it was virtually impossible not to believe in God, to one in which faith, even for the staunchest believer, is one human possibility among others" (3). Institutional and public secularization theses owe much to Émile Durkheim's notion that religion is a social practice with political and institutional (and therefore "profane") potency; see Émile Durkheim, *The Elementary Forms of Religious Life* (New York: Free Press, 1965), 22.

23. Cummings, *Mortal Thoughts*, 1–3, describes how Weber's theory of disenchantment has been used across disciplines. For a sharp reconsideration of disenchantment in a Reformation context, see Alexandra Walsham, "The Reformation and 'the Disenchantment of the World' Reassessed," *Historical Journal* 51, no. 2 (2008): 497–528, and for a recent collection on the topic of disenchantment in early modern drama, see Nandini Das and Nick Davis, eds., *Enchantment and Dis-enchantment in Shakespeare and Early Modern Drama: Wonder, the Sacred, and the Supernatural* (New York: Routledge, 2017).

24. Taylor, *A Secular Age*, 338, 376.

25. Taylor, *A Secular Age*, 543.

26. Victoria Kahn argues along similar lines: "It's too often forgotten that our ability to have a conversation about religious differences in the first place depends on the existence of a secular space of toleration. In the West, this secular space of toleration was the result of a lengthy and contentious historical process, one whose defining moment was what—with hindsight—we have come to call 'the early modern period' " (introduction to "Early Modern Secularism," special issue, *Representations* 105 [2009]: 1). See also de Grazia, "The Modern Divide," and Kathleen Davis, *Periodization and Sovereignty: How Ideas of Feudalism and Secularization Govern the Politics of Time* (Philadelphia: University of Pennsylvania Press, 2009).

27. Keith Thomas, *Religion and the Decline of Magic: Studies in Popular Beliefs in Sixteenth- and Seventeenth-Century England* (New York: Penguin, 2003), 48.

28. C. John Sommerville, *The Secularization of Early Modern England: From Religious Culture to Religious Faith* (Oxford: Oxford University Press, 1992).

29. Eamon Duffy, *The Stripping of the Altars: Traditional Religion in England, c. 1400–c. 1580* (New Haven, Conn.: Yale University Press, 1992).

30. Carl Schmitt, *Political Theology: Four Chapters on the Concept of Sovereignty*, trans. George Schwab (Chicago: University of Chicago Press, 2005).

31. Brad Gregory, *The Unintended Reformation: How a Religious Revolution Secularized Society* (Cambridge, Mass.: Belknap Press, 2012), 2. For a series of essays criticizing Gregory's position, see "Unintended Reformations," ed. David Aers and Russ Leo, special issue, *Journal of Medieval and Early Modern Studies* 46, no. 3 (September 2016).

32. As de Grazia points out, the historical teleologies of everyone from Hegel to Marx are maintained in contemporary scholarship, with its distinction between the "premodern" and the "early modern" ("The Modern Divide," 659–61).

33. Criticism of periodization has informed a good deal of the work published in such venues as the *Journal of Medieval and Early Modern Studies* and the ReFormations series published by the University of Notre Dame Press. See also Cummings and Simpson, *Cultural Reformations*, and Gordon McMullan and David Matthews, eds., *Reading the Medieval in Early Modern England* (Cambridge: Cambridge University Press, 2009). For recent work on periodization as related to Shakespeare and his contemporaries, see also Ruth Morse, Helen Cooper, and Peter Holland, eds., *Medieval Shakespeare: Pasts and Presents* (Cambridge: Cambridge University Press, 2013); John Watkins and Curtis Perry, eds., *Shakespeare and the Middle Ages* (Oxford: Oxford University Press, 2009); Katherine Steele Brokaw, *Staging Harmony: Music and Religious Change in Late Medieval and Early Modern English Drama* (Ithaca, N.Y.: Cornell University Press, 2016); and Jay Zysk, *Shadow and Substance: Eucharistic Controversy and English Drama across the Reformation Divide* (Notre Dame, Ind.: University of Notre Dame Press, 2017).

34. Harold Bloom, *Shakespeare: The Invention of the Human* (New York: Riverhead Books, 1999).

35. For representative arguments about Shakespeare's Catholicism, see Richard Wilson, *Secret Shakespeare: Studies in Theatre, Religion and Resistance* (Manchester, UK: Manchester University Press, 2009); E. A. J. Honigmann, *Shakespeare: The "Lost Years"* (Manchester, UK: Manchester University Press,

1985); and David N. Beauregard, *Catholic Theology in Shakespeare's Plays* (Newark: University of Delaware Press, 2007). For studies that align Shakespeare with English Protestantism, see Diehl, *Staging Reform*; Daniel Swift, *Shakespeare's Common Prayers: The Book of Common Prayer and the Elizabethan Age* (New York: Oxford University Press, 2012); and Graham Holderness, *The Faith of William Shakespeare* (Oxford: Lion Books, 2016).

36. Such arguments are made by Eric Mallin's *Godless Shakespeare* (London: Bloomsbury, 2007), which suggests that there is a hostility toward God in much of Shakespearean drama, and Richard McCoy's *Faith in Shakespeare* (New York: Oxford University Press, 2013), which argues that Shakespeare's plays privilege artistic faith over religious faith.

37. See, for example, Edward Said, "Introduction: Secular Criticism," in *The World, the Text, and the Critic* (Cambridge, Mass.: Harvard University Press, 1983), and Anidjar, "Secularism," 56–62.

38. See Sarah Beckwith, *Shakespeare and the Grammar of Forgiveness* (Ithaca, N.Y.: Cornell University Press, 2011).

39. See Steven Justice, "Did the Middle Ages Believe in Their Miracles?," *Representations* 103, no. 1 (Summer 2008): 1–29, a direct response to Taylor, and also Justice's "Eucharistic Miracle and Eucharistic Doubt," *Journal of Medieval and Early Modern Studies* 42, no. 2 (Spring 2012): 307–32.

40. See Sarah Beckwith, *Signifying God: Social Relation and Symbolic Act in the York Corpus Christi Plays* (Chicago: University of Chicago Press, 2001), and Nicole R. Rice and Margaret Aziza Pappano, *The Civic Cycles: Artisan Drama and Identity in Premodern England* (Notre Dame, Ind.: University of Notre Dame Press, 2015).

41. White, *Drama and Religion*, 169.

42. Dympna Callaghan and Suzanne Gossett, eds., *Shakespeare in Our Time: A Shakespeare Association of America Collection* (London: Bloomsbury, 2016).

43. Taylor, *A Secular Age*, 19; Cummings, *Mortal Thoughts*, 8.

44. Kastan, *A Will to Believe*, 7, 37.

45. Studies of hermeneutics in the Reformation include Brian Cummings, *The Literary Culture of the Reformation: Grammar and Grace* (Oxford: Oxford University Press, 2001); James Simpson, *Burning to Read: English Fundamentalism and Its Reformation Opponents* (Cambridge, Mass.: Harvard University Press, 2007); Shuger, *Habits of Thought*; Kimberly Johnson, *Made Flesh: Sacrament and Poetics in Post-Reformation England* (Philadelphia: University of Pennsylvania Press, 2014); Sophie Read, *Eucharist and the Poetic Imagination in Early Modern England* (Cambridge: Cambridge University Press, 2013); Ryan McDermott, *Tropologies: Ethics and Invention in England, c. 1350–1600* (Notre Dame, Ind.: University of Notre Dame Press, 2016); Zysk, *Shadow and Substance*; and Kristen Poole and Thomas Fulton, eds., *Reading Shakespeare and the Bible: Cultures of Interpretation in Reformation England* (Cambridge: Cambridge University Press, 2018).

46. Barbara Newman, *Medieval Crossover: Reading the Secular against the Sacred* (Notre Dame, Ind.: University of Notre Dame Press, 2013), 7.

47. David Loewenstein and Michael Witmore, eds., *Shakespeare and Early Modern Religion* (Cambridge: Cambridge University Press, 2014), 4.

48. Anthony Dawson, "Shakespeare and Secular Performance," in *Shakespeare and the Cultures of Performance*, ed. Paul Yachnin and Patricia Badir (London: Routledge, 1991), 83–97.

49. Arthur Marotti and Ken Jackson, eds., *Shakespeare and Religion: Early Modern and Postmodern Perspectives* (Notre Dame, Ind.: University of Notre Dame Press, 2011), 9.

50. Cummings, *Mortal Thoughts*, 15.

51. Dawson, "Shakespeare and Secular Performance," 84.

Part One

Defining a Secular Hermeneutics

Titus's Infinite Jest

William N. West

> If men could manage all their affairs by a definite plan (*certo consilio*), or if fortune were always favorable to them, no one would be gripped by superstition.
>
> —Spinoza, *Tractatus Theologico-Politicus*

Rethinking secularity in the age of Shakespeare means thinking about the range of meanings that our word *secular* has in relation to Shakespeare's playhouses and the culture they were part of, as well as in relation to ours. Many recent studies addressing the question of Shakespeare's secularity have intertwined it inextricably with the question of Shakespeare's religiosity and begin from assumptions that render these categories entirely too commensurable. In this essay, I want to see if I can rethink secularity in terms that do not make it a negative space cut out by the sacred, closer to its own terms. To sketch what those terms are, I speculate on the scene in *Titus Andronicus* in which Tamora visits Titus disguised as Revenge—as, that is, something worldly in the guise of something transcendent—in which the sacred and the secular seem to overlap. Tamora's certainty that she can tell the difference between her clear-sighted cunning and Titus's superstitious belief in Revenge is, I conclude, an index, if not a model, for how we might rethink secularity.

In what has been called a turn to religion in early modern studies, what is religious and what is secular are sometimes proposed as if they were zero-sum alternatives, with advances in one direction marked as retreats in the other. Perhaps the cloudiness of our category of the secular arises because our working definitions of secularity and secularism in studies of Shakespeare's age are predominantly privative: in their broad terms, the secular is just whatever is left over when you don't have religion, or sacredness, or numen. Max Weber's disenchantment (*Entzauberung*), Marcel Mauss's desacralization (*désacralisation*), Charles Taylor's great disembedding—these different names for the phenomenon of becoming secular all suggest that such movements are a stripping of the conceptual and affective altars. These and other loosely related claims have come to be known generally as the secularization hypothesis. Their argument is that the condition of secular modernity—a tautology in this case—is defined by a decline in the hegemony of religion, that the secular is what remains as religion withers.[1] This hypothesis has a long history, although it was first named in the early twentieth century. Radical thinkers of the eighteenth century understood Enlightenment to be the stripping away of ideologies, including religious ones, to reveal a world structured by rational human observation, common human sense, and free human interaction. Early twentieth-century scholars, from a different perspective, saw in the same historical changes a loss of meaningfulness, experiential richness, and community. As Hans Blumenberg summarizes, such discussions of secularity circle around the feeling that "something is absent, which is supposed to have been present before."[2] Secularism then assumes the shape of the hole left by the absconding of faith rather as a positive stance without reference to religiosity.

The secularization thesis has been increasingly challenged, or at least complicated, in fields like history, sociology, and philosophy, but it remains powerful in theater history and cultural criticism.[3] Here it can be powerfully nostalgic, and imaginary: secularity represents a reduction of a dazzling but missing glory of religious experience. When what is secular is characterized as privative, it is easy to talk about a richness that has disappeared from the world, hard not to refill the imagined gap with elements we imagine once patched it up. Even works that undertake to explore religious experience in secular terms, like William James's *The Varieties of Religious Experience* or Freud's *The Future of an Illusion*, struggle to find things to say about what secular experiences feel like. The word "religion"—*re*-ligion, "binding *over*, *again*," in a widely disseminated but incorrect etymology from *religare*, or "reselection," "redividing," even "rereading," in a less familiar but more accurate one from *religere*—seems to promise that we might regain what has somehow been lost.[4] Such approaches frame the secular as glancing back over its shoulder for approval at the sacred and do not see that secularity might present what is new rather than spending again what is already spent. Only if it is characterized positively and descriptively can secularity offer a form of experience and not just the overlooking of a form of experience.

In the introduction to their collection *Shakespeare and Religion*, Ken Jackson and Arthur Marotti usefully distinguish two ways of turning to religion in contemporary early modern scholarship: the historical and the philosophical or ethical.[5] The historical turn explores early modern religion as a powerful and independent motive not reducible to other frames of action, like politics or economics. The ethical turn addresses modern questions through religious modes of inquiry that are also not reducible to other modes of thinking, like problems of otherness, identity, and finitude. In an example offered by Jackson and Marotti, Julia Reinhard Lupton points out that religion as a "form of thinking" can "resist localization and identification with a specific time, place or nation."[6] Apparently conversely, Anthony Dawson notes that looking minutely at religious practices and beliefs reveals the "bracing intractability of the particular," a gesture that is valorized in other current critical contexts as well.[7] So characterized, the historical and ethical turns toward religion must overlap, if they do not actually conflict. But they may not so completely occupy the field. Ethical and philosophical questions, especially those on alterity and finitude, provide a crucial impetus toward religious thinking in early modernity and postmodernity alike. But that does not mean that, then or now, all attempts to address alterity and finitude draw on religious thinking. The "struggles between the universal and the particular" that Lupton eloquently locates in a religious form of thinking might also be called questions of "theory."[8] Religious thinking itself, though, or thinking religiously, can be a strong solvent for early modern writers: David Kastan has rightly observed that "religion provides Shakespeare with the fundamental language of value and understanding in the plays."[9]

In practice, both the historical and the ethical turns to religion present a weak obverse of the secularization hypothesis, associating plenitude with religion, and with secularity very little at all. The presence of religious content in Shakespeare, whether defined historically or ethically, seems incontrovertible (which of course does not say anything about whether religious thinking was rising, declining, or changing during the period). So does the importance of religion in this period, and so do claims that religious discourse is not readily reducible—at least not more readily reducible than other discourses—to any other way of talking, thinking, or acting. But in this case it also seems, conversely, that we might want to resist reducing or translating the discourses of the playhouse to the discourses of religion. Shakespeare and his contemporaries, especially his aristocratic sponsors and the bureaucracies of London and other towns where playing went on, certainly didn't. At the risk of being obvious, the plays performed by Shakespeare and his contemporaries were almost never identified as making explicitly religious claims, although they were often described and judged—usually harshly—in religious terms. But overt treatments of religious matters, like political ones, in performances were illegal.[10] While playing was zealously, if unevenly, regulated, it was certainly permitted, as it would not have been if Shakespeare's plays were recognized as religious or political in the full senses of the words.

A stronger version of the secularization hypothesis in the turn to religion argues that this so-called secularization covertly preserves religious structures and practices in disguised forms, drawing its strength from them. The most resonant claim from this camp is Carl Schmitt's, that "all significant concepts of the modern theory of the state are secularized theological concepts, not only because of their historical development . . . but also because of their systematic structure,"[11] but Ernst Kantorowicz's analysis of the doctrine of the king's two bodies and Max Weber's description of the Protestant work ethic also belong here, as well as New Historicist arguments that the theater drew its affective power from (as opposed to gathering its power in) the disenfranchisement of rituals sanctioned by the Roman Church. This strong secularization hypothesis amounts to an argument that people are thinking about God even when they don't say they are, and perhaps even when they say that they aren't. It makes it difficult to imagine secularity except as a regular set of alterations to an earlier condition, to be grasped as deviations from it. In other words, these approaches to religious discourse and religious thinking can overcode any other terms that either modern critics or early playgoers might have preferred to use. Methodologically, this seems dicey at least. Reading Kantorowicz, it can be hard to say if we are looking, with Schmitt, at a theological structure in secular garb or, with Hans Blumenberg, at a theological structure that has been "reoccupied" by secular content, perhaps "as a provocation," with the polemical aim of stealing fire from heaven.[12]

Scholars (re)turning to religion sometimes seem too quick to locate religious positions to Shakespeare's plays, often in excess of what the plays and their conditions of production own up to. They risk suggesting that the social importance of religion meant that it was not called into question by ideas that we might call secular, or that religious discourse provides the only, or the predominant, infrastructural coding of other structures of feeling and assuming its presence even when it is not explicit. This makes it hard even to articulate a proposal for secularity, since a religious sense can always be posited as co-opting it in the original reception of the plays. In any culture where religion is as powerful an institution and a discourse as it was in Shakespeare's age (powerful but not sovereign), it will inevitably organize a significant amount of symbolic activity, and provide flexible, developed models for making sense of other discourses and institutions. But such religious content is no more necessarily religious in function than good-bye (from "God be with you") is actually a blessing. It may be true that Shakespeare's plays had functions also associated with religious practices, communitarian or affective but not overtly confessional, or that patterns that occur in religious practices also appear onstage. But in that case I am not sure why we are invited to make an association with religion specifically, rather than with kinds of community or kinds of practice.[13]

In contrast to versions of the secularization hypothesis, we might try to think of secularity and religion as not convertible. In *The Legitimacy of the Modern Age*, Hans Blumenberg argues that the secularism that characterizes modernity is an entirely novel historical condition that develops in, and in response to, a tradition that is profoundly religious. For Blumenberg, the whole notion of a unified phenomenon of "secularity" is suspect. While many of the aspects of early modernity associated with its so-called secularization—differentiation of other spheres of authority, proliferation of religious positions, and the like—are historically accurate, Blumenberg argues that nothing is added by grouping them, and that in fact such grouping is misleading. These social changes interact collectively and may even reinforce one another, but they do not entail one another and thus do not represent a single condition but multiple transformations.[14] A single category of secularism is a kind of optical illusion. For Blumenberg the empirical course of secularization is the provision of new ways of responding—not always effectively—to old questions first posed under conditions of Christian hegemony. Following Nietzsche, Blumenberg suggests that individuals ask only those questions for which they are prepared with an answer, with the proviso that a present inherits many questions from its past for which the traditional answers no longer make sense.[15] While analogies cooperate, in other words, history doesn't—the passing on of questions from one generation to another is one factor that produces the dissonances of a new epoch. Contra Schmitt, Blumenberg argues that the awkward fitting of a nonreligious response to a question that can readily be answered in a religious framework does not make the response religious. On the contrary, it reveals the incongruence between them. What is important for Blumenberg is the transformative novelty of the responses to the newly impossible questions that are posed by the past to the present. They simply cannot be set aside but must be handled over and over, with different tools and in changed contexts.

Nietzsche's declaration "God is dead" is well known, but the aphorism is so striking that it is seldom cited in its full context (and for Nietzsche it bore revisiting and repeating, at least twice in *The Gay Science* and also in *Thus Spake Zarathustra*). In its earlier appearance in *The Gay Science*, Nietzsche first recounts how for centuries after the death of the Buddha passersby continued to point out his dreadful shadow in its cave. God, too, is dead, Nietzsche then proclaims—but as with the dead Buddha, the shadow of the dead God continues to be held in awe, "And we—we must still overcome his shadow!"[16]

It is as a Nietzschean shadow that religion continually reappears in scholarship on Shakespeare's plays, which do not, after all, display anything claimed as real divinity, doctrine, or the experiences of faith with anything like the precision or intensity or sincerity of many other works of the period, from Foxe to Herbert. They offer much that is enchanted or sublime without identifying it as religious: the transformation of Hermione, Prospero's spectacular magic, or the imagery of pilgrimage exchanged by Romeo and Juliet. But such moments were explicitly not religious to an Elizabethan, however much they may remind a modern viewer of what he or she imagines religious feeling to be like. Often indeed the plays specify that they are *not* divine or otherworldly, or that they gesture toward numinousness without touching it. They insist, invariably I think, on their distinction from religious discourse, even when they shadow it: they may be like it, but they are not the same as it. But we often see such moments like Nietzsche's shadow, fantastic traces that persist after their sources have faded. Herein lies a crucial resistance to the secular: the fear of giving up on the dead god, and an ongoing and utopian devotion to it as dead. If we could let the dead bury the dead, a secular position might not seem to be the haunted shadow of something more robust and vital. Is there a way *not* to make secularism and religion convertible, and so to let secularism stand on its own? I would like to try.

What shall we mean, then, when we use a word like "secular" or "secularity"? As Victoria Kahn, among others, has argued, the history of these words challenges our ability to offer a positive definition, since they were understood through early modernity as "the product of the distinction between the city of God and the city of man" that lay at the core of Augustine's politics.[17] Instead of looking for a definition of "secularity" or the "secular" that escapes its history, it might be more helpful to come up with a description of *what is secular*—that is, family resemblances that would neither be bound to an implied opposition to what is godly or sacred or religious nor lumped into a specious category.

In describing some of these shared resemblances, I draw on the old tactics of etymology. Etymologies can admittedly be devices for the kind of thinking that has been magniloquently called theologocentric, specifying (as etymologically their name does) the *true word* by referring it to its origins. I mean the etymologies of *saeculum* that follow instead as prompts, to spur thinking about what we might mean by choosing to use "secular" or "secularity." And etymologies can be worldly as well as logocentric and idealizing, relying on neither a primordial intensity of meaning nor even the gradually unlinking chain of a word's inheritances but introducing turbulence into its customary uses. Such worldliness can shake our accustomed categories and presumptions of meaning, among them the frontiers of secularity and religion.

Before being reinterpreted under Augustine's Christian dispensation, the Latin term *saeculum* named a variable measure of time, sometimes a generation, sometimes a life span, sometimes a hundred years, identified etymologically with sowing, cutting, reaping, or the limit of conceivable human age.[18] Varro, one of Augustine's favorite pagan sources—although Augustine does not cite him in reference to *saecula*—says a *saeculum* was the greatest length of time a man could hope to live, thus about a century. But these fixed counts of years were all qualified as "civil *saecula*," standardized by local conventions. Pagan authors also distinguished a "natural *saeculum*," which was the lifetime of the longest-lived person alive at the establishment of a new institution, like a colony, a city, a cult, or a dynasty.[19] An institution's first *saeculum* ended with that person's death; its next *saeculum* was calculated in the same way, from the end of the prior *saeculum*, and so on. Natural *saecula* measured human establishments, long-lasting but not eternal, with clear beginnings and foreseeable ends, by means of human lives. They thus had no preordained length but emerged from the accidents of human life and death. Any new institution thus generated and counted its own peculiar, concretely established, self-determined *saecula*. This kind of calculation is familiar in the epic tradition from *Iliad*, book 6, through the groves at Vallombrosa in *Paradise Lost*, where, without a murmur of sacrality, generations of humans are said to be as leaves, growing and falling. Neither linear nor cyclical, *saecula* are continually wearing out and continually refreshed, each time with a difference, over the rustle of their predecessors, which in time they join. History is not the primary condition of the measure taken of human affairs by *saecula*, if by "history" we mean something like circumstance or context. Existence in a world that is, among other things, temporal and finite, is. Transience is. Let transience stand, then, as a first positive feature of what is secular.

Another sense of what is secular, also taken from the Christian tradition, is that what establishes what is secular is *the world*. The natural *saeculum* as a time that is human without being individual is also, in a parallel etymology, the "world," a word that derives from old Germanic *werald*, a human's (*wer*) age (*ald*). *Werald* and its cognates regularly translate Latin *saeculum* in Old English and other early Germanic languages.[20] As defined in pagan sources, *saeculum* comes close to what Hannah Arendt calls "world" in *The Human Condition*: the environment in which humans dwell, not naturally given but wrought by human work and held in common, more durable than any person but not unending, for instance the institutions that natural *saecula* measure.[21] However we use it, and unlike "secularity," "world" is a positive category; even if one imagines another world, a better world, or a new world, the world does not become thereby a privation or negation of something else.[22] A "world" seems on the contrary to be radically and perhaps essentially immanent. We might think here of Wittgenstein's proposition that the world is all that is the case,[23] or of Stathis Gourgouris's that the worldliness of the ancient Greek view of life was its refusal to project anything otherworldly beyond it, making the world itself all in all: "If death is zero, then all life before it curiously becomes infinity and plenitude in every infinitesimal, ephemeral, and unreproducible moment. If the zero of death is undone by the promise of an eternal afterlife . . . death's zero expands backward all over life."[24] What is worldly is the infinite divisibility of moments that follow and fill that empty totalizing. "World" also seems to limn the folial, filial supersession of the generations of leaves and lives as its condition; the world is simply that renewing supersession itself rather than its outcome or its result. Thus, as a second positive mark of what is secular: worldly immanence.

In these terms, secularity is experienced only in a life that is passed through institutions in which humans partake communally, rather than by any single person. A third feature, then, is commonness. The *saeculum* is a precise but variable period measured by a human life span but exceeding any individual memory, since the longest-lived survivor of an institution would probably have been in infancy at its foundation. It thus marks human institutions using a contingent, particular biological life span as its measure. A *saeculum* also relies on human institutions for its calculation and its memorialization, since a *saeculum* outlasts any particular individual. What is secular is of lived experience without being confined to the particular experience of any one individual who has lived, a time uniquely and communally of humankind, perhaps, rather than eternity, a life span, or the *longue durée*. "If the world is to contain a public space," observed Hannah Arendt, "it cannot be erected for one generation and planned for the living only; it must transcend the life-span of mortal men."[25] Such an understanding of the *saeculum* as a time that is collectively but not personally human complicates the regular association of secularity with ideologies of individuation.[26] But what is secular is shared.

A fourth feature of what is secular is its resistance to prediction (or providence), its virtuality, and its disruptive irregularity. The earliest opposite term of *saecularis* was not *religiosus* but *regularis*, "conforming to a rule"; those priests were "secular" who lived outside a monastic order rather than within one.[27] This irregularity is why Erich Auerbach's *Poet of the Secular World* is, counterintuitively, Dante, whose work is obviously deeply and sincerely engaged with Christianity, a faithfulness not opposite what Auerbach recognizes as Dante's secularity.[28] For Auerbach, Dante's worldliness lies in the *Commedia*'s fidelity to the particularity of each figure that is represented in it. Their irreducible, untranslatable singularity, so distant from the intricate but generalizing allegoresis with which Dante is usually associated, is possible for Dante because his dead have taken up the positions that they will occupy for eternity; they are what Auerbach calls perfected, *vollkommen*—literally, "wholly arrived." But what has been perfected in each of them is the accumulating course of a worldly existence, singular, unique, literally extraordinary (as every individual exceeds what is ordered and ordinary). Furthermore, the eternal perfection of Dante's figures has been achieved by their worldly existence itself; their fully achieved or arrived perfection is at once what they have become and how they became that. What becomes eternal in Dante is what is of the world, realized and crystallized in a lasting essence, the perfection of human activity as an almost literal type that can stamp itself out again in the worldly actions of others, fulfilling nothing predetermined but coming more and more into its own unpredictable individuality. Such richly textured examples of what is secular go a long way in filling up the empty space of privation. I hope here too that etymology itself can be recognized as an example of what is secular and what is worldly—emerging in the transience of meaning, immanent, common rather than private, and finally unpredictable until it is achieved, as unpredictable and acute as Auerbach's association of the secular world with Dante.

The cost of Auerbach's counterintuitive innovation in finding the worldly in Dante's afterlives is that what is secular takes on many of the aspects of absoluteness and eternity and finally appears only in their guise, as the perfected figures of the dead. This world may be what produces the eternal world and what is eternized in it, but for Auerbach's Dante it is as another world that this world is preserved. I have argued elsewhere that what we might call religious thinking is marked by an attempt to part the world, and that in parting the world it departs from the world. It finds, that is, more in the world than just the world; it finds another world beyond itself.[29] Everything worldly becomes subject to its perfection, its *Vollkommenheit*, its final arrival at its inevitable, though not predestined or anticipated or providential, end. Worldly are ways of thinking or acting that escape (rather than resist) such partition, that remain in the world and do not try to go beyond it. Auerbach's eternity is made out of the secular world, as its clearest and fullest image. It takes the form, though, of a last judgment.

Standing against the idea of a last judgment is what Edward Said called secular criticism, a "worldliness" that couples a striving to recognize and acknowledge every vantage or experience that passes through a work of literature and a resistance to its reduction to finite systems that would render it predictable.[30] Said's gesture for worldliness sets itself against attempts to declare a "last (or for that matter the only) word" on a topic.[31] It is a way of holding argument open rather than deciding or foreclosing it, reasoning that offers itself to challenge. Auerbach's *Commedia*, too, suggests a way to keep accounts open even as it insists on their perfected closure. It is polyvocal and polyperspectival not only because of Dante's allegory—not, that is, as a multiple, determined recoding of what has already been expressed, as he described it to Can Grande—but because of the refracting points of view of its figures. Each incident in it, each figure, is more than doubled allegorically (and eschatologically), refracted more than fourfold by the unpredictable and apparently unlimited ways in which they illuminate and are illuminated. In its distinct levels of allegory, even its distinction between the world and eternity, vision and reality, the *Commedia* expresses external determining instances but also internal differences. From certain angles, then—and not immediately incorrect ones—and even granting its commitment to other kinds of closure, the *Commedia* develops a structure that is both complete and capable of multiplying indefinitely within its definite bounds, like the generations of leaves. The *Commedia* invites readers to imagine its worlds working infinitely *and* within their limits: like the universe, it is a book that is bound by love that continues to gloss and be glossed by love.[32]

What Auerbach and Said share in their understanding of worldliness is that the world's course is infinite despite its transience because of its multiplicity and its virtual if not actual incalculability. The incommensurable, incongruent, conflicting views of the world both scatter and secure it. It need make no other claim on any other infinitude or eternity; its transience and self-difference are already incalculable, without need of any externality. This description of worldlinesss sounds like what Arendt identifies as another particular condition of humanness: action. What distinguishes action from other kinds of human activity is that it has a beginning but no end. What will arise from an action is uncertain. For Arendt, action—the speaking of words and the doing of deeds—reveals a person; it "contain[s] the answer to the question asked of every newcomer: 'Who are you?' "[33] The world, in contrast, is for Arendt first of all collective: "Being seen and being heard by others derive their significance from the fact that everybody sees and hears from a different position . . . Only where things can be seen by many in a variety of aspects without changing their identity, so that those who are gathered around them know they see sameness in utter diversity, can worldly reality truly and reliably appear."[34] Such a worldliness does not entail, as secularization often held to, a loss of relationality and community; it might represent a broadening of what Said called horizontal affiliation.[35] It is this internal multiplication of relations and positions that produces the incalculability of a transient, finite world.

For Auerbach, Dante's intensely secular vision could come into focus only because Dante realized it as another world separated from the world, at once the fully achieved, represented world of the afterlives and the representing other world of the *Commedia* itself. But Auerbach could also imagine a similar lucidity in this world, the one we inhabit now, "a basic fabric of the world, perpetually weaving itself, renewing itself, and connected in all its parts."[36] In such a fictional world woven into the fabric of the world itself, rather than an inset box or mirror, "Dante's general, clearly delimited figurality, in which everything is resolved in the beyond, in God's ultimate kingdom, and in which all characters attain their full realization only in the beyond, is no more." This worldly fabric, according to Auerbach, infinite in its interconnections, beyondless, durable, and self-renewing, is Shakespeare's.[37]

Titus Andronicus is almost certainly not the play Auerbach was thinking of when he credited Shakespeare with introducing a new age and a new mode of figuration. He names Hamlet, Macbeth, Lear (the characters, interestingly, not the plays). But *Titus* also provides rich, clear, and concrete examples of what is secular, perhaps better ones than those Auerbach chooses, because they do not so easily slide into an alternative metaphysics of tragic humanism. Like *King Lear*, *Titus* reveals an anarchically pagan world, to which Olympian order is as alien as Christian ethics. The language of the opening scene is insistently religious, but the way religion's familiar terms are used is just as insistently worldly. Tamora's son Alarbus will be sacrificed "*ad manes fratrum*" (1.1.98)—"to the spirits of my brothers," as Lucius says—because Titus's sons "religiously . . . ask a sacrifice" (1.1.125). To ask religiously is to invoke the gods, but not to claim that the gods themselves are asking; it is a worldly demand, negotiated among mortals. Gods have no part in this maimed rite. It is required by the dead and the living, specifically in their familiality and mortality, "their brethren, whom you Goths beheld / Alive and dead" (1.1.122–23.). This distinction between gods and worldly spirits is one the Romans themselves made, if uneasily, and that Shakespeare could have known from the section of Plutarch's *Moralia* called *Roman Questions*.[38] The "piety" Tamora invokes to save Alarbus, "to fight for king and commonweal" (1.1.114), is likewise worldly. Words like "piety" and "religion"—or Tamora's "cruel, irreligious piety" (1.1.130)—are stripped of any claims to transcendence and drop to earth like the arrows Titus later aims at heaven (4.3).

But the world of *Titus* is godless rather than godforsaken. Its gods have not abandoned it and there seems to be neither nostalgia for their presence nor anticipation of their advent. To a person, the characters in the play act as if they live in a world that they have made, in situations that can be resolved or changed only by their own actions. The contentions over how to dispose first imperial power and then Lavinia present an almost schematic survey of ways of worldly action—threatening violence (1.1.4), claiming something by right of inheritance (1.1.5), seizing moral high ground (1.1.13), electing a leader by popular consensus (1.1.21), conceding the capacity to make a decision (1.1.53, 57), vowing, contracting, speaking forthrightly, seizing Machiavellian opportunity or applying *Realpolitik*—actions that share only an exclusion of appeals beyond the immediate actors of the scene and an utter unconcern for divine law or will. This world can accommodate with equal ease an almost ethnographic understanding of religion and a believer's faithful knowing. We observe the first when Aaron, who believes in no god, insists that Lucius swear to save Aaron's son, "because I know thou art religious" and "I know / An idiot holds his bauble for a god / And keeps his oath which by that god he swears" (5.1.74, 78–80); the second when, as he condemns Aaron to death by starvation, Marcus weakly refers to him as "an irreligious Moor" and "that misbelieving Moor" (5.3.120, 142), as though Aaron had no worse tricks than lack of faith and that alone were enough to bar him from human society. But the play allows no room for divine intercession and scarcely suggests that human beings expect it. Titus launches his arrows at heaven and into the palace of Saturninus because, as he says, Justice has left the world, "*Terras Astraea reliquit*" (4.3.4). But he is not offering a prayer or lament. Rather, he is quoting Ovid's *Metamorphoses*, as Lavinia had quoted it to expose Chiron and Demetrius as her rapists (4.1.47ff.), or as Titus had quoted Horace to threaten them, "*Integer vitae, scelerisque purus*" (4.2.20).[39] Citations like these are not messages from earth to heaven but worldly memories and references, conversations that rely on their shared, transient situatedness and their capacity to be resituated through and across uncertain affiliations—what I have been calling secular. The closest Titus comes to prayer is when his sons are being led to their deaths and he appeals to the stones, whose single virtue is their impassivity: "A stone is silent and offendeth not" (3.1.46). Even then Titus is clear that stones stand in not for the gods but for the tribunes' mortal, worldly powers.

The absence of the gods in *Titus* can best be discerned by comparing what is missing from the scenes in which Titus tortures a fly (3.2) and the scene in *King Lear* in which Gloucester cries, "As flies to wanton boys are we to the gods. / They kill us for their sport" (4.1.38–39). *King Lear* is sometimes also called a godless play, but its world has been abandoned by the gods and left in Nietzsche's shadow, where their absence is a cause for horror. Its piety is indeed cruel and irreligious. In *Lear* there are no flies: the flies are a figure for humankind before the excruciating heedlessness of the gods. In *Titus*, there are no gods. There are only flies and men, merciful or cruel, punishing or suffering, at different moments. In *Lear* the figure of the fly is an attempt to grasp an existential horror; in *Titus*, the actual fly substitutes for the body of Aaron, which Titus cannot reach. Its torture is Titus's contingent, brutal attempt to communicate the shambles of the world that he sees and that he and others have made of it.

I offer another example from *Titus Andronicus* of what is worldly—that is, what is immanent, common, transient without being historical, and *therefore* (not nevertheless) incalculable without recourse to any externality. Just before the play's catastrophe, when it seems that everything bad than can happen already has, Tamora contrives another cruelty against Titus:

> I will enchant the old Andronicus
> With words more sweet and yet more dangerous
> Than baits to fish. (4.4.88–90)

This intrigue is more instrumental than Tamora's or Aaron's previous plots. Tamora wants to convince Titus to invite his son Lucius to parley, so that she can "pluck proud Lucius from the warlike Goths" (4.4.109), whom Lucius is leading against Rome. What those sweet and dangerous words are is clarified in Tamora's next scene, when she visits the maddened Titus "disguised" with Chiron and Demetrius (s.d. 5.2.1) in "strange and sad habiliment" (5.2.1). They must neither be very good disguises nor readily recognizable ones, because Titus sees through them but is not able to name the figures they pose as ("I am not mad; I know thee well enough . . . For our proud Empress, mighty Tamora" [5.2.21, 26]). Tamora re-cues him:

> Know, thou sad man, I am not Tamora;
> She is thy enemy and I thy friend.
> I am Revenge: sent from th'infernal kingdom,
> To ease the gnawing vulture of thy mind,
> By working wreakful vengeance on thy foes . . .
> There's not a cave or lurking place, . . .
> Where bloody murder or detested rape
> Can couch for fear, but I will find them out
> And in their ears tell them my dreadful name,
> Revenge (5.2.28–40)

It seems that Titus believes what he sees, or what he is told, though he continues to express doubts, and doubts upon his doubts: "Good Lord, how like the Empress' sons they are, / And you the Empress! But we worldly men / Have miserable, mad, mistaking eyes" (5.2.64–66). But as Tamora departs without her sons, thinking Titus "credulous in this mad thought" (5.2.74), he declares, "I knew them all, though they suppose me mad, / And will o'erreach them in their own devices" (5.2.142–43). In the next scene, the last of the play, he does.

In this scene, both Titus and Tamora assert belief in figures of Revenge, Rape, and Murder as powers not of this world—that is, powers distinguished from those of "worldly men." Both are insincere. But both are also right, although neither believes in what he or she says. Revenge as such, Revenge as a figure, does not appear in this scene, or indeed in this play. Unlike in *The Spanish Tragedy*, it does not exist, certainly not as anything that could be "sent from th'infernal kingdom" or embodied onstage. But a worldly revenge comes about anyway when Titus in turn calls on Tamora's belief in her ability to deceive and convinces her to entrust her two ministers, Rape and Murder—that is, Chiron and Demetrius—to him. What comes about is what Tamora promises, and what she does not intend: empress, sons, and emperor will visit Titus for dinner, "And on them shalt thou ease thy angry heart" (5.2.119). The play's revenges take place through a series of moves and countermoves, none of which rise above any sort of agency that could be called earthly or human. In fact, they do not even rise to the level of unexceptional intentionality. They are, in short, thoroughly secular. How?

One way of understanding this next-to-last confrontation between Titus and Tamora, which prepares for the climactic banquet, is to see it as a clash of competing plots, with Titus getting the last laugh when he sees through Tamora's attempt to deceive him. But only Tamora has a plot for the future, the "determined jest" (5.2.139) of pretending to be Revenge. Tamora's premise is that a belief in otherworldly power like Revenge is "lunacy" (5.2.70); because Titus is mad, she believes that he will accept the idea of an embodied Revenge, and she believes that her own competent understanding of reality allows her to manipulate Titus's mad one. She believes, in other words, that "Whate'er I forge to feed his brain-sick humours" (5.2.71) is politic, cunning, worldly. But her confidence in her "determined jest" turns out to be as mad a belief as one in Revenge would be, and for the same reason: it posits something that is not tied to the world from within the world. Tamora believes that her jest of playing Revenge will determine Titus's responses to it. She imagines, in other words, a perfected Titus, one as complete and perspicuous as any of Dante's dead; her jest approaches Titus as if he were already determined by his history and that from that perfection she can determine his future. Her sure faith that she can successfully represent, grasp, and instrumentalize the world is Tamora's madness. It is a kind of minimal metaphysics: Tamora imagines that she can represent to herself the way Titus and the world will run. But belief in foresight is still faith in a kind of providence, even if it seems to be a human one: it fore-pictures a world within the world.

In contrast, Titus's actions are precisely *undetermined*. He assumes no model of the world but the world itself, within which he acts responsively. Although he knows what he is doing he does not imagine he knows what he will do next, because he does not presume what will happen next. Unlike Tamora's determinate jest, plotting a clear trajectory toward its outcome, Titus's actions in the scene are infinite jests (if I can rely on the etymon and press the synonym), acts without fixed aims, fired haphazardly into a future that set it ablaze. Titus does not, for instance, predict how Tamora or her sons might act; his actions respond to theirs and solicit actions again from them. Titus recognizes Tamora at his door ("I know thee well" [5.2.215]), but when Tamora says she is Revenge he follows her lead and makes his enemies into allegories:

> Lo, by thy side where Rape and Murder stands;
> Now give me some surance that thou art Revenge,
> Stab them, or tear them on thy chariot-wheels . . . (5.2.45–47)

Titus takes these names from Tamora's words that her task is to track down "bloody murder or detested rape" (5.2.37).[40] It is through Titus's charge that Chiron and Demetrius first assume their allegorical roles, although they enter "disguised" in some way (s.d. 5.2.1). When Titus asks her to confirm who they are, Tamora in turn follows him: "Rape and Murder, therefore callèd so / 'Cause they take vengeance of such kind of men" (5.2.62–63). The identities of Rape and Murder that will cover Chiron and Demetrius thus emerge from the accidents of the conversation that passes between Titus and Tamora. Titus's commitment is split between—or binds together—his immediate circumstances and an almost eschatological moment of vengeance. He navigates with reference only to these two points, not to any knowledge, control, or desire that might lead him from one to the other. He seems to have recourse neither to instruments with which to act, nor to fictions to project, nor concepts to think under. This may indeed be mad, but it also—in this scene—overreaches Tamora's belief that her determined jests allow her to outplot someone whose madness she thinks consigns him to belief in the supernatural.

I want to use this scene to propose a summary definition of the secular as a stance against the "re-" in "representation." What I mean by this is that this scene insists on the unrepresentability of what is to be performed—not, as we sometimes mean, that it is unrepresentable in retrospect but that it is unrepresentable before it is executed. It is, in other words, immanent; there is no breaking in of numinousness, no otherness that was not already included but incalculable. Tamora's attempt to predict Titus's actions achieves what she had wanted it to—it gets Titus to summon Lucius—but its very determination, as she calls it, exposes her to a revenge that falls outside the limits she imagined for it. Her attempt to bring something to presence again, in other words to re-present it, brings more of the world with it than she anticipated. In contrast, Titus's open-ended responses to Tamora set no limits; nothing seems wholly alien to them, any more than anything is wholly present to them. Tamora's approach, then, is *representational*, conceiving a world that is not a world. Titus's is *responsible*; that is, answering to the world, moment by moment, not representing it but acting within it. This is why it seems better to say that revenge comes about than that it is achieved. Titus's readiness is all. The best revengers' plans are simply the unswerving commitments they make to serve the times of the world, to answer to it until at last it bends to them: as Hieronimo promises, or threatens, in *The Spanish Tragedy*, "Why then I'll fit you."

Because Tamora chooses to stage Revenge for Titus, we can see Shakespeare's play figuring itself as a comment and reproduction of Kyd's great precursor. A similar reperformance, or revision of how performance works, takes place in *Spanish Tragedy*, between on the one hand

Hieronimo's masquelike productions earlier in the play, whose labeled, allegorical figures are illegible to their viewers before Hieronimo's expert decoding of them reduces them to their lapidary moral, and, on the other, the performance of violence with which the play ends, as interpretation is rendered not just impossible but gratuitously beside the point.[41] *The Spanish Tragedy* takes place under the knowing eye of Revenge but works toward its catastrophe behind the backs of its characters. That determining position is the one that Tamora desires but cannot occupy. Tamora imagines herself to have the same kind of provident knowledge that Hieronimo as playwright pretends for himself, that Revenge displays, and that Kyd as playwright possesses. Titus as character and *Titus Andronicus* as play reject both the mastery that sees what lies ahead and another kind that sees that it cannot see.

In the epigraph to this argument, Spinoza associates the desire for a definite plan with superstition: the incapacity of certain counsel, or perhaps determined jest, pushes humans into imagining kinds of control and understanding that they do not have. *Titus* likewise shows how attempts to determine action from outside it fall short, or to one side—and also how this hamartia, this missing of the mark, calls forth repercussions that are not fully accountable before they have taken place. In place of representation, foreplanning, sure reason, determined jest, *Titus* advances as its worldly alternative a responsible acting—acting in response to the world and to others in it, attuning one's deeds and the world as it is together, transforming both. This careful description of the unpredictability of things without seeking their rupture outside them is what I would call secular thinking. To be sure, unpredictability is sometimes thought as the advent of the Other, and religious thinking is sometimes invoked as a way of coming to terms with alterity and unpredictability. But although religious thinking imagines what is unpredictable as housed in something extraordinary, ultimately it models the extraordinary on us.

Some echoes of worldly outcomes for plays in the time of *Titus* can be discerned in this account by an English observer, Henry Crosse:

> at a Play, . . . a man is not wearied be it never so tedious, because they . . . with great alacrity doth swiftly run over in two hours space, the doings of many years, galloping from one country to an other, whereby the mind is drawn into expectation of the sequel, and carried from one thing to an other with changeable motions, that although he were unacquainted with the matter before, yet the cunning Art he seeth in the conveyance, maketh him patiently attend the Catastrophae.[42]

What interests me is Crosse's description of how the play extends infinitely, indeterminately, into the future. The playgoer is delighted to follow the play, even though he does not know where it is going; he is "carried from one thing to an other with changeable motions . . . although he were unacquainted with the matter before." A play's catastrophe is anticipated but unknown; nevertheless, the "conveyance" of the play, its transient forward motion, will get you there. In this a play resembles the apocalypse of revealed religion—except that it has not been revealed, and there is no sense that its eventuality is determined from the outside. Its ends result from its own apparently infinitely extensible working out. In this strange description, the play has no outside not only because it engages all the senses and absorbs the attention but also because its rules and boundaries are entirely its own. If there is something to be called secular, it is this ongoing and mutual responsibility to circumstance, of the playgoer to the play and the play to the playgoer. I am skeptical of the claim that performance itself must be secular; indeed, in the past few decades performance has reached repeatedly for transcendence. But *Titus* shows how performance *can* be secular, and how a rejection of re-presentation can emerge in a medium that is predicated on iterability and reenactment. Plays can remind us what being in the world feels like: their transience, uncertainty, attention without expectation, our lack of mastery in them even as we respond.

I do not propose this as Shakespeare's theory of secularity, or even of his attitude toward secularity. I doubt that Shakespeare could have articulated the premises such a theory would demand, or that he would have been interested in working one out (I think it is more likely that Shakespeare could have had a theory of worldliness). I do not even propose it as a Shakespearean theory of secularity. But I think it might demonstrate one way for us to continue to address the concern of secularity in Shakespeare, which is properly ours—that of our own moment, that of our own shared world, that of our many perspectives on it. This is not Shakespeare's concern, but our own.

Notes

1. For compact surveys of the history of the secularization hypothesis and some challenges to it in sociology and other fields since Weber, see Victoria Kahn, "Introduction," in "Early Modern Secularism," special issue, *Representations* 105 (2009): 1–8, and Brian Cummings, *Mortal Thoughts: Religion, Secularity and Identity in Shakespeare and Early Modern Culture* (Oxford: Oxford University Press, 2013), 1–18.

2. Hans Blumenberg, *The Legitimacy of the Modern Age*, trans. Robert M. Wallace (Cambridge, Mass.: MIT Press, 1983), 4; first published in German in 1966 under the title *Die Legitimität der Neuzeit.*

3. As Cummings has argued, the history of aesthetics and aesthetic objects is also bound up with the problem of secularization; perhaps that is why the model persists differently in fields of study that take such object and practices as their primary focus (*Mortal Thoughts*, 8–10).

4. See Giorgio Agamben, "In Praise of Profanation," in *Profanations*, trans. Jeff Fort (New York: Zone Books, 2007), discussed in William N. West, "Humanism and the Resistance to Theology," in *The Return of Theory in Early Modern Studies*, ed. Paul Cefalu and Bryan Reynolds (New York: Palgrave Macmillan, 2011) 167–91.

5. Ken Jackson and Arthur F. Marotti, *Shakespeare and Religion: Early Modern and Postmodern Perspectives* (Notre Dame, Ind.: University of Notre Dame Press, 2011), 1–21. This develops their discussion in "The Turn to Religion in Early Modern Studies," their introduction to a special issue of *Criticism* 46 (2004): 167–90.

6. Julia Reinhard Lupton, "The Religious Turn (to Theory) in Shakespeare Studies," *English Language Notes* 44 (2006): 145–49; quoted in Jackson and Marotti, *Shakespeare and Religion*, 3.

7. Anthony B. Dawson, "Claudius at Prayer," in *Religion and Drama in Early Modern England: The Performance of Religion on the Renaissance Stage*, ed. Jane Hwang Degenhardt and Elizabeth Williamson (Burlington, Vt.: Ashgate Publishing, 2011), 235.

8. Ian Hunter, "The History of Theory," *Critical Inquiry* 44 (2006): 78–112, sees "theory" as it was practiced in the second half of the twentieth century as a purely secular exploration of the problem of the irruption of alterity.

9. David Scott Kastan, *A Will to Believe: Shakespeare and Religion* (New York: Oxford University Press, 2014), 6. Kastan's forceful statement is part of an argument that Shakespeare is worldly, but of a world that depends heavily but not exclusively on religious thinking to make sense of itself.

10. Elizabeth's proclamation of May 16, 1559, required the licensing of plays for performance and included the charge that "none . . . be played wherein either matters of religion or of the governance of the estate of the commonwealth shall be handled or treated" (quoted in Tanya Pollard, ed., *Shakespeare's Theater: A Sourcebook* [Malden, Mass.: Blackwell Publishing, 2004], 303). This of course does not mean that the plays were neither religious nor political in wider senses, only that they were not generally recognized as intervening in religious or political debates.

11. Carl Schmitt, *Political Theology: Four Chapters on the Concept of Sovereignty*, trans. George Schwab (Chicago: University of Chicago Press, 1985), 36; first published in German in 1922 under the title *Politische Theologie*.

12. Blumenberg, *Legitimacy*, 104.

13. Anthony Dawson has subtly traced the specific secularity of early modern playing, including its borrowing and lendings of religious forms; see Anthony B. Dawson and Paul Yachnin, *The Culture of Playgoing in Shakespeare's England: A Collaborative Debate* (Cambridge: Cambridge University Press, 2001); Anthony B. Dawson, "Shakespeare and Secular Performance," in *Shakespeare and the Cultures of Performance*, ed. Paul Yachnin and Patricia Badir (Aldershot, Hampshire, UK: Ashgate Publishing, 2008), 83–97; and Anthony B. Dawson, "The Secular Theatre," in *Shakespeare and Religious Change*, ed. Kenneth J. E.

Graham and Philip D. Collington (Houndmills, Basingstoke, UK: Palgrave Macmillan, 2009), 238–60.

14. Taylor makes a similar claim that a theory of immanence does not require a humanism, although these are often linked.

15. Blumenberg, *Legitimacy*, 48.

16. *Die fröhliche Wissenschaft*, Aphorism 108: "Gott ist todt: aber so wie die Art der Menschen ist, wird es vielleicht noch Jahrtausende lang Höhlen geben, in denen man seinen Schatten zeigt.—Und wir—wir müssen auch noch seinen Schatten besiegen!" Cummings, *Mortal Thoughts*, 5–6, discusses a different appearance of the phrase in *Fröhliche Wissenschaft*, §125. It also appears at §343 and in *Also sprach Zarathustra*. See Lacan's comment that God is not (safely) dead but hazardously Unconscious; *The Four Fundamental Concepts of Psychoanalysis*, trans. Alan Sheridan (New York: Norton, 1978), 27, 59.

17. Kahn, "Introduction," 1.

18. From, respectively, Lewis and Short's *Latin Dictionary*; Pokorny, *Indogermanisches Wörterbuch* (the first three senses); and Varro, *De lingua latina*, 6.11.

19. Censorinus, *De die natali*, XVII. I have also referred to the articles on *saeculum* in *Der neue Pauly* and William Smith, *A Dictionary of Greek and Roman Antiquities* (London: Murray, 1875).

20. Eric Hayot, *On Literary Worlds* (Oxford: Oxford University Press, 2012), 53, mentions this etymology. The *OED* confirms it and notes the use of "world" and cognates to translate *saeculum*; s.v. "world."

21. On distinguishing "world" and "earth," see Hannah Arendt, *The Human Condition* (Chicago: University of Chicago Press, 1958), 134. Arendt also distinguishes "secular" from "worldly," although clearly she is thinking of secularity in terms of the secularization hypothesis: modernity did not gain this world when it lost the other world of religion; modern secularism loses both worlds in a fever of introspection (254, 320). Edward Said uses both "secular" and "worldly," apparently interchangeably; see *Humanism and Democratic Criticism* (New York: Columbia University Press, 2004), 61, where he clarifies that "secular" is particularly concerned with time and history and "worldly" with a real world of experience. But these concepts are in practice for Said nearly fungible.

22. "Another world" as an afterlife is attested in Old English, often as a "world to come" (*OED*, s.v. "world"); "other world" is also attested in Old English (*OED*, s.v. "other world"). Miles Coverdale uses "better world" in *A goodly treatise of faith, hope, and charite* (Southwark: James Nicholson, 1537); the earthly "new world" appears in English in 1549 (*OED*), and it is the title, in Latin, of Amerigo Vespucci's 1503 pamphlet *Mundus Novus*.

23. The first proposition of the *Tractatus Logico-Philosophicus*.

24. Stathis Gourgouris, *Lessons in Secular Criticism* (New York: Fordham University Press, 2013), 73.

25. Arendt, *Human Condition*, 55.

26. This association is noted, e.g., in Cummings, *Mortal Thoughts*.

27. Du Cange, *Glossarium infimae et mediae latinitatis*, s.v. *saecularis*.

28. Erich Auerbach, *Dante als Dichter der irdischen Welt* (Berlin: de Gruyter, 2001). The word that is translated in the published English title as "Secular" is a third term, *irdisch*, that Auerbach translated into English as "earthly." For Auerbach's translation, see James I. Porter's introduction to *Selected Essays of Erich*

Auerbach, trans. Jane O. Newman (Princeton, N.J.: Princeton University Press, 2014), xxi, as well as the lengthier discussion of what Auerbach meant by this braid of terms, xvii–xxvi.

29. West, "Humanism," where I cite Agamben, "every separation . . . contains or preserves within itself a religious core" (74), and Régis Debray's still more capacious claim that "the work of organization is by its very nature 'religious,'" where "organization" assumes partition and division as a necessary antecedent (quoted in Graham Hammill and Julia Reinhard Lupton, "Sovereigns, Citizens, and Saints: Political Theology and Renaissance Literature," *Religion and Literature* 38, no. 3 [Autumn 2006]: 3).

30. See Said's introduction and conclusion to *The World, the Text*; he develops his argument in *Humanism and Democratic Criticism*. As Gourgouris observes, Said never offered a definition of secular criticism, preferring to exemplify it—perhaps in keeping with its antireductive stance.

31. Said, *Humanism and Democratic Criticism*, 48.

32. *Paradiso*, 33.85–90. My discussion is influenced here by John Ahern, "Binding the Book: Hermeneutics and Manuscript Production in *Paradiso* 33," *PMLA* 87, no. 5 (October 1982): 800–809.

33. Arendt, *Human Condition*, 178.

34. Arendt, *Human Condition*, 57.

35. Said, "Introduction," 16–20. On the recurrent conflation of secularism and individualism in accounts of modernity, see Cummings, *Mortal Thoughts*.

36. Erich Auerbach, *Mimesis: The Representation of Reality in Western Literature*, trans. Willard R. Trask (Princeton, N.J.: Princeton University Press, 1946), 327; first published in German in 1946 under the title *Mimesis: Dargestellte Wirklichkeit in der abendländischen Literatur*.

37. Auerbach, *Mimesis*, 327.

38. In a question of human sacrifice, Plutarch asks how Romans make this distinction, while acknowledging that they did; while the gods did not accept human sacrifices, human lives could be offered to the spirits of the mortal dead (question 83). This same question is noted by Gary Kuchar in "Decorum and the Politics of Ceremony in Shakespeare's *Titus Andronicus*," in Jackson and Marotti, *Shakespeare and Religion*, 46–78, 49–50, who sees it as a sign of Roman hypocrisy in the play.

39. *Metamorphoses* 1.150; *Odes* 1.22.1.

40. In Q1, these nouns are lowercase, while all other references to rape, murder, and revenge after Tamora declares to Titus "I am Revenge" are capitalized, suggesting their precipitation from actions into allegorical entities. Folio capitalizes these and all other occurrences.

41. See William N. West, "'But This Will Be a Mere Confusion': Real and Represented Confusions on the Elizabethan Stage," *Theatre Journal* 60, no. 2 (May 2008): 217–33. Gourgouris might see in this Kyd's play's difference from itself reproduced in Shakespeare's play as a difference from Kyd and a difference perceived between Titus and Tamora.

42. Crosse, *Vertues Commonwealth* (London: Thomas Creed, 1603), Q2r-v; I have modernized the spelling.

Secularity Meets Wonder Woman in *All's Well That Ends Well*

Kent Cartwright

One might doubt that secularization has completed itself historically, or ever could, since, as a reaction against sectarian assumptions and principles, secularism would seem always to be in conversation with religion.[1] If that is so, we might think of secularization as a movement along a bipolar continuum from religion toward worldliness: such a linear image would capture the sense that the secular and the religious are parts of a whole. But we might modify that image with a more dynamic one of the permeability and fluidity of these forces, the secular and religious washing into each other—overwhelming, mixing, or receding—the dominant position perhaps shifting, as the introduction to this volume so eloquently argues. In England, secularization supposedly began in the early modern period, and perhaps no theater piece captures the complex interplay between a religious worldview and an incipiently secular one better than Shakespeare's *All's Well That Ends Well* (ca. 1605). The play, especially in its treatment of wonder, negotiates precariously between the worldly and the spiritual, drifting toward the former but deeply invested in the latter, changing emphasis with the narrative currents. A comparison of *All's Well* with Counter-Reformation Italian comedy helps to put these qualities in relief.

As Brian Cummings observes, "Both in the past and in our own society, the secular and the religious, far from being incommensurate, intersect in creative and profound ways."[2] Nonetheless, in Elizabethan England, he argues, "all of life was religious," in the sense that religion defined "a way of life in the round" rather than a category that could be differentiated from other categories of life, such as the exclusively secular.[3] C. John Sommerville, although making an often-noted case for secularization in early modern England, refers approvingly to scholars who see the differentiation of the religious from the secular as developing throughout the course of the seventeenth century, but with traditional patterns of thought still in place circa 1600.[4] Likewise, Anthony Dawson, who views the early modern theater as "secular," still acknowledges that "religious ways of thinking and feeling saturated the whole period."[5] Although Cummings's claim for a religious "way of life in the round" has the ring of truth, it is hard to know what that means precisely. Some early modern activities must certainly have been experienced as more directly religious, or less so, than others. The New Science, of course, had already implanted the idea of natural systems that work according to mathematical principles, and even before that the Renaissance was heir to a long medieval debate about the relative distance between divine will and natural law.[6]

Regarding Shakespearean theater, Dawson has posed one of the most cited arguments that it was essentially secular.[7] He sees early modern drama as characterized by a heteroglossia (in Bakhtin's usage) of competing voices of different registers arriving from different perspectives (e.g., class and gender) that make any final didactic or authoritative message impossible. Drama is rife with unmediated and jockeying points of view. Shakespeare and his contemporaries, Dawson further argues, appropriate biblical or other religious allusions only to misconstrue them and to make them, as with other voices, subservient to the aesthetic design of the play—an essentially secularizing gesture. In a thoughtful rebuttal, Paul Stevens objects that Dawson's argument (along with Sommerville's) reflects an exaggerated emphasis on individualism in Protestantism (Stevens thus downplays the power of competing voices) and insists that "the early Reformation theater of Foxe and Bale," popular biblical drama in the commercial playhouse, and seventeenth-century works such as *Comus* give evidence that plenty of early modern drama could subsume polyphony to an overarching, even didactic, religious message.[8] He has a point. Yet pace Stevens, one might respond that polyphony occurs in late medieval morality plays, as in the struggle between carnival and Lent in *Mankind*, and that polyphony even features in John Bale's rigorously polemical plays.[9] Thus, one wants to acknowledge a general truth in Stevens's argument yet to resist it in particular applications, so that the generalization always admits of exceptions and the critical terrain remains uneven. To complicate the matter further, the polyphony of voices in Shakespeare can sometimes be those of different confessional positions—the ghost of Hamlet's father, for example, talks of the Catholic doctrine of purgatory, while Hamlet expresses views closer to those of Protestant reformers—so that a specific play's heteroglossia might be itself fundamentally religious.[10] Thus, on the one hand Dawson's position can be qualified, and, on the other, Stevens does not rebut it entirely. "The degree to which" Shakespeare can be "characterized as a religious playwright remains," as David Loewenstein and Michael Witmore declare, "subject to debate" (3).

As the views of Dawson and Stevens suggest, at stake in the debate about secularization is an understanding of the nature of Shakespearean drama, including how any message in a play fractures or coheres according to the play's forms of discourse, how its aesthetic structure and intentions override or reinforce religious effects, and even how individualism is valued. Thus, the claims for religiousness or secularity might be very different from play to play. While both Nathaniel Woodes's *The Conflict of Conscience* (1581) and Marlowe's *Doctor Faustus* (1592?), for example, may reflect the paradoxes of Calvinist theology, *The Conflict of Conscience*'s ambivalence is far more grounded in a confessional dilemma than is the existential ambiguity of *Doctor Faustus*.[11] Although the religious/secular debate remains difficult to arbitrate on a macro level, it can be vibrantly interesting at the level of the individual drama, and comparisons can be revealing.

In *All's Well That Ends Well*, the tension between the spiritual and the worldly constitutes a central critical issue. These contrary pulls are often negotiated or elided in other of Shakespeare's comedies, but *All's Well* sets them at odds. As Helen Wilcox puts it, the remedies to the comedy's problems "may be perceived to derive from either heavenly or human intervention; both interpretations are signalled by the play."[12] *All's Well*'s denouement stops short of clarifying matters, for its abruptness makes the lovers' newfound amity and the redemptive prospects of "heavenly or human intervention" feel fragile. Indeed, while the ending achieves a hard-won resolution, it leaves room for skepticism and melancholy, the first the intellectual, the second the emotional mode of secularization. The play's action portrays the main character, Helen, as a "woman of wonder" (to use Louise George Clubb's evocative term), a character who possesses miraculous skills, who calls forth powerful emotional responses from others, and who apparently confirms values of personal virtue and faith in providence but whose confessional or doctrinal associations remain blurry and metaphorical.[13] Helen's wondrousness, we might note, appears to be not only of the spirit but also of the body. In that regard, *All's Well* embraces a Counter-Reformation sense of a preternatural female presence that inspires wonder, but it does so in a way that renders the character's wondrousness difficult to classify, multivalent, even contradictory. The effect becomes especially clear when *All's Well* is set against late sixteenth-century Italian comedies similarly experimenting with wonder.

Wonder can function as something of a baggy-monster term. Peter G. Platt helpfully distinguishes between an Aristotelian concept, in which wonder constitutes a pleasurable state of doubt that pushes one in the direction of factual or logical certainty (and thus dispels the activating wonder), and an incipient Renaissance notion in which wonder constitutes a state of rapt suspension in the face of what cannot be rationally or empirically explained.[14] The first version points toward secularity; the second toward religiosity. Wonder in Shakespeare's romances, Platt argues, favors the transcendental perspective, the experience of something that exists beyond rational explanation. Shakespeare's earlier comedies, it seems to me, often play with the difference between the Aristotelian concept and the rapturous view: in a play such as *The Comedy of Errors*, for example, a rational authority figure, the Duke, interposes himself among the squabbling and misinformed parties in order to sort out the evidentiary truth, but in *Errors*, rationality can never fully dispel the aura of quasi-religious mystery that surrounds the day's events.[15] We have it both ways—and thus Shakespearean comedy offers a useful arena for exploring these values.

The accommodations of early Shakespearean comedy, however, yield to the internal conflicts of *All's Well That Ends Well*, for the play's almost self-conscious discourse of wonder amounts to a struggle between wonder's quotidian version and its spiritual one. That struggle results not in a Catholic rhapsodizing of the transcendent, as happens with the woman of wonder of late sixteenth-century Italian comedy, but in a difficult secularizing of wonder. The spiritual dimension of wonder is acknowledged and claimed in *All's Well*, but it carries a whiff of nostalgia. Meanwhile the experience of bodily, especially sexual, existence gains prominence. For the purposes of this essay, I would treat *All's Well* as differentiating the claims of the body (i.e., of the Pauline natural man) from the claims of the spirit (of the Pauline new man), as if they were demarcating the separate domains of the secular and the religious rather than expressing what Cummings calls "a way of life in the round."[16] Of course, the opposition between godliness, on the one hand, and the world, the flesh, and the devil, on the other, certainly can arise within a religious worldview (as it does in late medieval morality plays). Yet in *All's Well* those terrains are becoming distinct: libidinal claims seem to fall outside the province of confessional claims (at least in the Clown's tone-setting view), and Helen's behavior reflects that divergence when she actively repudiates her love obsession over Bertram by going on a pilgrimage (although it will give way, in turn, to a more worldly quest).

All's Well, that is, showcases the tension between "the sacralizing and secularizing impulses within texts."[17] In the first act, Helen declares a kind of crypto-Catholic "can-do" attitude in endeavoring to win Bertram:

Our remedies oft in ourselves do lie
Which we ascribe to heaven. The fated sky
Gives us free scope, only doth backward pull
Our slow designs when we ourselves are dull. (1.1.218–21)[18]

Heaven favors the bold, and malleable fate gives way to human initiative—hardly the kind of sentiments one would expect to read in, for example, the writings of the Puritan apologist William Perkins. Helen does not sound like a Calvinist (especially before the age in which Protestantism made the world safe for capitalism).[19] People fail at new and seemingly "impossible . . . attempts," she continues, because they do not imagine or believe that those undertakings can be accomplished (226). In her own attempt, Helen intuits the support of a "power" that causes her love to "mount" and to reach for the "bright particular star" that is Bertram (222, 88). The immediate context of her remark suggests that the "power" she has in mind is divine, but her sense of that force is posed as a question: "What power is it . . . ?" (222).

The answer could turn out to be a power more earthly than heavenly, as Helen's conversation with Parolles suggests. "How might one do," Helen asks Parolles, to lose one's virginity "to her own liking" (152–53).[20] The play's sequence of scenes puts Helen's desire to win Bertram in parallel with the Clown's desire to take a wife: "I think I shall never have the blessing of God till I have issue o' my body" (1.3.24–25). But the Clown's invocation of God is immediately rendered ironic, for he adds, "I am driven on by the flesh, and he must needs go that the devil drives" (29–30). The Clown develops that thinking further, for, in a suggestive comment, he explicitly separates confessional ideology from the affairs of the body—in this case, cuckoldry: "For young Chairbonne the puritan and old Poisson the papist, howsome'er their hearts are severed in religion, their heads are both one: they may jowl horns together like any deer i'th' herd" (52–55). Some matters, the Clown makes clear, render the era's confessional distinctions and boundaries irrelevant; certain aspects of natural man simply follow their natural course and defy religious categories.

For its part, Helen's wondrousness occurs as sometimes of the body and others more divine. The difficulty of finding a purchase is compounded by her famously elusive character. Various critics have commented on Helen's changeable taffeta identity, which, in the first half of the play, vacillates between a worldly self-assertion and a spiritualized self-effacement. She creates and re-creates herself in response to others. To be saved from despair and called into action in the first two acts, says Alexander Leggatt,

Helen "needs to be teased, as she is by Parolles . . . ; challenged, as she is by the Countess; insulted, as she is by the King."[21] Helen's sense of self appears to change according to social situation and influence, while her motives are subject to progressive revelation or reformulation—or they are made opaque. As Susan Snyder points out, the play as it advances tends to "decharacterize" Helen (i.e., to render her motives unknowable), empowering contradictory views of her identity.[22] One example is Helen's unexplained decision in Florence to abandon her pilgrimage, along with its implied self-critique of her previous behavior, and to undertake a new plot to win Bertram. Similarly, the periodic celebration of Helen's inherent goodness by numerous credible characters intermittently refocuses the audience's view of her from a subject to an object—an "ideologically acceptable" one, even perhaps "a channel of heavenly grace."[23] Helen's opacity makes the source of her power as divine or secular a matter of mystification (and, in this respect, she contrasts strikingly with comparable wondrous women in late cinquecento Italian comedy).

We can gain perspective by considering how wonder itself plays out in *All's Well*. How do characters understand Helen's wondrousness and the secular or spiritual orientation that it might imply? Helen possesses a formidable goodness that earns admiration, but her magnetism compels characters to scrutinize her physical responses, her body, in a way that makes her appear something more, as if touched with heavenly grace. "I have hopes of her good that her education promises," says the Countess; "She derives her honesty and achieves her goodness" (1.1.39–40, 44–45).[24] Helen, that is, possesses a core of integrity, refined into virtue by education. From that modest opening, the sense of Helen's affective power grows, for a few scenes later the Countess adds that Helen "herself without other advantage may lawfully make title to as much love as she finds" (1.3.102–3). Helen's virtues transcend the values of property or finances ("advantage" is glossed as monetary interest) and lawfully entitle her to "love," of which she is owed "more . . . than is paid" (104). When the Steward reveals having overheard Helen's exclamations of love for Bertram, "delivered in most bitter touch of sorrow" (117), the Countess's compassionate support is instant and unequivocal (see 128–35): "Her eye is sick on't, I observe her now" (136). Indeed, the Countess expresses a keen attunement to Helen's bodily passions, to the way words "strive upon [her] pulse," to her sudden paleness, "salt tears," and blushing "cheeks" (169, 172, 176). She seeks to see into "the mystery of [Helen's] loneliness" (171) to infer its cause.[25] Helen's obvious passion and her obstinate reserve, her "mystery," call forth the Countess's engagement, as if Helen possessed some heightened or extraordinary quality that demands response.

In her scene of meeting with the King, Helen becomes linked directly with "wonder." Lafeu is brimming with enthusiasm for her as "a medicine / That's able to breathe life into a stone" (2.1.70–71). The King suffers from a physical malady, but Lafeu's image evokes multiple associations, including resurrection from a stony tomb. Yet Helen's ability to "araise King Pépin" or to give "Charlemagne a pen in 's hand," enabling him to "write to her a love-line" (74–76), depicts the maiden unequivocally as sexually arousing.[26] Moments later Lafeu refers to himself as "Crissid's uncle," and the King, who notices Helen's beauty ("fair one" [97]), declines Helen's ministrations by declaring that he will not "prostitute" his "malady" (95, 119). Helen herself says that she would "venture" being accused of "a strumpet's boldness" to help the King (168–69), while her healing will have the effect of making him "lust[y]" (2.3.26; cf. 42), so that he might find a "maid" toothsome again (see 2.3.42–44). While Helen's energetic passion had suggested an evocative sublimity for the Countess, Lafeu and the King respond to Helen's beauty and vigor as a matter of sexual allure.

But, rather differently, Lafeu also declares himself "amazed" by "her sex, her years, profession, / Wisdom, and constancy" (2.1.81–82). The King takes up Lafeu's tone and speaks of her as an "admiration" on whom he will spend his own "wonder" (86–87; the first instance of "wonder" in the play). When, taunted by the King, Helen wells up in response, she invokes distinctly religious imagery: "Holy writ in babes hath judgement shown"; "miracles" (136, 139). She now represents herself as "inspirèd merit" offering "the help of heaven" (146, 150), and the King hears in her mild voice the "powerful sound" of "some blessèd spirit" (174, 173), as if her effect had transformed before his very eyes and ears. Her influence on him is strongly visceral, while he wonders if the cause is divine. Helen's willingness to risk the traducing of her "maiden's name" and to suffer death under the "vilest torture" if she fails (170, 172) constitute a radical denial of the claims of femininity and of the body; that denial has the air of courting quasi-religious martyrdom. Yet her venturing of her life is so extreme that it guarantees her entitlement to the King's gift of her husband of choice, and it now turns her earlier hyperbole—"There is no living, none, / If Bertram be away" (86–87)—into a deadly serious statement. Lafeu, echoing the King, sees in Helen something like Counter-Reformation evidence against the Protestant belief that "miracles are past" (2.3.1).

Helen's ability to arouse the King and Lafeu shifts itself between the sexual and the metaphysical. When challenged by the King as a quack physician, Helen suddenly responds with a new "certainty and confidence"

(2.1.167; see also 157), takes on a vividness of presence (as she had before the Countess), and rises in speech with the incantatory power of chant: "The greatest grace lending grace . . ." (see 158–66). Snyder observes that this poetic speech of exalted allusions, rhymed lines, and parallel clauses has been, in some modern productions, delivered with such hallucinatory effect that "spectators sometimes speak of *seeing* the King's cure, which in fact takes place off-stage" (see Snyder's commentary note at 2.1.158–66). Indeed, the play may intend to create the theatrical illusion that Helen charms away the King's malady with her vigorous and sensual charisma, even before she administers her heavenly medicines. Although *All's Well* has put the claims of the body and of human intervention in tension with those of the spirit and divine intervention, and although Helen seems sometimes erotic and sometimes numinous, the effects of sexuality and the effects of transcendence, at the crucial moment, become indistinguishable from one another in the consuming experience of wonder.[27] We cannot tell sexiness from godliness.

From here, however, something happens to the idea of wonder. To be sure, Helen never forfeits her power to attract others and inspire admiration; her charm sways the First Lord, Diana, and the Widow. Nonetheless, as the play progresses, the overt celebrations of Helen as a woman of wonder tend to occur when she is recollected as dead. The last scene offers the most notable example. The King wants to bury the memory of Helen like an "incensing relic" (5.3.25), like a Catholic devotional object that incites painful memories but also exudes a holy perfume. The perfume of an "incensing relic" bespeaks a divine presence that hovers on earth and bridges the gap between the temporal and the spiritual.[28] Helen is distilled here into her nonsexual numinous mystery, the two aspects of her wonder separated. Between those nostalgic reminiscences and Helen's actual return, however, a heteroglossic tangle of accusations, squabbling, anger, humiliation, folk riddling, and exasperation intervenes, aimed largely and successfully at achieving the real-world humiliation of Bertram. The spiritualizing of Helen is well over by the time she returns from the dead in the denouement, although it is the play's most wondrous moment and inevitably charged with religious valence. Helen in the end is far too proactive, morally relativistic, and earthy to be a true Counter-Reformation woman of wonder. Yet Shakespeare seems to want to accomplish something nonetheless magical: to wash this opportunistic, secular heroine in the authentic glow of "incensing relics." If Helen stands for a new kind of female figure, then the play may be a form of Shakespearean blessing. Yet of course, nothing is ever quite that simple or clear, as the hurried form of the ending suggests.

Some perspective on the puzzle of Helen's wondrousness can be found by comparing her with two female characters from Italian comedies of the second half of the sixteenth century: Carizia in Giambattista Della Porta's *Gli Duoi Fratelli Rivali* (*The Two Rival Brothers*), circa 1590, and Drusilla in Girolamo Bargagli's *La Pellegrina* (*The Female Pilgrim*), circa 1568. These plays reflect a late cinquecento resurgence of Counter-Reformation sentiment. That development aimed to reinforce the clarity of Catholic faith by renewing emphasis on Providential design, personal free will, and the individual's intimate, even ecstatic, relationship with God, as seen in the writings of Saint Theresa of Ávila and Saint John of the Cross. Louise George Clubb, in her influential discussion, compares Carizia and Drusilla, as embodiments of Counter-Reformation values, to Helen from *All's Well* and to Isabella from *Measure for Measure* (Clubb's argument is that Italian conventions in drama influenced Shakespeare's playwriting).[29] In these instances, the female inamorata of earlier Italian comedy has transmuted into a figure who "functions as a vehicle for [an] idea" (Clubb 67), but not as an allegory. The wonder woman shows "remarkable intrinsic worth" and assumes "an extra-fabular reality" as a "thing enskied and sainted" (68). Carizia, in *The Two Rival Brothers*, for example, displays a self-effacing virtuousness and a generosity and forgiveness towards others that seem to draw the favor of Providence.[30] Her beloved, Don Ignazio, celebrates her "air of majesty and of wondrousness"; "she made beautiful beauty itself" (1.1, p. 59).[31] Carizia is "so dazzling a spectacle of beauty" that, in a public appearance, she has "ravished . . . the eyes and hearts of all observers"; "tongues fell silent, spirits hung suspended . . . everyone gazed and was amazed at an unheard-of loveliness" (1.1, p. 59). This is beauty made unearthly, evoking rapture. The play contains much more of such awed language towards Carizia, who appears only twice (in 2.3 and 5.4) and who expresses herself reasonably and modestly (she calls herself a "poor creature" who "live[s] humbly in [her] station" [2.3, p. 107]), and who behaves with a disarming sincerity. Like Helen (and Hero in *Much Ado About Nothing*), Carizia suffers humiliating rejection, in this instance from Don Ignazio (who has been cruelly lied to), seems to die heartbroken, but returns at the end as if from the grave—more authorizing of her wondrousness—to forgive those who have attempted to destroy her. Although it contains a variety of voices, *The Two Rival Brothers* is a play where heteroglossia certainly does not displace the overarching religious message.

The true lover Don Ignazio may beatify Carizia, but his malevolent brother, Don Flaminio, strives to conquer her in order to serve his lust: "The more that chastity of hers makes me suffer, the more it makes me love her" (1.2, p. 69). "I want to make every effort to induce her to take me as her lover," he declares; "I am determined not to live without her, or," he adds for good measure, "her sister" (2.9, p. 137). When Flaminio hears that Carizia is betrothed to Ignazio, he becomes frantic with jealousy and upends the prospective wedding much in the destructive manner of Don John's plot against Claudio and Hero in *Much Ado About Nothing*. Della Porta emphatically distinguishes the man who seeks Carizia to satisfy his carnal appetite from the man who pursues her as a figure of divine beauty. Don Ignazio's ennobled love affords him a vision of Carizia's wondrousness that his brother's frenzied obsession can never achieve.

Della Porta's approach to the woman of wonder differs decisively from that of Shakespeare. Shakespeare, instead of separating lust and adoration into different suitors, combines and mixes those responses early in the play, within both Lafeu and the King, so that the effects of lust and adoration are difficult to distinguish from each other. Even when Helen is praised as divine, furthermore, the language never reaches the level of florid rhetorical exultation that typifies late Renaissance Italian comedy. In *The Two Rival Brothers*, wonder occurs as ecstatic and quasi-religious; in *All's Well That Ends Well*, wonder is as likely to be secular as it is spiritual.

Drusilla, the pilgrim of Bargagli's *La Pellegrina*, "bears a strong generic resemblance to Helena," argues Clubb (77). Drusilla, in disguise, arrives in Pisa putatively as a pilgrim but secretly in search of Lucrezio, whom she had clandestinely married in Spain three years earlier but who apparently has forsaken her and become engaged to another woman. Like Bertram misinformed about Helen's condition, Lucrezio believes that Drusilla has died. For her part, Drusilla demonstrates a self-sacrificial humbleness in her willingness to give up Lucrezio when she believes that he loves another woman, and, in her disguise as a pilgrim, she even undertakes to help Lucrezio ("I wish nothing better than to place myself at your service" [2.7, p. 86])[32]. Along with exercising exemplary self-effacement, Drusilla stands as a model of female constancy in her devotion to Lucrezio, as well as of chastity in her prior refusal even to kiss Lucrezio before their marriage was publicly acknowledged. Her sexual purity is contrasted with the illicit sexual indulgence of the unmarried Lepida, who has become pregnant by her tutor, even though she is betrothed elsewhere. Much of the play's comic action revolves around Lepida's stratagems to hide her condition and avoid forced marriage (Lepida does possess the virtue of devotion to her beloved).[33] The two female characters intersect when Drusilla is called upon to diagnose Lepida's presumed madness (a metaphor for her behavior).

Like Helen, Drusilla exhibits special medical skills, and other characters increasingly seek her advice. In doing so, they become charmed by her spiritual radiance, for Drusilla, again like Helen, has the power of attracting people, of commanding their attention, and of inspiring their affection. Lucrezio, although failing to recognize Drusilla in her disguise, is nonetheless awed by her "noble aspect," her "noble presence," and her "kindness of heart" (2.7, p. 84). Even the hard-nosed and randy female innkeeper, Violante, calls Drusilla "saintly" and "a truly kind person" (3.2, p. 90). Likewise the nurse, Giglietta, calls Drusilla a "kind soul" and recounts her "really genuine" sigh denoting love, which, Giglietta insists to Violante, reflects Drusilla's devotion to "spiritual matters" rather than to those of the flesh (3.7, p. 104). Drusilla, argues Clubb, is not only "nunlike" but also "active and articulate . . . dispensing wisdom, blessing, and scrupulous example" and possessing "a saintly Counter-Reformation rigor" (78). She is "a thing apart . . . a combination of enterprising independence with moral and intellectual superiority," qualities that derive from "the *commedia grave* figure of the woman as an embodiment of spiritual values" (79).

Drusilla's character and her story line overlap with those of Helen. Helen, shamed to think that she has driven Bertram into the perils of war and caused his resolution never to return home while she is there, steals away from Roussillon for a self-mortifying pilgrimage to Saint James Compostela. On her way, she arrives at Florence, but remains there when she discovers Bertram's presence; this incidental convergence contrasts with Drusilla's pilgrimage, which stops off intentionally in Siena, where Drusilla hopes to find Lucrezio.[34]

The contrast between these two parallel narratives sharpens especially in relation to sex. Helen pursues Bertram with the kind of trick, or *beffa*, that was typical of earlier, decidedly farcical and secular Italian comedy, yet here the deception is turned to serious purposes. Helen's bed-trick plot emerges as full-blown, without any prior revelation to the audience of her motives or intentions. She must overcome the ethical resistance of the Widow, who fears the "staining" of her "reputation" (3.7.7–8). Helen persuades her by bribing her with a purse of gold: "Let me buy your friendly help" (15). She will later pile on more money. Helen's stratagem has the effect of encouraging Bertram to attempt adultery and to betray his family heritage by forfeiting the ring passed down from father to son in "some four or five descents" (24). Rings, of course, symbolize female sexuality.[35] Helen avoids delving too closely into the ethics of her action by calling it "lawful" (30, 45, 46): "Wicked meaning in a lawful deed, / And lawful meaning in a wicked act, / Where both not sin, and yet a sinful fact" (45–47). We have thus entered into the domain of worldly, secular compromise, where good ends are claimed to justify unethical means, where succeeding necessitates the pragmatic moral casuistry of "all's well that ends well." Whatever the truth of that claim, Helen's moral vision is diametrically opposed to that of Drusilla, who never asserts herself or reveals herself to Lucrezio as long as she believes that he loves another, her self-abnegation bespeaking her devotion. That Drusilla could undertake a bed trick, as Helen does, is unimaginable.

In *The Female Pilgrim*, the character who engages in duplicitous sex, Lepida, is sharply distinguished from the truly nunlike Drusilla. Drusilla's eventual reuniting with Lucrezio—who has always been in love with her—expresses the triumph of her irresistible and saintly character and patient devotion, while Helen's success is based pragmatically on sex. In the climax of both *The Female Pilgrim* and *All's Well*, the heroines appear to the beloved as if wondrously returned from the dead, but only Helen returns pregnant. *The Female Pilgrim* replays the difference between *All's Well* and *The Two Rival Brothers*, for Drusilla, like Carizia, compels a profoundly spiritualized desire, while, in contrast, sexuality is addressed through lesser characters. Sex in the two Italian comedies occurs as secular and worldly, concupiscent; it stands in opposition to true, chaste religiosity, which triumphs ecstatically. In *All's Well*, as noted, religion and sexuality are presumably allotted discrete domains, only to have their effects made indistinguishable. Wonder in Italian *commedia grave* breathes of heavenly ether, but in *All's Well* it remains ultimately bound up with the secularized body and its carnal claims. *All's Well*'s secularizing of wonder—the relentless encroachment of the secular upon the transcendent aspect of wonder—becomes not only an effect but also a theme, standing in opposition to the Italian comedies' Counter-Reformation sacralizing of wonder. Clubb makes a significant contribution in identifying the woman-of-wonder figure and its late sixteenth-century religious context. Yet despite Clubb's likening of these characters, Helen's wondrousness occurs as distinctly more worldly and compromised than that of her Italian counterparts.

The problem of wonder in *All's Well* comes into relief in the strange aesthetic dissatisfaction created by the play's ending. As *All's Well* pushes toward its close, Helen is decharacterized, sanctified, and made an object of nostalgic and sentimental pathos. The First Lord describes her "austere sanctimony" in pilgrimaging and her death of "grief," so that "now she sings in heaven" (4.3.50–53).[36] The Countess speaks of "the death of the most virtuous gentlewoman that ever nature had praise for creating" (4.5.9–11). The King says, "We have lost a jewel" (5.3.1), and Lafeu recalls Helen's "astonish[ing]" beauty, her "captivat[ing]" words, and her "dear perfection" that subdued all hearts (see 5.3.15–19). Bertram, for his limited part, views Helen as "she . . . Since I have lost, have loved" (53–54), and the King in response consigns Helen regretfully to oblivion: "Our own love, waking, cries to see what's done, / . . . / Be this sweet Helen's knell, and now forget her" (65–67). Helen becomes an "incensing relic," fading in memory as from a lost and more miraculous world.

The play, however, restores Helen in its most powerful and affecting moment, when, believed dead, with eulogies long done, she enters the stage to the shock of all. "Is't real that I see?," asks the King; "No . . . but the shadow of a wife," responds Helen, who can come fully into being only when acknowledged by Bertram (306–7). But the ending is famously unsatisfying, and its religious potentiality proves impossible to realize fully. After the immediate consternation of the revelation, the play completes itself in just twenty-eight more lines, in which Bertram and Helen have one speech each, making up four lines of negotiation about the implications of the evidence for what Helen claims, with Bertram not even speaking directly to her: "BERTRAM If she . . . / HELEN If it appear . . ." (315–18). Of course, this emotionally truncated hurriedness is only the last of a series of dissatisfactions that the audience has already experienced. In the more than two hundred lines that precede Helen's entrance, Bertram has compounded lie upon dishonorable lie about how he received Helen's ring (the King begins to suspect him of murder) and about his relationship with Diana, whom he traduces as "a common gamester to the camp" (188). Even Parolles proves more honest than he. Furthermore, Diana, at first bathed in honest righteousness, has so extended the proceedings by her evasive and riddling answers that the King completely reverses his opinion: "Take her away. I do not like her now. / To prison with her" (280–81). And even as the truth unfolds, lurking in the background is the fact that Helen has satisfied the conditions of what was only a mock contract with Bertram, the terms of which were not meant literally, as Helen has taken them (see 311–14).

The ending of *All's Well* could hardly be more opposite in tone from that of *The Two Rival Brothers* or of *The Female Pilgrim*. Regarding *Pilgrim*, Richard Andrews notes the "refined emotional suffering" of the lovers throughout the play and the ending's "final almost orgasmic relief of tension when the false assumptions are removed."[37] Drusilla and Lucrezio have an extended, emotional denouement (5.7) of reunion, recognition, and explanation, saturated with enough sentiment to allow the spectators to enjoy the lovers' profound feelings vicariously:

> LUCREZIO: . . . Now I recognize you. My sweet Drusilla, my divine Drusilla, so you weren't dead?
> DRUSILLA: I was dead because I was deprived of you. . . .
> LUCREZIO: Drusilla, my only love! I wept and sighed so much for you! . . .
> . . . .
> LUCREZIO: I can't stop hugging you . . . (5.7, p. 145)

Helen, Carizia, and Drusilla all return from the dead, but only with the latter two are emotions allowed to dilate fully and completely.[38] Andrews notes that *The Female Pilgrim* focuses on "the close exploration of emotions with which the audience are to sympathize, rather than on intrigue or subversion," while *All's Well*, we might say, does the opposite, concentrating in the denouement on intrigue, subversion, and puzzlement rather than on depths of empathy-inducing feeling: emotions trapped in mind games rather than released into sublimity.[39]

In comedies, audience members (and readers) develop desires on behalf of characters. Comedy employs dramatic irony, sometimes called discrepant awareness—the superiority of the audience's knowledge of relevant details compared with that of the protagonists—so that the ending constitutes that occasion in which everyone's knowledge is brought into equivalence. In our empathy towards comic characters, we want them to know what we know.[40] With *All's Well*, the main protagonist who lacks understanding, and eventually information, is Bertram—less so Helen, who generally knows as much as we do.[41] (The business of dramatic irony is staged as a play within the play, in the subplot of Parolles and the drum, where it is as uncomfortable as it is amusing). Bertram, the King, and the Countess need to learn the essential truth about Helen, not only that she is not dead but also that she has fulfilled the technical requirements that Bertram had set; nonetheless, the process of getting at the truth through witnesses and accusations pushes the audience close to a disengagement of sympathy. Bertram's crudeness and protracted hypocrisy lower him further and further in our esteem; Diana's temporizing riddles turn tiresome; what remains of Helen is a ring. When she reappears, what we want for her, and what the play denies, is a form of protracted emotional acknowledgment and embrace of her by Bertram that reflects all that she has undergone to achieve reconciliation, an ending on which a future can be built, an ending, that is, on the elevated emotional level of the endings in *The Two Rival Brothers* and *The Female Pilgrim*. While the play has first increased and then finally dispelled the knowledge deficit, it has not resolved the emotional deficit. *All's Well* denies us not the evidence of Helen's wondrousness but the satisfaction of the feelings that go with it, which have been expended earlier in the nostalgic sanctifying of Helen as *dead*. The celebration of her wondrousness has been disassociated, to a significant degree, from her revivification. The last scene gives us wonder, metaphoric incense, but first disperses and then foreshortens its impact. It is as if the quasi-religious language of nostalgic wonder could be brought close, but not too close, to the circumstances of Helen's reanimation. Religion and secularity are bound to each other here, but separated by layers of gauze.

In relation to secularity and spirituality, the denouement of *All's Well* falls on the side of secularity, revealed especially when one contrasts it with the emotionally exalted, numinous endings of the two Italian analogue comedies. The play valorizes wonder but also makes it confusing, for it becomes associated incommensurately with sanctity, sex, nostalgia, and finally a rabbit-out-of-the-hat stage surprise. It is never allowed to be an expression of unadulterated religious transcendence, and it is not allowed at the close to become sufficient; we know that because we long for wonder (and without it may feel melancholy). That is not to say that *All's Well* is a failed comedy or a bad play; hardly so, for it continues to be produced with great success.[42] The comedy seems calculated to make the experience of wonder partially available and partially deferred; we are made to wish for more—more integration of past and present, nostalgia and reality, religion and secularity. By the conclusion, Helen is a revenant but not so much a Counter-Reformation female saint in the mode of Carizia and Drusilla. We have landed in the secular world of nonimmaculate pregnancies, implied contracts, transactional relations, withheld emotions, and ends-justified means, where the promise of wonder must be made good by smarts and superior intel. Yet there is something ambitious in Shakespeare's treatment of this admirable, enterprising, and flawed new woman. The playwright gives her quick-wittedness, along with the kind of assertive, even manipulative, freedom that would shatter the image of the nunlike Drusilla. Helen may be rendered opaque and made to play fairy-tale games, but the play is driven by her knowing realism. She arrives at the end flawed and earthy but trailing clouds of the ancient glory, the hint of incense, of something both here and not here, the reminder of a spiritual mystery that still adumbrates and gives value to the worldly. *All's Well* has a Counter-Reformation glow, but, as Dawson would argue, it has too little doctrinal authoritarianism and too many voices to be fundamentally religious. Nor is it wholly secular. Rather, secular action manages to proceed pragmatically but to retain a distant religious aura; it feels Aristotelian and paradoxically a bit rapturous. Helen, as the secularized wonder woman, offers to extend the possibilities of wonder itself.[43]

Notes

1. *The Oxford English Dictionary* defines "secularization" as "the conversion of an ecclesiastical or religious institution or its property to secular possession and use; the conversion of an ecclesiastical state or sovereignty to a lay one" (*n.* 1a); or, "The giving of a secular or non-sacred character or direction to (art, studies, etc.); the placing (of morals) on a secular basis" (*n.* 2); *The Oxford English Dictionary Online (OED)*, accessed by subscription. The *OED* defines "secular" as "belonging to the world and its affairs as distinguished from the church and religion" (*adj.* 2a). The final distinction between "religious" and "secular" may depend on the cultural practices and perceptions of a particular historical period.

2. Brian Cummings, *Mortal Thoughts: Religion, Secularity and Identity in Shakespeare and Early Modern Culture* (Oxford: Oxford University Press, 2013), 4–5; see also 1–18.

3. Brian Cummings, "Afterword," in *Shakespeare and Early Modern Religion*, ed. David Loewenstein and Michael Witmore (Cambridge: Cambridge University Press, 2013), 304.

4. C. John Sommerville, *The Secularization of Early Modern England: From Religious Culture to Religious Faith* (Oxford: Oxford University Press, 1992), 96; see also Sommerville's full discussion of secularization in the arts, 82–97.

5. Anthony B. Dawson, "The Secular Theater," in *Shakespeare and Religious Change*, ed. Kenneth J. E. Graham and Philip D. Collington (New York: Palgrave Macmillan, 2009), 238.

6. On that latter subject, see Kellie Robertson, *Nature Speaks: Medieval Literature and Aristotelian Philosophy* (Philadelphia: University of Pennsylvania Press, 2017).

7. See Dawson, "The Secular Theater"; see also Anthony B. Dawson, "Shakespeare and Secular Performance," in *Shakespeare and the Cultures of Performance*, ed. Paul Yachnin and Patricia Badir (Aldershot, Hants, UK: Ashgate Publishing, 2007), 83–97. See also Tom Bishop, "Othello in the Wilderness: How Did Shakespeare Use His Bible?," in Graham and Collington, *Shakespeare and Religious Change*, 196–214.

8. Paul Stevens, "*Hamlet*, *Henry VIII*, and the Question of Religion: A Post-Secular Perspective," in Loewenstein and Witmore, *Shakespeare and Early Modern Religion*, 236–41.

9. On medieval drama, see, for example, Anthony Gash, "Carnival Against Lent: The Ambivalence of Medieval Drama," in *Medieval Literature: Criticism, Ideology, and History*, ed. David Aers (New York: St. Martin's Press, 1986), 74–98. On Bale, see Katherine Steele Brokaw, *Staging Harmony: Music and Religious Change in Early English Drama* (Ithaca, N.Y.: Cornell University Press, 2016), 50–85. Sixteenth-century drama as a whole moves away from any overt, tidy moral or sectarian didacticism, partly from the influence of humanism; see Kent Cartwright, *Theatre and Humanism: English Drama in the Sixteenth Century* (Cambridge: Cambridge University Press, 1999).

10. See Loewenstein and Witmore's introduction to *Shakespeare and Early Modern Religion*, 1–19.

11. On the similarities between these two plays in terms of Calvinist theology, see David Bevington, "Christopher Marlowe's *Doctor Faustus* and Nathaniel Woodes's *The Conflict of Conscience*," in *The Oxford Handbook of Tudor*

Literature, 1485–1603, ed. Mike Pincombe and Cathy Shrank (Oxford: Oxford University Press, 2009), 704–17.

12. Helen Wilcox, "Shakespeare's Miracle Play? Religion in *All's Well That Ends Well*," in *All's Well, That Ends Well: New Critical Essays*, ed. Gary Waller (New York: Routledge, 2007), 143. Wilcox offers an excellent analysis of the play's basic ambivalence.

13. See Louise George Clubb, "Woman as Wonder: Theatergram of Italian and Shakespearean Comedy," in *Italian Drama in Shakespeare's Time* (New Haven, Conn.: Yale University Press, 1989), 65–89. Eric Nicholson, interestingly, places Helen in relation to divalike Renaissance actresses, especially in Italy: Shakespeare "assimilated the widespread continental European notion that female actors were extraordinary, enchanting, and even a touch superhuman" ("Helen, the Italianate Theatrical Wayfarer of *All's Well That Ends Well*," in *Shakespeare and the Italian Renaissance: Appropriation, Transformation, Opposition*, ed. Michele Marrapodi [Farnham, Surrey, UK: Ashgate Publishing, 2014], 172).

14. See Peter G. Platt, *Reason Diminished: Shakespeare and the Marvelous* (Lincoln: University of Nebraska Press, 1997), 1–18. T. G. Bishop emphasizes wonder as an intense emotional experience induced by a situation of undecidability or in-betweenness (*Shakespeare and the Theatre of Wonder* [Cambridge: Cambridge University Press, 1996], 1–41).

15. One can find the same device in subsequent Shakespearean comedies such as *A Midsummer Night's Dream* and in early Tudor comedies such as *Gammer Gurton's Needle* (ca. 1553).

16. "The natural man receiveth not the things of the Spirit of God . . . neither can they know *them*, because they are spiritually discerned" (1 Corinthians 2:14 [King James Version]). Paul suggests a religious view of life in which certain ways of being are excluded.

17. The phrase is borrowed from Bishop, "Othello in the Wilderness," 196.

18. This and subsequent citations refer to William Shakespeare, *All's Well That Ends Well*, ed. Susan Snyder (Oxford: Oxford University Press, 1994).

19. On the classic Catholic-Protestant debate over free will, see Ernst F. Winter, trans. and ed., *Erasmus–Luther: Discourse on Free Will* (New York: Continuum, 1989).

20. Thus, Helen's use of "mount" at 222 is open to multiple connotations.

21. Alexander Leggatt, "Introduction," in *All's Well That Ends Well*, ed. Russell Fraser (Cambridge: Cambridge University Press, 2003), 30.

22. See Snyder, *All's Well That Ends Well*, 39–40: "A crucial question of motivation is left in doubt when Shakespeare has Helen apparently announce a pilgrimage to Santiago de Compostela in Spain and then arrive in central Italy in the town where she knows Bertram to be."

23. Snyder, *All's Well That Ends Well*, 37. Snyder also wryly observes that critics who overidealize Helen may be practicing the same kind of sanctification that Helen does toward Bertram (37–38).

24. See Fraser, *All's Well That Ends Well*, for the editing of 1.1.39–41, which seems preferable to Snyder's version.

25. Helen encourages the image of her Viola-like, self-contradictory mysteriousness as she responds to the Countess, "O then give pity / To her . . . / That seeks not to find that her search implies, / But riddle-like lives sweetly where she

dies" (213–17), forcing the Countess to drag out of her the information about her plans.

26. Leggatt, "Introduction," says that "Shakespeare adds to Boccaccio a surprising, seemingly irrelevant, undercurrent of sexuality in Helen's curing of the King" (31), yet also that "another element in Helen's cure of the King . . . is the power of heaven" (32).

27. Wilcox notes, after the King's cure, Helen's statement, "Heaven hath through me restored the King to health" (2.3.65) and its paradoxical inconsistency with her earlier, "Our remedies oft in ourselves do lie / Which we ascribe to Heaven" ("Shakespeare's Miracle Play?," 142–43).

28. "Incensing" here has a secondary connotation, the inflaming of an individual with passion, especially anger, at Bertram's treatment of Helen and her demise (*OED*, s.v. "incense," v2 3a).

29. See Clubb, "Woman as Wonder." See also Michele Marrapodi, "The 'Woman as Wonder' Trope: From *Commedia Grave* to Shakespeare's *Pericles* and the Last Plays," in *Shakespeare and Renaissance Literary Theories* (Farnham, Surrey, UK: Ashgate, 2011), 175–99.

30. Clubb, "Woman as Wonder," 74–77.

31. Quoted, here and subsequently, from Giambattista Della Porta, *Gli Duoi Fratelli Rivali / The Two Rival Brothers*, trans. and ed. Louise George Clubb (Berkeley: University California Press, 1980). Page numbers are cited because the edition lacks line numbers.

32. References are to Girolamo Bargagli, *The Female Pilgrim (La Pellegrina)*, trans. Bruno Ferraro (Ottawa: Dovehouse Editions, 1988). As with *The Two Rival Brothers*, page numbers are cited because the edition lacks line numbers.

33. The play contains various comments, especially by lower-class characters, about the sexual infidelities and contrivances of women.

34. Although critics have noted that Florence is not on the way from France to Spain, nothing in the play beyond the dubious pilgrimage route gives evidence that Helen has followed Bertram to Florence intent on winning him back, although she does instantly seize the opportunity when it arises.

35. See Gordon Williams, *A Glossary of Shakespeare's Sexual Language* (London: Athlone, 1997), 260.

36. In the spirit of mystifying Helen, the audience never learns how the false rumor was spread of her arrival at Saint James and her subsequent death, nor how Helen herself seems to know that she is "supposed dead" (4.4.11).

37. Richard Andrews, *Scripts and Scenarios: The Performance of Comedy in Renaissance Italy* (Cambridge: Cambridge University Press, 1993), 227.

38. The same difference obtains with Shakespeare's source, William Painter's story of Giletta of Narbonne, in *The Palace of Pleasure*, translated from Boccaccio's *Decameron* (printed in Snyder, *All's Well That Ends Well*, 225–32): "The Count, knowing the things she had spoken to be true and perceiving her constant mind and good wit and the two fair young boys, to keep his promise made and to please his subjects and the ladies that made suit unto him to accept her from that time forth as his lawful wife and to honour her, abjected his obstinate rigour, causing her to rise up, and embraced and kissed her, acknowledging her again as his lawful wife" (232).

39. Andrews, *Scripts and Scenarios*, 228.

40. For a fascinating argument that dramatic irony in Elizabethan and Jacobean drama can reflect, and gain energy from, the desire of Protestants to know whether or not they are elect, see Claire Elizabeth McEachern, "Two Loves I Have: Of Comfort and Despair in Shakespearean Genre," *British Journal of Aesthetics* 54, no. 2 (April 2014): 191–211.

41. However, Helen never witnesses or is made to know of Bertram's embarrassingly dishonorable attempt to lie about the ring and Diana.

42. For a favorable discussion of the play from a theatrical point of view, see Gary Waller, "From 'the Unfortunate Comedy' to 'this Infinitely Fascinating Play': The Critical and Theatrical Emergence of *All's Well, That Ends Well*," in *All's Well, That Ends Well: New Critical Essays*, ed. Waller, 1–56.

43. One might speculate that a project of Shakespeare's comedies, especially when the late romances are included, is the charting and wary exploring of those numinous experiences, variations on wonder and wondering, that lie in the shifting ground between the quotidian and the religious.

Wooing Words

Secularizing Language and the Language of Secularism in *Much Ado About Nothing* and *Romeo and Juliet*

Tobias Döring

Hermeneutics is the art of reading, traditionally practiced and perpetuated to interpret scripture. In George Steiner's memorable words from *Real Presences*, an interpreter is "a decipherer and communicator of meanings. He is a translator between languages, between cultures and between performative conventions. He is, in essence, an executant, one who 'acts out' the material before him so as to give it intelligible life."[1] As suggested in these phrases with their threefold repetition of "between," hermeneutics is a way to cross or bridge a distance, some intervening space or obstacle that hampers the communication of meaning and so must be overcome. Without the gap, no need for hermeneutics would arise. Yet it is precisely this same interspace that makes interpretation a precarious and risky process, not easily predicted or controlled. For it is never really certain what meanings an interpreter deciphers and communicates. Translating between languages, between cultures, and between performative conventions does not always bring to life a fixed and given script, as Steiner's vision of the "executant" would suggest. Instead of reconfirming or reiterating a stable and familiar message, hermeneutic acts may also lead to doubts, uncertainties, and unforeseen results. This is why hermeneutics has historically also become allied to attempts at questioning the holiness—indeed the wholeness—of formerly inviolable texts.

Nineteenth-century philology provides a case in point. When David Friedrich Strauß, the German Protestant theologian and Hegelian philosopher, published his *Life of Jesus* in the 1830s, he scandalized the pious public by demonstrating simply the effects of careful reading. He subjected the Gospels to the kind of hermeneutic scrutiny first learned in classical philology a generation earlier with Friedrich August Wolf's

Prolegomena ad Homerum (1795),[2] which questioned both the textual integrity of the Homeric epics and the historical existence of a single writer as their originating author—just as Strauß's reading questioned the historical account the Gospels give us of the life and deeds of Jesus. His reasoning was grounded in the ever-growing distance between contemporary religious faith and the perpetuated texts on which it founds itself. As he argued in the introduction, the difference between then and now, between foundational monuments and current intellectual culture, between written records and contemporary critical consciousness could not remain without effect on Christian articles of faith and so would lead contemporaries, sooner or later, to put holy books in doubt.[3] That is to say, his hermeneutic criticism emphatically acknowledged the interpretable interspace and, rather than taking the scripts to be interpreted for granted, scrutinized their own condition. Should we therefore, by the force of such examples, postulate a close, perhaps even a necessary connection between hermeneutics and secularization?

According to the understanding suggested in the present volume, the meaning of "secular" cannot readily be fixed, determined, or debated unless we pay attention to the cultural transactions it enables or is subjected to—transactions, above all, with its antonym, "sacred."[4] These transactions are, in an important way, related to hermeneutic acts that are, in turn, largely shaped by the social actors who perform them. The secular, in this sense, is not something given, once and for all, but continues to be made and remade in specific circumstances by specific people and the cultural practices they share, including also practices of criticism.[5] *Das Leben Jesu, kritisch bearbeitet*, as the full title of Strauß's study reads in the original German, already emphasizes the philosophically critical approach he chose. In one of the most influential uses of the term for our time, Edward Said has described the secular as resulting from a particular critical activity, an effect of reading, a perspective taken or a choice made in current engagements with literature. What he called secular criticism emerges from a "critical consciousness" that is "a part of its actual social world and of the literal body that the consciousness inhabits," "steeped in the reality" and "in specific circumstances."[6] Exemplified by Erich Auerbach and his exile in 1940s Istanbul, this sort of criticism "deals with local and worldly situations," Said argued; it is "always situated," "skeptical, secular," and "reflectively open to its own failings."[7] That is to say, secular criticism begins by acknowledging the critic's own position vis-à-vis the texts he or she reads, especially the critic's constitutive *distance* from these texts—as in the case of Auerbach in Istanbul—before venturing toward their interpretation. In contrast then to Steiner's "real presences" in literature and the overt religious quality of hermeneutics Steiner seems to envisage by turning critics into authors' acolytes, Said qualifies literature and criticism in clearly worldly terms. In his rethinking, the secular emerges as a process of positioning and repositioning through interpretive acts. Its transaction lies in giving to critical articulations and ideas a local, worldly habitation.

I set out here to discuss such hermeneutical transactions by exploring some of the concrete verbal acts by which these transactions unfold. What Said calls the actual social world is constituted by the language that constructs and shapes this actuality—especially in the context of early modern theatrical performance, which in the age of Shakespeare relied not on elaborate stage design or illusionistic practices but on spoken words. What effects they may have when uttered on a public stage and how their utterance may implicate religious rites is the chief interest of my subsequent discussion. I focus on two short but celebrated scenes of verbal action in Shakespearean drama, one from comedy (*Much Ado About Nothing*) and the other from tragedy (*Romeo and Juliet*). In each case, the plot involves a friar—that is, an executant of religious rites—and an exchange of words meant to bring about some changes in the world; "doing things" with words, in J. L. Austin's sense.[8] The putative success, or failure, of these speech acts offers us some indication as to the cultural transactions they perform. Thus, the stage of Shakespearean theater may turn into a platform on which to test notions of the secular in relation to hermeneutics because the theater is always, in Said's sense, reflectively open to its own failings, especially to the fact of failing or void speech acts when performed on the stage.[9]

At this point, it is useful to recall Steiner's exact wording. In addition to what he calls a decipherer and communicator of meanings, the interpreter for him is also a performing actor who "acts out" a given script. In a curious hermeneutic twist, the phrasal verb "act out" introduces possibilities of feigning, fiction, and pretense, as with the imagined world the playhouse offers to spectators. One reason, arguably, to see early modern theater as secular lies precisely in acknowledging the "as if" of playacting, which places all the acts and actions we observe into a different frame: players on the stage may actually kiss, but they never actually marry, murder, mourn, or bury—all these are actions that an actor might play and that the playhouse represents, but only displaced into modes of would-be action. It is this "as if" that Shakespearean drama constantly invites us to appreciate—and critically acknowledge as a crucial gap—not least by means of such internal stage managers and metatheatrical figures as friars and their frequent scheming.

Anthony Dawson has explored such a connection between secularity and theatrical performance. He argues that Shakespeare's theater, "by orchestrating different languages and voices," has helped "to separate religious language from its ideological center, appropriating it for different uses; in doing so it reinforced the secular foundation on which it is built—its separateness from religious culture."[10] This separateness, we might add, becomes especially evident or prominent whenever what is being staged appears to be so close to a religious ritual that it might almost look like one. At such points it is crucial that we recognize, again following Dawson, "how different the religious content appears when it is transported onto the public stage,"[11] where it is juxtaposed with other kinds of language altogether—like marriage vows juxtaposed with jealousy in *Much Ado* or holy pilgrimage with sexual desire in *Romeo and Juliet*. In these contexts, religious content is repositioned in the framework of playing such that none of its speech acts can be sincere or serious anymore. So when ceremonial practices or sacred terms are thus recycled and reused for entertainment purposes, as I suggest they are in these two plays, we realize that the Shakespearean theater is not only a platform but also an agent of the secular: not simply showing but actively promoting early modern transformations of religious culture. The theater renders this form of secularity precisely by means of the interpretative acts it engenders: rather than simply reflecting a fixed or given secular idiom, the early modern playhouse takes a seemingly sacramental event and reinterprets it by staging it anew. The secularization happens in that very act of staging and appropriation.

For this reason, it is just these points where stage and church practice seem to converge that become so alluring and attractive to consider, especially in the fluid process of theatrical representation. It would be misleading to think of the secular as separated from all ritual procedure. The original context of the term, as a period or "age," was in fact closely associated with it, since "the succession of *saecula* was marked with ritual,"[12] as the editors of a recent volume on the philosophical and political dimensions of the secular explain: "Already in the ancient usage of *saeculum* there is reference to both the natural conditions of life and the civil institutions of ritual and calendar."[13] For this reason, if for no other, it is problematic to think of the secular simply as an absence, or reduction, of all things religious—what Charles Taylor critically refers to as "a subtraction story."[14] Secularism is not a neutral position, with no ideological import or importance of its own. Even the Weberian narrative of disenchantment, so often involved in general accounts of secularization, continues to rely on points of reference in some earlier religious culture.[15] But not only is the secular necessarily defined with reference to religion, the very notion of secularization, we should note, was originally introduced to describe a process *within* the medieval church, when members of the clergy departed from their religious order so as to take up office elsewhere and serve as priests in worldly, local parishes.[16] As Cummings and Simpson remark, the "very notion of 'secularity' itself, after all, turns out to be the product of long *religious* histories."[17] In this way, secularism cannot be taken, in any uncomplicated sense, as the opposite term to religion nor can any opposition between these two be taken simply for granted. In order to rethink the secular in the age of Shakespeare, therefore, we may have to rethink the entire concept.[18]

For this purpose, I begin with a look at my two key examples, before turning to broader secularization debates and some issues of language efficacy. The final section of the essay gauges, as we begin to rethink Shakespeare's secularism, what religious possibilities remain and what new ones are put forward.

In an influential reading of John Milton's *Lycidas*, Stanley Fish noted that the speaker of this poem demonstratively identifies the failures of just the tradition on which he wants to draw—in this case, pastoral elegy—so as to put himself in its place: "If, in some sense, he can do no better," Fish observed, "at least he is able to recognize a false surmise when he sees one."[19] The point refers to the conventional rites of mourning to which the poem's speaker summons "every flower that sad embroidery wears"[20] only to suggest that, in fact, no flower ever does wear sad embroideries, thus revealing all such supposed rites of natural mourning as "false":[21] the ritual gesture is performed appropriately, but its true import is no longer believed and so denounced as hollow. Following Fish's argument, we might question other ritual performances, too. What, for instance, about marriage vows: would we recognize a false nuptial when we saw one?

Historically, the answer to this question had some bearing on the process and debates of secularization, so it is remarkable to see marriage rites and their correct performance debated in one of Shakespeare's romantic comedies, *Much Ado About Nothing*. In the wedding scene, when Claudio and Hero stand before the Friar, Benedick makes just this point: "This looks not like a nuptial" (4.1.67),[22] he observes, commenting on the heated exchange of words between the infuriated bridegroom, the would-be bride, and her exasperated father. But what, in fact, allows for such an observation? No doubt, at this point in the scene it should be obvious even to the most casual observer that the proper ritual procedure befitting a wedding has been derailed. The ceremony to be performed hardly moves past its opening actions, and even these are cast into doubt.

At the outset, Leonato orders the Friar to "be brief" and just use what he calls "the plain form of marriage" (4.1.1–2)—that is, without preliminaries and ceremonial ado. The Friar follows suit and starts directly with the crucial question to the bridegroom, only to be told that the conventional formula he uses requires emendation:

> FRIAR: You come hither, my lord, to marry this lady?
> CLAUDIO: No.
> LEONATO: To be married to her, Friar. You come to marry her.
> (4.1.4–7)

This wedding ceremony already looks quite inauspicious, even though Leonato tries his best to mend it. To the audience, of course, it is clear why the supposed bridegroom refuses to take up his role, defecting from the ritual before it has properly begun. But considering the Friar's office and the awareness of the other ceremonial participants, the wording is suggestive. The linguistic update Leonato offers marks a difference between the active and the passive voice and so points us to tricky questions historically discussed in contemporary theology. These questions address what the part of a participant or worshipper in any ceremonial act might be: would he or she actively perform their role with true conviction? Or would he or she simply let it happen passively, perhaps going through the motions of a given ritual procedure? The distinction is subtle and hard to make out, especially in the Elizabethan church, which placed more emphasis on outward conformity than inner thought. So could the church recognize a false believer when it saw one? As Ramie Targoff explains, the "established church certainly could not control the worshippers' internal focus on the service," so that it rather "sought to combat visible manifestation of distraction."[23] The problem was especially acute in public prayer, where worshippers had to determine "when they must pray on their own behalf, and when the minister's prayers represent them."[24] The issue therefore turns on questions of representation—questions that are relevant here in three respects.

First, it was often noted by reformers that standard forms of prayer, like other ritual acts, may encourage inattention. In his posthumously printed *Treatise of Prayer* (1640), George Downame describes the problem as follows:

> And theretofore we must take heed that the speech of the mouth do not go before but always follow the conceit of the mind. For many times it cometh to passe, that as the musicians singers will run over

> a song which he hath been used to play although his mind be otherwise occupied, so in prayer the tongue will run over that form of words which it hath been used to utter, though the mind be roving about other matters. But this ought not to be so.[25]

Even though he argues for "a set form" to "be preferred before" an "extemporall prayer,"[26] too much reliance on representative set forms, on routine procedures, and given wordings may clearly have adverse effects. For just this reason, Protestant polemics against Popish ritual loved to single out the constant "mumbling" in church as a point of particular criticism, especially Latin mumbling.[27] Following or vocalizing the mere sounds of ecclesiastical language without attending to the words, as in Downame's vivid description, would induce churchgoers to chime in with ornate ceremonial utterances without ever comprehending what they actually say. Thus (ironically, for its Catholic-Italian setting), the keyword "plain" in Leonato's opening instruction to the Friar also serves as admonition in favor of the comprehensible and plain language that the English church reformers championed.[28]

Second, issues of representation were widespread in the English Reformation, whether in the context of the Eucharistic Controversies or in that of episcopal organization and administration. At the same time, secular transactions in the early modern period can be described as movements that increasingly distrusted religious representation and representativeness, instead placing greater emphasis on individual and personalized faith. Such a transaction could be described, in John Sommerville's words, as a "change from a religious *culture* to a religious *faith*."[29] The distinction has a special point: even though the realm and public scope of the religious may be reduced or marginalized in this process, its impact or potential use is not. As a private faith, religion has changed its locus but retained its force. Secularization, in this sense, should be seen not as a process of loss or subtraction, but as a transformation and a shift in emphasis from an all-pervasive, general, and representative religious culture to various more specialized and specified uses of religion. To understand nonsecular societies, Sommerville invites us to imagine a people "whose religious rituals are so woven into the fabric of their society that they cannot separate religion from the rest of their activities, *they often not even have a word for their commerce with occult powers*."[30] Conversely, to have such words and to discuss such commerce and its proper form implies that secularization must be under way.

Third, if we ask ourselves how early modern theater relates to such developments, we should recall that *representation* has a theatrical dimension, too. In *Much Ado*, the would-be wedding is soon followed by a would-be funeral (act 5, scene 3), which takes place without a corpse and therefore is specifically void.[31] But no matter what peculiarities or shortcomings these two ritual scenes may have, both religious ceremonies are principally staged as mere representations of the real thing. As spectators in the playhouse, we are constantly aware that nothing sacramentally efficacious happens in them, or through them, because we know we are watching a show. In this sense, the theatrical performance figures forth a seemingly sacramental event at the same time that it reminds us of its secular transformation. In the late sixteenth century, it would have been quite impossible, indeed illegal, to have actual religious words or rites recognizably performed in the playhouse.[32] But even if any of the ritual acts we witness had looked like a nuptial or a funeral, in fact nobody ever gets married (or buried) on the stage. In J. L. Austin's terms, the relevant speech acts are only cited here, not really used.[33] What follows, then, for the secular transactions at stake and their hermeneutic premises? Before tackling this question, let us consider another example, this one from *Romeo and Juliet.*

In *Romeo and Juliet*, Shakespeare's other Italian drama dominated by a scheming and inventive Friar, we are shown what happens when a plot involving a feigned death goes wrong. But we are never shown the "holy act" (2.5.1) of matrimony by which the "holy church incorporate two in one" (2.5.37). Instead, the actual marriage ceremony takes place offstage, not witnessed by anyone. What we do see is the first and fateful meeting of the "star-crossed" lovers, presented in the following dialogue:

> ROMEO: If I profane with my unworthiest hand
> This holy shrine, the gentle sin is this:
> My lips, two blushing pilgrims, ready stand
> To smooth that rough touch with a tender kiss.
> JULIET: Good pilgrim, you do wrong your hand too much,
> Which mannerly devotion shows in this;
> For saints have hands that pilgrims' hands do touch,
> And palm to palm is holy palmers' kiss.
> ROMEO: Have not saints lips, and holy palmers too?
> JULIET: Ay, pilgrim, lips that they must use in prayer.
> ROMEO: Oh, then, dear saint, let lips do what hands do:
> They pray; grant thou, lest faith turn to despair.
> JULIET: Saints do not move, though grant for prayer's sake.
> ROMEO: Then move not while my prayer's effect I take. [*He kisses her.*]
> (1.4.204–217)

We observe here how the first physical contact, their kiss, is prepared and produced by means of a verbal exchange resonant with sacramental meanings that call to mind the ritual acts denied to English worshippers in the reformed Elizabethan church. With "saints," "pilgrims," "holy palmers," "holy shrine," and intercession, the multivalent speech acts all recall, or possibly reactivate, several of the forms and practices of "mannerly devotion" that were outlawed a generation earlier. If Juliet is figured as a "saint" or statue, she turns Romeo's ardent acts of passionate devotion into a version of idolatry—and a willful idolatry at that. Elsewhere in this volume, the post-Reformation fates of medieval idols, hymns, and effigies are explored in greater detail.[34] But the short dialogue from *Romeo and Juliet* already shows that whatever sacramental remnants still abound in English cultural memory may now be gathered in the playhouse and employed so as to stage an unmistakably erotic encounter, culminating in a kiss. Should such a reinterpretation be seen as an act of outright blasphemy or, instead, as a more complex secular transaction?

Romeo's opening line speaks of profanation, suggesting a determined move away from notions of the sacramental. The "profane" is not, in fact, fully synonymous with the "secular." Both terms suggest some departure from the sacred, though the former casts this departure in spatial terms whereas the latter casts it in temporal terms. Etymologically, "profane" means "outside the temple" and so derives from rites and acts of worship for which a special place has been assigned and consecrated.[35] Everything placed inside this location—the "shrine"—must be dedicated to the holy cause, hence comply with its demands. Anything or anyone placed outside is "profane"—that is to say, they cannot participate in the rites practiced there. They may cross the threshold to the sanctum only under strict conditions often regulated in some *rite de passage*, the physical and formal movement from profane to sacred space.[36] In this sense, the sacred is a category of emplacement. As Claude Lévi-Strauss said with regard to holy objects, their being in their place is what makes them sacred.[37] As a social institution and part of a popular entertainment industry, therefore, the early modern playhouse is desacralizing insofar as it displaces ritual objects and content from one location to another and, it follows, from one signifying context to another.

Placing and emplacement thus emerge as crucial factors in investigating the hermeneutics of the sacred—just as much as they do for thinking about the cultural transactions of the secular.[38] Wedding ceremonies are paradigmatic: where is the appropriate place for matrimonial rites—in a church or in some other public space? The choice depends on whether marriage is considered mainly a religious, perhaps even a sacramental, affair or rather a civil bond and social institution. But to pose the question according to this strict opposition may already be a problem; it points us to relevant debates waged during the English Reformation. While the controversies over marriage were never as strong on this question as on key points like the Eucharist, they were nonetheless taken up. For example, Article 25 of the Thirty-Nine Articles of 1563 stated that only two sacraments remain in the English Church. Yet while denied sacramental status, matrimony was still to be solemnized by means of ceremonial procedures in front of an altar and by a given form of words in the *Book of Common Prayer*. The prayer book provided an order for public ceremony, which was often celebrated in church even though, as David Cressy and Lori Anne Ferrell remind us, in law a couple could also be married by a private exchange of vows.[39] Eminent Protestant authorities like Thomas Becon and Martin Bucer also wrote on the issue of marriage, negotiating its civil and contractual, as well as sacramental and ecclesiastical, emphases. In *De Regno Christi*, Bucer seems to favor a social model of marriage, whereas Becon never questions the propriety of the church's jurisdiction over marriage.[40]

An even more radical position that marriage was no business of the church's at all, rather a matter for civil authority, was also articulated at the time—though remaining, as Cressy puts it, "isolated" and thus anticipating much later developments in the history of secularization.[41] In nineteenth-century Germany, for instance, with Bismarck's newly founded Prussian state, this question formed the major battle line of the so-called *Kulturkampf*—that is, his programmatic conflict with Catholicism in attempting to stem its influence on social life: whether marriage was legitimately made outside, and without, the church. As a result of this battle, the introduction of civil marriage has rendered wedding service as an adjunct or a festive supplement—the clearest marker of a secularization process that strictly delimits, and reduces, the church's administrative power over central areas of human life by shifting authority to other institutions, like the registry office, sanctioned by the state.

Crucially, however, even die-hard nineteenth-century secularists still recognized the need for ceremony and for ceremonial language to be used on such occasions—not unlike the authors of the *Book of Common Prayer*, who also retained certain ceremonies without advocating their sacramental efficacy. In Victorian England, it was George Jacob Holyoake who championed, popularized, and organized secularism through his many activities. However, he concludes his book on *The Origin and Nature of Secularism* (1896) with a chapter he titles "Secularist Ceremonies" and opens with the observation that "certain ceremonies are common to all human society" and should therefore be continued even under secular auspices.[42] This is why he offers unbelievers viable alternatives to the ritual and wording used in church, so as to invent the sort of ceremony that could well be performed without standing in front of an altar. The marriage service, in particular, is to be reinvented and reworded because in church, according to his hermeneutics, "it contains things no bride could hear without a blush, if she understood them," so that "the Secularist naturally seeks for other forms of speech"; that is, for a more appropriate and comprehensible idiom.[43] The language of secularism, according to this testimony by one of its most prominent proponents, thus continues early modern Protestant campaigns against mumbling.

In Holyoake's own language, secularism is defined as "a code of conduct" and "a mode of instruction," which seem to share some crucial aspects with the code and mode of classic rhetoric: "He who is afraid to know both sides of a question cannot think upon it. Christians do not, as a rule, want to know what can be said against their views . . . Thus the Christian cannot think freely, and is against others doing it."[44] Polemics aside, what this description essentially suggests is to see secularism as a version of the old rhetorical exercise of an argument *in utramque partem*—"to know both sides of a question"—an exercise, moreover, with clear affinities to the dialogical two-sidedness of drama. In the theater, any declaration of belief or doctrine comes across principally as the declaration of a character onstage and is therefore difficult to take or understand as absolutely given, without thinking of the possibility that there are always other sides as well. This is why the theater can never *state* religious doctrine, only *stage* it—an ambivalent procedure that renders all religious utterances made in the playhouse questionable because they may always be disowned as just the one side of performance. And this is why, in my view, theatrical language holds such intriguing possibilities for the language of the secular: because it constantly reminds us of its partial, dialogic, or—in Bakhtinian terms—heteroglossic character, one that resists attempts to see or take any statement as exclusive, final, or absolute.

Rather than understanding secularity in terms of the diminishment of religious culture we should perhaps see it on its own terms as questioning the scope and force of religious language by insisting, like language in the theater, on a larger dialogue with dissenting views and voices. The language of secularization, then, is dialogic language in performance and in hermeneutic contact also with its opposite, the counterview or other side to any given question. What, however, follows from this for the secularization of language?

Let us return, with such contexts in mind, to the fundamental issues of language and religious ritual in English Reformation contexts. In Sommerville's study, he argues that, as part of the early Tudor reconstitution of the church under Henry VIII, "language was among the first things to be secularized."[45] This comment refers to the change from Latin to the English vernacular, which was both a precondition and a consequence of sixteenth-century Protestant transactions. Generally speaking, the foundation of any new religious practice should perhaps always be combined with the assertion, or at least strong commendation, of a new language.[46] Put otherwise, a religious reformation is in some sense a linguistic reformation.[47] But especially the early modern Protestant Reformations—both in England and on the Continent—with their stress on the vernacular, have long been understood to gain much of their cultural force from linguistic issues, following Martin Luther's revolution, which, in the phrase of Robert Stillman, was "semiological as well as theological."[48] In fact, Protestant attempts to change the language may never have gone far enough. As Machiavelli cannily observed in the *Discorsi*, when Christianity once tried to supersede the classic pagans and erase all memories of their old faith, it still kept the classic language it inherited from them—namely, Latin—and adopted it for the new church.[49] In doing so, it also kept alive many theological concepts it would rather have dismissed. Such a point would not be lost on sixteenth-century reformers. Their hermeneutic efforts to translate liturgical texts may also have been driven by the need to find an uncontaminated truth, superseding the older, Romanist religious legacies they found problematic. So if the change from Latin to English, in Sommerville's terms, also "changed English religion from a matter of practice to a matter of thought" and thus, in his sense, from religious *culture* to religious *faith*, such a secularizing linguistic move would also be of consequence for a contemporary understanding of what words can do in the world.[50]

To situate this large debate on verbal power, translation, and the efficacy of utterances in concrete terms, we may find pertinent—though necessarily quite localized—examples in the two Shakespearean plays. When, for instance, Hero praises Benedick and wonders why her cousin Beatrice so much resents him, she conjures up the verbal action of a witch: "I never yet saw man, / How wise, how noble, young, how rarely featured, / But she would spell him backward" (3.1.59–61). When Benedick, much later, tries to put his love for her into appropriate words, he famously despairs in trying to compose a poem: "Marry, I cannot show it in rhyme. I have tried. I can find out no rhyme to 'lady' but 'baby'; an innocent rhyme. For 'scorn,' 'horn'; a hard rhyme. For 'school', 'fool'; a babbling rhyme;

very ominous endings. No, I was not born under a rhyming planet, nor I cannot woo in festival terms" (5.2.30–34). Both these speeches, though mundane or casual in the their motivation and occasion, highlight verbal power and so raise the question of what, if anything, the sound and shape of words might mean or do. In particular, their references to witchcraft and to the ominous efficacy of rhyming are highly resonant in contemporary debates on language and the force of words. Hero's caustic comment about witches who work their conjuring by uttering names or prayers backward and so reverse the given order is based on a "commonplace of scholarly demonology: that witches did everything backwards" and that witchcraft, generally, is "an act of pure inversion."[51] But her comment also implies the underlying notion that utterance matters and that some verbal signifiers, used by certain speakers under certain circumstances, function as a spell, with an impact on reality that is potentially changed by it. Such a magical understanding of words and sounds and their effects also underlies the comic desperation Benedick displays when contemplating rhyme words and their "ominous endings." For rhyme operates precisely in an area where given meanings of familiar words are dangerously sliding into other meanings, by virtue of the chant of language that enchants its users: the similarities of sound suggest semantic similarities and even social bonds, which may well be illicit and are, at any rate, not easily controlled. Rhyme may sound like "babbling" and yet be "ominous" because it often seems the echo of another sense.

This point is relevant, above all, for the fateful verbal exchange cited earlier between Romeo and Juliet. Their dialogue not only unfolds in rhymes but also, as has been well noted, assumes the pattern of a sonnet, complete with three quatrains and, right before the kiss, the couplet. Unlike Benedick's, Romeo's wooing here is clearly manifest "in festival terms": not only does he activate the lexicon of sainthood, pilgrimage, and holiness from the repertoire of the old church but he also employs a poetic form, translated and adapted from Petrarchan practice, strongly associated in its formative Italian version with religious worship.[52] Or rather, both Romeo and Juliet, the wooer and the wooed, are cast in verbal and poetic roles by which the language form they share, on the level of the outer communicative system, assumes the traditional form of courtship and signals to the audience their shared fate and social bond by means of linguistic binding.[53] The rhymes function like a spell, as if to charm the two protagonists henceforth to act under verbal magic. This is the kind of language that makes a difference in the world and brings about what it refers to, as in sacramental formulas or ritual utterances like marriage vows, whose force the play here seems to draw on. Whether or not their willful use of such a language for erotic purposes may be a profanation, their rhyming and their sonneteering work as a dramatic act of reenchantment.

As a matter of fact, rhyming was, like mumbling, a point of attack against Catholic worship. In Reformation debates and polemics, the linguistic forms of traditional church service were routinely criticized on this account, and satirists like Luke Shepherd made prominent use of silly rhymes to ridicule papist worship.[54] Protestants generally preferred prose for prayer and, with the notable exception of the Psalms, decided "to abandon verse as a vehicle for public devotion."[55] Rhyme often operates like—or indeed *as*—a magic force in language, uncannily productive in establishing likeness and equivalence. Yet as in the debates on witchcraft, while many Protestant writers ridiculed the language of Catholic ceremony, they did not fully deny its effects. For even in rejecting verbal elements like rhyme in ritual utterance, they acknowledged their potential force. As Stuart Clark argues, "the Protestant accusation that Catholicism was a religion based on witchcraft arose from questioning the sense in which specific religious rituals could be said to be efficacious."[56] Yet the witches' verbal power manifest in conjuring turned out to be hard to disown: "I conjure thee *Sibylia* by all the rail of words aforesaid, and by their vertues and powers, I charge and bind thee by the virtue thereof": what Reginald Scot cites in his *Discoverie of Witchcraft*.[57] This along with what Marlowe stages in his history of a Doctor Faustus who congratulates himself on the "virtue" in his words and "the force of magic" and his "spells"[58] are strong examples of Protestant language users trying out the magic power—or, as they say, the "virtue"—of specific words that they, on theological principle, should reject.[59] That is to say, the problem of efficacy in words and rites continued to trouble and to haunt reformed language. The problem also has particular bearings for the use of language in the theater, where, according to the constitutive "as if" of playacting, speech acts function without real force.

Or so we would like to believe. In contrast to the general assumption that words onstage are merely mentioned and never actually used, we need only remember the oft-recounted anecdote about an early seventeenth-century performance of *Doctor Faustus* where the uttering of magic spells onstage seems to have been so effective that all of a sudden, as the players noted with dismay, one devil too many was among them on the stage—at which point they broke off their show and, "contraye to their custome," as the source says, spent the night in prayer.[60] Even if this anecdote is untrue, its popularity suggests that the utterance of magic spells, even in the theater, can bring about some real change and make an impact on reality; perhaps the early popularity of Marlowe's drama arose precisely from the fascination that conjuring and its performative potential held for Elizabethan audiences. As Andrew Sofer argues, "in plays such as *Doctor Faustus*, conjuring models a performative speech act that threatens to blur the distinction between theatre and magic."[61] Wooing may well be a different speech act, and yet plays of courtship, such as *Much Ado* or *Romeo and Juliet*, still offer strong occasions to investigate the same issue and the same performative blurring, since wooing is, like conjuring, a test case for the force of verbal acts to achieve worldly ends and influence a person's behavior. To woo someone "in festival terms" means also to try out these terms and see what change, if any, they might bring about. Courtship may in general be tantamount to rhetoric, as Kenneth Burke suggested in his reading of *Venus and Adonis*, but especially a comedy of courtship that announces all its verbal action to be "about nothing" is certainly well suited to exploring how "much ado" some words onstage still make.[62]

In a chapter titled "Language, Signs, and Magic," Thomas M. Greene considers early modern debates on language and identifies two major different theoretical positions, which he calls disjunctive as opposed to conjunctive and which he traces in some central issues like the Eucharistic Controversies.[63] While disjunctive theories assume a clear distinction between words and things and between literal language and figurative language, conjunctive theories assume that words are equivalent to things, can be substituted for them, and indeed share their referent's essence because they are, or may be, consubstantial. In a cautious but decisive move, Greene then argues for a "rough homology" between this split in language theories and "the Catholic-Protestant" split, a homology that clearly helps explain the often-noted cultural alliance between Catholic practices and magical ones just as the Protestant routine rejection of, yet endless fascination with, magical speech acts. In this way, Shakespeare questions Protestant, and in Sommerville's sense, secular theories of language, disjunctive notions that strictly distinguish *verba* from *res* and bar verbal utterances from efficacy. Even if, as argued earlier, the playhouse is a dialogic, multilingual, heteroglossic space in which religious language can only ever play one part among many, the playhouse is also the thing wherein to rehearse the rhymes and forms of ritual language and find out how strong, if at all, their force may still be going. Wooing words, in the double sense of this phrase, is what *Romeo and Juliet* or *Much Ado About Nothing* engage in.

Strauß's *The Life of Jesus* was first translated into English in 1846 by Mary Ann Evans, better known as George Eliot, who led most of her life with a married man whom she referred to as her husband. When she died, there was some discussion about whether she should be interred in Westminster Abbey, given her significance as a major writer. Yet her well-known skepticism against the church and Christian faith eventually ruled against it.[64] Her burial thus became a secular transaction. Later George Jacob Holyoake, an old acquaintance, arranged to have his grave in Highgate Cemetery immediately next to hers, with a bust of himself looking toward her. Her gravestone reads, "Here lies the body of George Eliot," followed in the next line by her married name, "Mary Ann Cross." It seems as if this double inscription, placed in a memorial but civic context, testifies to the ways in which marriage is a figure for the worldly power of names and words.

Julia Reinhard Lupton reconsiders ongoing debates on secularism and political theology and proposes to see marriage as the central trope for the contract between religious and political discourses: "To what extent," she asks, "do the contracts that bring communities into being operate laterally, as an equalizing force among persons now conceived as citizens, and to what extent do these contracts embody a heteronomous element of sheer jurisdiction, coming from above in a stroke of exceptional violence?"[65] On the basis of the foregoing discussion I suggest that, prior to such political hermeneutics, we need to establish first by what means the stage sets up a space of norms, or at least pretends to do so, and what the relevant dimensions of this space might be. It is the force of words and verbal acts, I argue, that is crucial for this purpose and crucially put to the test in theater. And it is the trope that, in a comedy like *Much Ado* or a tragedy like *Romeo and Juliet*, serves precisely to mediate or "marry" the literal and figurative dimensions of theatrical language, the factual and the fictional power of words onstage, the foundational and vacuous force of speech acts in the playhouse. When in act 4 of *Much Ado* the simple and "plain form of marriage" founders, we begin to realize that the relationship between these two dimensions is so complex that their particulars will need a lot of recounting afterward.

In a sense, this recounting is what I have tried to supply with this essay. When Ben Jonson coined his famous phrase and praised Shakespeare as "not of an age but for all time," he was placing the work of his colleague and rival strictly outside the realm of the "secular," which, following its early Latin usage, first appeared to signify a temporal or calendric unit[66]—roughly, in fact, what Jonson called an age. In this sense, to historicize Shakespearean texts means to secularize them, to embed them firmly in his "age," as suggested also by the title of the present volume. On the other hand, any current engagement with Shakespearean texts must in some way disembed them from this given context since—like Auerbach and his engagement with the Western canon—we are no longer of his age but of another place and time, necessarily reading, hearing, speaking and seeing otherwise, from a distance and from a critically different hermeneutic position. I have tried in my discussion to negotiate between these two positions. To rethink the secular in the age of Shakespeare, we must rethink the terms of our debate, in the self-reflexive manner proposed by Said's secular criticism, while also thinking of the ways in which these very terms pose the issue of debate in the first place. According to Taylor, secularism has contributed to what he calls the great disembedding; that is, a reconstitution in practices of the self, outside the social vectors previously taken for granted.[67] The playhouse, I have argued, functions as an institution of such disembedding, as well as of provisional reembedding. It is a social space where terms and means of other practices of self and of society can be tested and rehearsed.

The secular, in Shakespearean theater, is less a given than a possibility that goes along with, as well as against, other possibilities staged in it. What I earlier referred to as the "as if" of playacting is also the "what if" of play watching. Following a show, spectators are constantly prompted—and, in some cases like Shakespeare's *Henry V*, openly called upon—to imagine, to suppose, and to conjecture. There is always, we are made to realize, more than meets the eye and more than one meaning involved. This is why the versatility of words to do and mean so many different things at once is often played out with such relish, especially in bastard words like rhymes and puns, whose illegitimate ambiguities translate into pragmatic differences when placed into a social context.

I cite one last example from *Much Ado*. When in act 1 Don John, "the bastard" (4.1.186), confers with his henchmen to hatch the plot against his brother, he utters the celebrated line, "If I can cross him any way, I bless myself every way" (1.3.55–56). Here he manages to moralize two meanings in one word, offering a hermeneutic challenge to interpreters. In the religious context defined by the Church of England, to cross oneself would have been seen as a particularly problematic, potentially recusant gesture of opposition. Yet Don John's remark rather plays with the alternative meaning of "to cross" in the sense of "to frustrate or thwart." The recusant reference is thus undercut—indeed crossed—by his sinister intent only to be reinstated with "bless myself" at the end of his quip. Whichever context we apply, the meaning shifts and the pragmatic uses vary. In Steiner's phrase then, any interpreter who tries to "act out" this material must give it differently intelligible forms of life. This is the hermeneutics of the playhouse.

If, according to Sommerville, nonsecular societies do not even have the words for the religious culture that pervades them, the cultural work of early modern playwriting and of performance may indeed be to provide such words and concepts and thus to make articulate, or articulable, what has long been going on, holding up the mirror less to nature than to the notions of nature generally entertained. The point is to render ritual observable and so offer a perspective that turns participants into spectators. *Wooing* words, in the sense of "words that have the power to reach out to others and to win them for the speaker's point of view," therefore are the kind of words that work best in the theater; at the same time, wooing *words*, in the sense of "trying to find and use the kind of language that makes a difference in the world," is an activity that the early modern theater might have shown, and perhaps taught, its spectators, reinterpreting social realities. The hermeneutic difference is slight but crucial, and it helps to account for the transactions of the secular.

Notes

1. George Steiner, *Real Presences* (London: Faber, 1989), 7.
2. For a brief account of the Homeric question, see Albin Lesky, *Geschichte der griechischen Literatur* (Bern: Francke, 1971), 50–59.
3. "Wo immer eine auf schriftliche Denkmale sich stützende Religion in weiteren Raum- und Zeitgebieten sich geltend macht, und ihre Bekenner durch mannigfaltige und immer höher steigende Entwickelungs- und Bildungsstufen begleitet: da thut sich früher oder später eine Differenz hervor zwischen Geist und Form jener alten Urkunden und zwischen der neuen Bildung derer, welche an dieselben als an heilige Bücher gewiesen sind. Diese Differenz . . . tritt . . . selbst an den wesentlichen Inhalt heran, und es wollen auch die Ideen und Grundansichten solcher Bücher der fortgeschrittenen Bildung nicht genügen" (David Friedrich Strauß, *Das Leben Jesu: Kritisch Bearbeitet* [Tübingen: Osiander, 1835], 1:1).
4. For a critical discussion of the "sacred" and its interrelations with notions of the secular, see the introduction to *Performances of the Sacred in Late Medieval and Early Modern England*, ed. Tobias Döring and Susanne Rupp (Amsterdam: Rodopi, 2005).
5. See also the essay by William N. West in the present volume.
6. Edward W. Said, *The World, the Text, and the Critic* (Cambridge, Mass.: Harvard University Press, 1983), 16.
7. Said, *The World*, 26.
8. J. L. Austin, *How to Do Things with Words* (Oxford: Clarendon, 1975).
9. For the critical debate on this point between Jacques Derrida and the speech-act theorists, see Jonathan Culler, *On Deconstruction: Theory and Criticism after Structuralism* (London: Routledge, 1983), 115–20.
10. Anthony B. Dawson, "The Secular Theater," in *Shakespeare and Religious Change*, ed. Kenneth J. E. Graham and Philip D. Collington (New York: Palgrave Macmillan, 2009), 243.

11. Dawson, "The Secular Theater," 257.
12. Craig Calhoun, Mark Juergensmeyer, and Jonathan van Antwerpen, eds., *Rethinking Secularism* (Oxford: Oxford University Press, 2011), 8.
13. Calhoun, Juergensmeyer, and van Antwerpen, *Rethinking Secularism*, 11.
14. Charles Taylor, "Western Secularity," in Calhoun, Juergensmeyer, and van Antwerpen, *Rethinking Secularism*, 39.
15. In his recent book, Akeel Bilgrami even speaks of "Secular Enchantment"; see *Secularism, Identity, and Enchantment* (Cambridge, Mass.: Harvard University Press, 2014), 99–214.
16. See Calhoun, Juergensmeyer, and van Antwerpen, *Rethinking Secularism*, 8.
17. Brian Cummings and James Simpson, introduction to *Cultural Reformations: Medieval and Renaissance in Literary History* (Oxford: Oxford University Press, 2010), 7.
18. See the contribution by William N. West in the present volume.
19. Stanley E. Fish, "*Lycidas*: A Poem Finally Anonymous," *Glyph* 8 (1981): 13.
20. John Milton, "Lycidas," in *The Poems of John Milton*, ed. John Carey and Alastair Fowler (London: Longmans, 1968), l. 148.
21. Milton, "Lycidas," l. 152.
22. All citations from Shakespearean texts according to The Norton Shakespeare (Third Edition), eds Stephen Greenblatt, Walter Cohen, Suzanne Gossett, Jean E. Howard, Katharine Eisaman Maus, Gordon McMullan (New York: Norton 2016).
23. Ramie Targoff, *Common Prayer: The Language of Public Devotion in Early Modern England* (Chicago: University of Chicago Press, 2001), 39.
24. Targoff, *Common Prayer*, 40.
25. George Downame, *A Godly and Learned Treatise of Prayer* (Cambridge: Roger Daniel, 1640), 86.
26. Downame, *Godly and Learned Treatise*, 138.
27. See Carla Mazzio, *The Inarticulate Renaissance: Language Trouble in an Age of Eloquence* (Philadelphia: University of Pennsylvania Press, 2009), 22.
28. See Brian Cummings, *The Literary Culture of the Reformation: Grammar and Grace* (Oxford: Oxford University Press, 2002), chap. 5.
29. C. John Sommerville, *The Secularization of Early Modern England: From Religious Culture to Religious Faith* (Oxford: Oxford University Press, 1992), 3; emphasis added.
30. Sommerville, *Secularization*, 4; emphasis added.
31. See Tobias Döring, *Performances of Mourning in Shakespearean Theatre and Early Modern Culture* (London: Palgrave, 2006), chap. 5.
32. See Debora Shuger, "Civility and Censorship in Early Modern England," in *Censorship and Silencing: Practices of Cultural Regulation*, ed. Robert C. Post (Los Angeles: Getty Research Institute, 1998), 89–110.
33. But see the deconstructive move against this neat distinction, as discussed in Culler, *On Deconstruction*, note 9.
34. See the chapters by Angela Heetderks and Emma Maggie Solberg in the present volume. For another careful study on the use of saints in the Church of England and their continued fate in Puritan theology, see Janel Mueller, "The Saints," in Cummings and Simpson, *Cultural Reformations*, 166–87.

35. See Andrew Spicer and Sarah Hamilton, eds., *Defining the Holy: Sacred Space in Medieval and Early Modern Europe* (Aldershot, Hants, UK: Ashgate Publishing, 2005).
36. See Edward Muir, *Ritual in Early Modern Europe* (Cambridge: Cambridge University Press, 1997), 20.
37. Claude Lévi-Strauss, *Das wilde Denken*, trans. Hans Naumann (Frankfurt am Main: Suhrkamp, 1973), 21.
38. See Jonathan Smith, *To Take Place: Toward Theory in Ritual* (Chicago: University of Chicago Press, 1992).
39. David Cressy and Lori Anne Ferrell, eds., *Religion and Society in Early Modern England: A Sourcebook* (New York: Routledge, 2005), 61.
40. See John Witte Jr., *From Sacrament to Contract: Marriage, Religion, and Law in the Western Tradition* (Louisville, Ky.: Westminster John Knox Press, 1997), 143.
41. David Cressy, *Birth, Marriage, and Death: Ritual, Religion, and the Life-Cycle in Tudor and Stuart England* (Oxford: Oxford University Press, 1997), 295.
42. George Jacob Holyoake, *The Origin and Nature of Secularism* (London: Watts, 1896), 212.
43. Holyoake, *Secularism*, 212.
44. Holyoake, *Secularism*, 8, 18.
45. Sommerville, *Secularization*, 44.
46. See Robert E. Stillman, *Philip Sidney and the Poetics of Renaissance Cosmopolitanism* (Aldershot, Hants, UK: Ashgate Publishing, 2008), 93.
47. For more elaborate and substantial discussion of this complex issue, see the following studies: Cummings, *Literary Culture*; Timothy Rosendale, *Literature and Liturgy in the Making of Protestant England* (Cambridge: Cambridge University Press, 2011); and Sophie Read, *Eucharist and the Poetic Imagination in Early Modern England* (Cambridge: Cambridge University Press, 2013).
48. Stillman, *Renaissance Cosmopolitanism*, 93. See also Brian Cummings's introduction to *The Book of Common Prayer* (Oxford: Oxford University Press, 2011), ix–lii.
49. Niccolò Machiavelli, *Discorsi: Gedanken über Politik und Staatsführung*, trans. Rudolf Zorn (Stuttgart: Kröner, 1977), 181–82.
50. Sommerville, *Secularization*, 48.
51. Stuart Clark, *Thinking with Demons: The Idea of Witchcraft in Early Modern Europe* (Oxford: Clarendon Press, 1997), 13, 15.
52. See Michael R. G. Spiller, *The Development of the Sonnet: An Introduction* (London: Routledge, 1992), 56.
53. For the term "outer communicative system" and its use in drama analysis, see Manfred Pfister, *Das Drama: Theorie und Analyse* (Munich: Fink, 1984).
54. See Janice Devereux, ed., *An Edition of Luke Shepherd's Satires* (Tempe, Ariz.: Arizona Center for Medieval and Renaissance Studies, 2001). See also my brief discussion of Shepherd's satires in *Performances of Mourning*, 173–76.
55. Targoff, *Common Prayer*, 66.
56. Clark, *Thinking with Demons*, 534.
57. Reginald Scot, *The Discoverie of Witchcraft*, ed. Hugh Ross Williamson (London: Centaur Press, 1964), 338.

58. Christopher Marlowe, *Doctor Faustus*, ed. David Scott Kastan (New York: Norton, 2005), 15.

59. See my discussion of the Protestant Sidney and his engagement with efficacious language in his sonnets: "Beginning to Spell: Sidney's *Astrophil and Stella* and the Crux of Protestant Poetics," *Poetica* 45, no. 1/2 (2013): 67–84.

60. Marlowe, *Doctor Faustus*, 181.

61. Andrew Sofer, "How to Do Things with Demons: Conjuring Performatives in *Doctor Faustus*," *Theatre Journal* 61, no. 1 (March 2009): 2.

62. Kenneth Burke, *A Rhetoric of Motives* (Berkeley: University of California Press, 1969), 212–21.

63. Thomas M. Greene, *Poetry, Signs, and Magic* (Newark: University of Delaware Press, 2005), 34.

64. See Nancy Henry, *The Life of George Eliot: A Critical Biography* (London: Wiley, 2014), 264, from which the information in this paragraph is taken.

65. Julia Reinhard Lupton, *Citizen-Saints: Shakespeare and Political Theology* (Chicago: University of Chicago Press, 2005), 11.

66. Calhoun, Juergensmeyer, and van Antwerpen, *Rethinking Secularism*, 8.

67. Taylor, "Western Secularity," 49.

Part Two

Political and Social Secularities

"Of Government the Properties to Unfold"

Governmentalities in *Measure for Measure*

Jennifer R. Rust

Measure for Measure opens with a cryptic inquiry into the nature of government posed by the governor himself. In the play's first lines, the Duke of Vienna addresses this inquiry to his deputy, Escalus:

> Of government the properties to unfold
> Would seem in me t'affect speech and discourse,
> Since I am put to know that your own science
> Exceeds in that the lists of all advice
> My strength can give you. Then no more remains
> But this: to your sufficiency, as your worth is able,
> And let them work. The nature of our people,
> Our city's institutions and the terms
> For common justice, you're as pregnant in
> As art and practice hath enrichèd any
> That we remember. (1.1.3–13)

The Duke not only introduces government as a dominant preoccupation of the play but also obfuscates his agency with regard to it: the action modifying "the properties of government" is deferred until the end of the line and suspended in the infinitive ("to unfold"). In the third line, the Duke identifies himself as the evident source of any "discourse" of "government," but at the same moment, he declares his own inability to "affect" this discourse, to "unfold" the map of proper character of government. In this syntax of failing mastery, the Duke disavows a "discourse" of government despite what "seems" to be the case. While the Duke evades easy clarity in his initial "speech" of government (so much so that editors have speculated that some of the Duke's lines are missing), he hints at how its nature will be conceived in the subsequent play.[1]

"Government" is a "discourse" but also something grasped by means of a "science," a field of knowledge. Encompassed within this science of government is what the Duke calls "the nature of our people" as well as the "city's institutions" and the "terms for common justice." As the Duke intimates, institutions stand between nature and the law. "Institutions" aspire to shape both terms, but they further require adept "art and practice," which amount to the strategies of the wise governor. However, in the Duke's initial address the mood is interrogative, hesitant: government is not something known in advance but is instead something far more provisional, a process rather than a determination.

Critical responses to the Duke's governmental agenda in the play tend to stabilize its tentativeness, but these readings also align his motives and aims with various schemes of secularizing interpretation. They emphasize the Duke's ultimate ability to impose his vision of good governmental order upon the world of the play; they share a faith in the Duke's absolute power, a power that is understood in predominantly secular terms. One approach takes its cue from the references to a "discourse," "art," and "practice" of government that pepper the Duke's opening speech, discovering in the Duke's practice a Foucauldian aspiration to total state power.[2] This is the tendency of several influential New Historicist or cultural materialist political interpretations of Shakespeare inflected by Foucault's thought of the 1980s and early 1990s. While the characteristics of these arguments vary, they tend to emphasize several factors: a surveillance-state setting, an "omniscient" Duke, a biopolitical concern with controlling the unruly sexuality of Vienna, and religious practices such as confession marshaled as "mere politic device[s]" in the service of this state and its ruler.[3] These secularizing analyses of the play read it as an allegory of emergent forms of secular state power. These readings stand in strong contrast to an equally prominent tradition of "King James Versions" or Christianizing allegories of the play.[4] In the "King James" tradition, the play is understood largely as a reflection (or even celebration) of the historical ruler's divine-right ideology. As an idealized parallel to James I of England, the Duke appears as a secular ruler who successfully absorbs and commands forms of power formerly associated with the ecclesiastical sphere.

These apparently contrasting critical approaches to the play correspond to two influential models of secularization. The account of religion as a "politic device" of power evokes the celebrated "disenchantment of the world" thesis attributed to Max Weber, while the divine right allegory resonates with Carl Schmitt's claim in *Political Theology* that "all modern theories of the state" are secularized theological concepts—the political is the theological translated into a new idiom.[5] Giorgio Agamben emphasizes the distinction between these two thinkers of secular modernity, who were separated by generational, political, and confessional sensibilities: "While, for Weber, secularization was an aspect of the growing process of disenchantment and detheologization of the modern world, for Schmitt it shows on the contrary that, in modernity, theology continues to be present and active in an eminent way." For Schmitt, secularization "concerns a particular strategic relation that marks political concepts and refers them back to their theological origins."[6] Despite their apparent differences, both models reach the same outcome when they are applied to *Measure for Measure*: the theological sphere is either evacuated by or buried within a burgeoning state power, and, as a result, government as a mode of secular political power supersedes religion as the dominant paradigm of order by the end of the play.

In this essay, I want to resist the urge to stabilize and secularize the tentativeness that marks the Duke's governmental discourse at the beginning of the play. The most crucial forms of government in the play are pastoral forms not comprehensible in purely secular terms. Pastoral government and various resistances to it are prominent motifs that run throughout the play and must be understood as more than "mere politic devices" in the world of the play. Pastoral government destabilizes any opposition between the secular and the sacred: it interweaves these two orders, persistently marshaling human conduct toward a horizon of salvation that transcends the immediately given world. In order to illuminate the dynamic of pastoral government in *Measure for Measure* and to challenge claims that the play represents a process of secularization as it is often understood, I draw upon elements of Foucault's work that postdate the peak of his influence in Shakespeare studies. According to Foucault's account in his 1977–78 lectures *Security, Territory, Population*, modern governmentality emerges from the medieval pastorate as, paradoxically, the by-product of an intensified Reformation spirituality.[7] For Foucault, the Reformation was "much more a great pastoral battle than a great doctrinal battle," a struggle over the desirable means of governing the lived practices of individual and communal conduct toward salvation.[8] In this context, the secularity of early modern government is only relative, and it is certainly neither the product of a disenchantment of religion nor its transfer between church and state (as in the models of secularization derived, respectively, from Weber and Schmitt). It is rather the side effect of a late medieval and early modern proliferation of forms of religious conduct—experiments in alternative forms of pastoral government—that threaten to overwhelm political government and in response to which it must innovate and adapt.

The governmental challenge that the Duke confronts at the beginning of *Measure for Measure* is this Reformation-era proliferation of forms of extreme religious conduct, a challenge that he attempts to answer not with a robustly secular model of government but with a series of tentative experiments in pastoral government. The challenge lies not in the overexuberant sexuality of the city, despite appearances, but in the rise of severely ascetic forms of conduct that zealously seek to govern this exuberance. The play conspicuously marks this ascetic zeal, which is inspired by the governmental enthusiasms of the Reformation and embodied in the distinct figures of the Puritan Angelo and the Catholic novice Isabella. When the Duke adopts the guise of a pastor to curb the excesses of ascetic government represented by these figures, he ironically contributes to the proliferating governmentalities that vex the world of the play. Rather than securing a new secular order or accomplishing a smooth transfer of power from ecclesiastical to political realms, the Duke's ministrations fail as acts of pastoral government; this pastoral failure in turn implies that the Duke ultimately fails to establish any stable government at all, whether pastoral or political. The nature of this failure becomes clear through Foucault's analysis of pastoral government and the Reformation struggle around it, and this historical context provides the framework of analysis for a rereading of the play.

In *Security, Territory, Population*, Foucault defines "governmentality" as a modern phenomenon properly dating from the eighteenth century but genealogically related to the far older practices of government associated with the Christian pastorate.[9] While the modern governmentality of the state is concerned with political economy and the management of populations toward prosperity and health, pastoral governmentality is preoccupied with the spiritual and moral guidance of an "economy of souls" toward a transcendent horizon of salvation.[10] What these two forms of governmentality share is an emphasis on strategically directing properties inherent in individuals and communities, rather than imposing externally determined laws. In its focus on immanent processes, government must be distinguished from sovereignty: "Whereas the end of sovereignty is internal to itself and gets its instruments from itself in the form of law, the end of government is internal to the things it directs . . . it is to be sought in the perfection, maximization, or intensification of the processes it directs, and the instruments of government will become diverse tactics rather than laws."[11] To clarify this claim in terms of the specific case of pastoral governmentality, the end of this form of government is ultimately the spiritual salvation of the flock, but its governmental tactics focus on shaping the everyday conduct of both the individual and the group, "perfecting" and "intensifying" this conduct to achieve the larger goal of salvation for all.

Foucault argues that the paradigm of governmentality places the relationship between politics and theology at the level of the minister rather than that of the sovereign. In a move reminiscent of the *Annales* school's deemphasizing of the "great man" approach to history, Foucault's analysis marginalizes traditional sovereign figures. The "fundamental problem" of religion and politics does not concern the Pope or the Emperor but "that mixed figure, or the two figures who . . . share . . . the same name of minister . . . The minister, with all the ambiguity of this word, is perhaps the real problem and where the relationship between religion and politics, between government and the pastorate, is really situated."[12] The minister is a figure for governmentality par excellence: he is that quasi-sacred administrator-pastor, whose qualities later appear in the doctor, public health official, or director of social policy. The minister is a ligature between pastoral power and populations, between the state and its constituents. In modern usage, "minister" as a verb signifies both providing intimate care for another (including serving or healing) and enforcing rules and performing religious duties.[13] Now more commonly used with the prefix "ad-" (meaning "to" or "toward," a prefix that can imply heightened passivity among those being ministered to), "to minister" signifies the activity of implementing policies that intervene between individuals and institutions to make the state or church function as a collective body. The medical and sacramental dimensions of the term are fully available by the mid-fifteenth century.[14] Foucault's emphasis on the minister as a political-theological figure recalls his celebrated reference to Ernst Kantorowicz's "remarkable analysis" of the king's "double body" at the beginning of *Discipline and Punish*.[15] While Foucault distances himself from a political theology centered on the sovereign figure, he does not take leave of political theology altogether. Instead, he attempts to reorient its focus toward the ministrations of power on the abject "least body."[16] From the perspective of *Security, Territory, Population*, this ministerial activity is contiguous with the governmentality of the pastor. It is the minister who really has two bodies; he is potentially the pastor within an economy of salvation and the functionary of the political state.

The ministerial pastor is concerned first and foremost with the realm of conduct. Conduct has a "double dimension."[17] It involves the governance and direction of both the individual and the collective; thus the pastorate is equally concerned with the spiritual health and salvation of the individual and the community.[18] From the early church into the sixteenth century, the pastorate developed a host of strategies to govern the conduct of its flock; these governing strategies inevitably also inspired forms of resistance, which emerged as modes of counter-conduct challenging the authority of the orthodox ecclesia. Forms of counter-conduct "redistribute, reverse, nullify and partially or totally discredit pastoral power in the systems of salvation, obedience, and truth."[19] Counter-conduct practices are *not* opposed to Christianity as such; they actually activate radical dimensions of the Christian tradition, including "eschatology, Scripture, mysticism, the community, and ascesis."[20] Because they remain within the field of Christianity, counter-conduct activities can always be reintegrated into established pastoral structures. Thus, according to Foucault, the Reformation did not result in a total breakdown of the pastorate but rather "a formidable reinforcement of the pastorate in two different types"—a "more meticulous" yet "hierarchically supple" Protestant pastorate and a hierarchically stringent Catholic, Counter-Reformation pastorate.[21] In neither case, however, did the response to the counter-conduct revolt result in a rejection or erasure of religious activity. Counter-conduct does not generate a more secular world but more concentrated collective and individual forms of religious activity.

In early modern Europe, counter-conduct revolts redoubled the force of pastoral government rather than dissolving it into secular neutrality. Foucault argues that the Reformation opened new fields of governmentality not by effacing pastoral government but precisely by intensifying it. He claims that the upheavals of the sixteenth century produced a "proliferation" of questions of conduct. These questions were taken up by an intensified post-Reformation pastorate but also by an emergent "public domain," where these questions began to become politicized: "[T]he problem also arises of how and to what extent the exercise of the sovereign's power can and must take upon itself these previously unacknowledged tasks of conduction." Nonetheless, Foucault eschews the narrative of a secularizing transfer when he says, "[T]here was not a transition from the religious pastorate to other forms of conduct . . . In fact there was an intensification, increase, and general proliferation of this question and of these techniques of conduct. With the sixteenth century we enter the age of forms of conducting, directing, and government."[22] The Reformation and Counter-Reformation thus enhanced pastoral government in various forms—an enhancement visible in devotional innovations, intensified spiritual direction of adults, and more direct interventions in the education of children. In addition, and more significantly, these practices vastly expanded the overall field in which questions of government arose. Just as Foucault emphasizes a "proliferating economy" of discourses of sexuality in *The History of Sexuality*, he highlights the proliferation of discourses on conduct and government in general in the early modern period in these lectures on governmentality.[23] The dynamic of proliferation and intensification described in the governmentality lectures implies certain consequences for the thought of the secular as such. The vast increase of discourses of government—including especially pastoral government—challenges efforts to identify a straightforward, linear transition from secular to sacred forms of governance in this period. As a result of this discursive profusion, the emergent governmentality of Reformation Europe must be understood as constitutively intermingled with sacred and secular elements.

As we turn back to Shakespeare's play, it is important to bear in mind that the situation of Reformation England has an additional layer of complexity not fully captured in Foucault's account, which is focused largely on the general European context. On the one hand, the English sovereign (Henry VIII) advanced the Reformation for primarily political reasons, at least initially. On the other hand, this Reformation involved a substantial dismantling of the pastoral institutions of the medieval church (such as friaries and monasteries) without effectively replacing them in the new Church of England. Thus, the English sovereign becomes deeply involved in questions of religious conduct from the earliest stages of the Reformation. However, because it lacks an adequate infrastructure for pastoral government, his regime is underequipped to deal with the wave of counter-conduct unleashed by this Reformation. *Measure for Measure* stages the difficulties encountered in this unique and paradoxical situation.

The governmental complexity specific to *Measure for Measure* is particularly illuminated by Foucault's account of the interrelation of ascesis and monasticism in the larger tradition of pastoral government; this account clarifies the governmental implications of the prominent monastic and ascetic motifs in the play. Ascesis (the practice of strict self-control and bodily discipline) is a particularly pointed example of the paradox of Christian counter-conduct and pastoral governmentality. Foucault underscores this paradox by noting the common association of "asceticism with the very essence of Christianity."[24] However, ascetic conduct can also represent a challenge to the Christian pastorate. The nature of this challenge is clarified by the emergence of monastic institutions in the church: "the appearance of a communal and hierarchized life according to a rule imposed in the same way on everyone."[25] Foucault portrays asceticism as an assertion of spiritual self-government that disputed the authority of the pastoral government of the church: "whenever and wherever pastoral counter-conducts develop in the Middle Ages, asceticism was one of their points of support and instruments against the pastorate."[26] The development of monasticism aimed to curb ascetic excesses of the sort we see in Angelo and Isabella. Ascetic rigor becomes a form of counter-conduct. It announces a desire for other forms of government with implications that extend beyond the strictly ecclesial sphere and impinge upon broader social and political orders.

Foucault's schematic, broadly drawn characterization of counter-conduct and governmentality in the sixteenth century can be further grounded with a few instances that illustrate both the allure of ascetic habits in an early modern devotional context and the challenges such asceticism posed to extant and emergent forms of spiritual and political government.[27] Asceticism has a complex and sometimes vexed role in both Protestant and Counter-Reformation discourses. Saint Ignatius of Loyola's personal struggles with ascetic urges appear as a significant stage in a larger conversion process that culminates in the founding of the Society of Jesus in the early 1540s.[28] Ultimately, in Ignatius's rhetorical reconstruction of his life, his *Acta* (commonly translated into English as his "Autobiography"), ascetic renunciation is cast as an attractive mode of conduct, an appealing imitation of the saints and of Christ that must nonetheless be overcome because it poses great temptations to indulge in exorbitant, self-regarding behavior.[29] A parallel anti-ascetic discourse can be found in the preface to Richard Hooker's *Laws of Ecclesiastical Polity* (1593).[30] In defense of the established Church of England, Hooker presents a polemical account that attributes the potential for a divisive asceticism to the followers of Calvin. Hooker's account demonstrates how a reformed strain of ascetic conduct appeared as a political and social threat to good government in late sixteenth-century England. Hooker assimilates Calvinism to Anabaptism as he casts Protestant extreme asceticism as attractive but also dangerous insofar as it is liable to transform suddenly into an ungovernable licentiousness that foreshadows larger social chaos. For Hooker, the Anabaptist experience reveals a slippery slope leading from reformed asceticism to polygamy to civil war and social breakdown.[31] From the perspective of Hooker's moderate, politically sanctioned Protestantism, extreme asceticism is as distempered as extreme license, despite its apparent appeal to apostolic purity.

In various confessional discourses during the sixteenth century, then, the ascetic imperative—a mode of conduct with a long tradition in

Christianity—exerts renewed appeal in a climate of generalized religious turmoil. Sixteenth-century ascetics present a challenge on multiple levels. They contest government by previously acknowledged forms of pastoral power; they dispute traditional ways of ordering conduct toward salvation and they also threaten the harmony of civil society in an era in which religious, social, and political forms of government are intertwined. *Measure for Measure* dramatizes this ongoing historical struggle in the microcosm of a fictional Vienna, where several ascetic characters assert themselves in ways that implicitly endanger the established government, inspiring in response alterations in the relationship between pastoral and political governance. The convergent pressures of Catholic and Protestant ascetic counter-conduct produce a politically reconstituted pastorate in the play; the distant possibility of a secular state emerges from this pressurized context not as a positive prospect but as a negative capability.

Measure for Measure refracts the early modern ascetic into two stage characters that together enact a governmental challenge to both pastoral and political governments. Insofar as he mediates between the ascetic Catholic Isabella and the ascetic Puritan Angelo, *Measure*'s Duke imaginatively inhabits a space similar to that of the English Church government, although, unlike Hooker, Shakespeare's play is distinctly skeptical of the pastoral legitimacy of this avatar of "ecclesiastical polity." In this context, the ascetic--and not the louche libertine, such as Lucio--represents the true trial of the governor. This may seem a counterintuitive claim given that audiences usually accept the oft-stated premise that the Vienna of *Measure* is overwhelmed by an epidemic of sexual vice. However, closer scrutiny of the text reveals the Duke's contradictory rationales for putting the ascetic Angelo in charge of the city, rationales that are significantly uttered in a pastoral setting--evidently a monastery--as a warrant for taking on a monastic guise.

While much has been made of the Duke's purportedly omniscient role as a false friar and confessor, it is less frequently noted that the Duke himself appears early in the play in the pose of a penitent undergoing confession, enumerating his many sins of omission as a governor to an actual friar (1.3). Before the Duke inhabits the guise of a pastor, he is shown to be subject to pastoral power himself, responding to the questioning of his own spiritual director, Friar Thomas, who, like the audience, is evidently perplexed by the Duke's motives for abandoning his rule of Vienna: "No, holy father, throw away that thought. / Believe not that the dribbling dart of love / Can pierce a complete bosom" (1.3.1–3). Even as the Duke himself adopts the posture of the ascetic in denying concupiscence, he expresses the aspiration to live in the intensified pastorate of the monastery: "My holy sir, none better knows than you / How I have ever loved the life removed" (1.3.7–8). This scene does not present a corrupt or absurd pastorate: we are indeed invited to identify with a pastoral perspective, as Friar Thomas acts as a reasonable spokesman for a potentially skeptical audience (a point that places the play at a notable distance from more prevalent anti-Catholic representations of friars in Reformation England), particularly in his mild effort at correcting the Duke's conduct as a lax governor: "It rested in your grace / To unloose this tied-up Justice when you pleased" (1.3.31–32). Friar Thomas's questioning reinforces the sense that the Duke is a ruler who cannot manage his subjects' conduct.[32]

In this context, the most unmanageable form of conduct is not that of the worldly sinners but of the ascetic Angelo, who seems otherwise free from pastoral governance. While the Duke laments his inability to control a city overrun with "headstrong weeds" (1.3.20), a figure evocative of riotous fleshly vice, his ultimate rationale for adopting the "habit" (1.3.46) of a "true friar" (1.3.48) concerns the threat of Angelo's asceticism: "Lord Angelo is precise, / Stands at a guard with envy, scarce confesses / That his blood flows, or that his appetite / Is more to bread than stone" (1.3.50–53). The Duke dwells upon Angelo's radical denial of the body, his implied monomaniacal drive to imitate the example of Christ in the desert to an exorbitant, individualistic degree. Julia Lupton's affiliation of Angelo with a long tradition of hermetic Christian asceticism also reinforces such a reading (when he confronts Isabella, "Angelo . . . is also . . . the hermit tempted by the *diable en femme*").[33] This image of ascetic excess represents the final gambit that the Duke uses to persuade Friar Thomas, a representative of the more tempered communal asceticism of the monastery, to allow him to adopt the "habit" of a brother. The Duke argues that this change of costume is necessary to correct such an outlier. It is common to read the Duke's adoption of the guise of the Friar as a redoubling of his sovereign power with spiritual authority; the larger context of the scene, though, suggests it might be more apt to see something of a strategic retreat here, a signal that the Duke perceives his most urgent challenges as a ruler coming from fields usually governed by pastoral power.

Thus, at the outset of the play the Duke appears as a governor ironically inadequate to the efflorescence of governmentalities that surround him. The excess of illicit sexual activities is only a superficial problem; the more profound challenges are the ascetic models of government embodied by Angelo and Isabella as representatives of intensified Protestant and

Catholic spiritual regimes.[34] Of course, Angelo and Isabella enter into conflict with each other, and Angelo severely lapses from his initial high ascetic posture, moving from one extreme to another, while Isabella's fate is more complex. Nonetheless, at the start of the play, they each articulate severe forms of ascetic governmentality. In their urgent ascetic discourses, they aspire to orient their own worldly conduct (and potentially that of others) toward vividly imagined horizons of transcendent salvation and divine justice.

Angelo articulates a form of ascetic governmentality tinged with a reformed sense of divine election in the early scenes of the play. Prior to his fall into lechery, Angelo articulates an ideal of law that absolutely coordinates earthly government to a scheme of godly justice. He explains this position to Isabella early in their initial interview:

> The law hath not been dead, though it hath slept:
> . . . .
> Now 'tis awake,
> Takes note of what is done, and, like a prophet,
> Looks in a glass that shows what future evils,
> Either raw, or by remissness new conceived
> And so in progress to be hatched and born,
> Are now to have no successive degrees,
> But ere they live, to end. (2.2.93–101)

The law that governs quotidian existence is reimagined in Angelo's rhetoric as a biblical prophet with a fierce and strict instrumental agency. This divinely ordained law not only foresees but also actively cuts off crimes before they are even committed. The precognitive agency of this law (imaged as a prophetic "glass" or mirror) is necessarily transcendent as it strikes *before* transgressions become material events. Angelo's language casts the law and its attendant governmentality as intrinsically ascetic insofar as the "evils" that it seeks to prevent are metaphorized in terms of a natural cycle of conception, pregnancy, and birth; they are "newly conceived" and would be destined to be "born" without the abortive agency of the law, which ensures that "ere they live," they "end" or die.

Isabella's complementary Counter-Reformation asceticism is highlighted in her first lines in the play, in a scene (1.4) immediately juxtaposed with the Duke's fretful complaints about the "precise" Puritan Angelo (1.3). In terms of dramatic structure, the convent would seem to complement the monastery as a site of communally mediated asceticism, but Isabella is portrayed as striving to outdo the rule of the order she is about to join, underscoring the sense of a burgeoning ascetic governmentality in Vienna:

> ISABELLA: And have you nuns no farther privileges?
> FRANCISCA: Are not these large enough?
> ISABELLA: Yes, truly. I speak not as desiring more,
> But rather wishing a more strict restraint
> Upon the sisterhood, the votarists of Saint Clare. (1.4.1–5)

The convent is explicitly posed as site of government, a place governed by clear rules of conduct; however, this pastoral framework is also marked as deficient from Isabella's stridently ascetic position. Isabella's stringent attitude is frequently marked as echoing Angelo's own rigidity, and my reading is generally in concord with such views. Critics who want to read Isabella's portrayal as a species of antimonastic satire will, however, also insist on a difference between them: while Angelo is supposedly "self-reliant," Isabella's austerity demands "external restraint."[35] In this passage, though, Isabella asserts herself ("I speak") in an individualistic vein, challenging as insufficient the rule of the "sisterhood," the community of the convent. While she ultimately affirms this rule ("Yes, truly"), she also articulates a desire for an intensified ascetic experience ("more strict restraint"), placing herself somewhat at odds with the communal boundaries of the order. Isabella's initial contradictory stance reinforces the pervasive sense of ascendant, individualistic asceticism in the early scenes of the play, amplifying the challenges represented in Angelo's ascetic posture.

The Duke's answer to the challenge presented by the ascetic governmentalities embodied in Angelo and Isabella is to take on the habit of a friar, the mendicant cousin of the monk—a mode of religious conduct that sought to govern the excesses of asceticism, as Foucault argues. A friar is not exactly a monk, however; mendicant orders live in religious community but are far from cloistered. Instead, we might understand friars as bringing the total liturgical and sacramental form of life of the monastery into the secular world of the laity.[36] From the perspective of the Catholic pastorate--admittedly highly contested in Reformation England--friars ideally expand access to the sacraments and spiritual direction, although even in Catholic contexts their work could be seen as controversial and disruptive.[37] Friars are relatively secular ministers of the Church insofar as they circulate in the everyday world, but they are also always agents of an established form of pastoral governmentality. In becoming a friar, the Duke aspires to adapt pastoral governmentality to the agenda of political government, but the habit never really fits. The Duke's performance as a friar is far from the seamless, devious guise of surveillance assumed by earlier Foucauldian critics, nor is it an affirmation of a divinely anointed ruler's good government of souls.[38]

The Friar-Duke conforms to neither of these models of secularization. Instead, Shakespeare's play stages a failure of secularization in the sense of a Schmittian transfer of functions from Church to State. The Duke, as Friar, consistently sabotages his own efforts at pastoral government. Unlike the play's figures of ascetic governmentality, the Duke is persistently preoccupied with government as solely a matter of ordering worldly, immanent existence; he is notably much less concerned with orienting those whom he governs toward any salvific horizon. While the Duke's version of pastoral government may emphasize communal goods over individual desires, it tends to lose sight of salvation as a transcendent end. Indeed a good measure of the comedy in the play emerges from the Duke's repeated failures as a pastor. Ironically, the Duke's habit as a friar actually comes to underscore the *difference* between the Duke's government and serious pastoral government. At the least, the Duke's experience posits an unstable, if not impossible, passage between these modalities of government. I turn now to a more detailed review of the Duke's activities in the office of friar in order to demonstrate that the instability of the Duke's government is inherently linked to his inadequate pastoral strategies.[39]

The failure of the Duke's pastoral care appears most clearly when he attempts to assume to role of confessor and spiritual adviser. The first notable instance of the Duke's ineffective government occurs in his pseudopastoral exchange with Juliet, Claudio's unhappy partner:

> DUKE: Then was your sin of heavier kind than his.
> JULIET: I do confess it and repent it, father.
> DUKE: 'Tis meet so, daughter. But lest you do repent
> As that the sin hath brought you to this shame--
> Which sorrow is always toward ourselves, not heaven,
> Showing we would not spare heaven as we love it,
> But as we stand in fear—
> JULIET: I do repent me as it is an evil,
> And take the shame with joy.
> DUKE: There rest.
> Your partner, as I hear, must die tomorrow,
> And I am going with instruction to him.
> Grace go with you. *Benedicite! Exit.*

> JULIET: Must die tomorrow? O injurious law,
> That respites me a life whose very comfort
> Is still a dying horror! (2.3.30–44)

The Friar-Duke demands that Juliet repent not for reasons of social shame or self-love but from true respect for "heaven," the realm of salvation. Juliet, however, interrupts this effort to govern her stance toward a transcendent end with a terse, equivocal interjection that evidently embraces "shame" while repenting "evil."[40] Juliet cuts short the Friar-Duke's rhetoric and undercuts his pose of spiritual authority, drawing the audience's attention to the Friar-Duke's failure to govern her conduct toward a salvific horizon. While the Friar-Duke evidently accepts her formulation and departs with a parting "*Benedicite!*" he also interjects the unwelcome news that Claudio "must die tomorrow," a phrase that destabilizes his blessing with an imminent reality that affects Juliet in a devastating way. As Juliet echoes the Friar-Duke's words, she finds her "life" transformed from "comfort" to "dying horror." The Friar-Duke's blunt death notice drastically undoes whatever spiritual comfort he may have provided in the prior exchange. We learn nothing further about the state of Juliet's soul, but we are left with the uneasy sense that the Duke's unexpectedly blunt emphasis on the deathly function of the law has accomplished precisely the opposite of sound pastoral government. This is only one of the earliest inklings that the Duke's governmentality, although disguised "like power divine" (5.1.361) for much of the play, is decidedly oriented toward immanent, rather than transcendent, economies.

The counterpart to this episode of dismal pastoral governance is the Duke's attempted consolation of Juliet's partner, Claudio, at the beginning of act 3. Critics stretching back to Samuel Johnson have noted problems with the Duke's pastoral discourse in 3.1.[41] In the Arden edition of *Measure for Measure*, J. W. Lever aptly asserts, "The Duke's description of the human condition eliminates its spiritual aspect and is essentially materialist and pagan."[42] Building on these insights, I want to emphasize that the materialism of the Duke's *ars moriendi* is a sign of his larger failure to marshal a credible version of pastoral governmentality. Rather than working as a form of secularizing disenchantment that reinforces his sovereign power, this pastoral failure reinforces a more general sense of disoriented government in the play.

The Friar-Duke's opening exhortation—"Be absolute for death" (3.1.5)—emphasizes the earthly world apart from any passage toward an afterlife. Pastoral governmentality is always concerned with conduct in this world; however, it should also orient this life toward salvation. The absence of any suggestion of salvation in the Friar-Duke's discourse persistently distorts his otherwise clichéd *ars moriendi* tropes. This tendency is most evident in those parts of the speech that actually come closest to evoking a transcendent reality. For example, the Friar-Duke admonishes Claudio, "A breath thou art, / Servile to all the skyey influences" (3.1.8–9). Insofar as these lines allude to astrology, they both refer to a heavenly sphere and contain it within an earthly frame of reference. The "skyey" heavens are defined only in terms of the earthly influences; they remain part of the material world rather than a trope for the transcendent horizon of salvation. A similar point can be made about "breath," which sometimes works as a metaphor for spirit, but in this context is identified sheerly with bodily exhalation. "Servile" further implies bondage to the stars as material determinants, not signs of a higher and freer spiritual realm. This inexorable state of material being is subject to perpetual disintegration in the Friar-Duke's discourse as he proceeds to present a version of pagan Epicurean cosmos, invoking the concept of atomism to dissolve the illusion of an integral person: "Thou art not thyself, / For thou exist'st on many a thousand grains / That issue out of dust" (3.1.19–21).[43] This personal disarray is not the product of conflicting passions within the soul but is essentially projected into material being. In the Friar-Duke's disconsolate consolation, being is reduced to an "after-dinner's sleep" (3.1.33): again, the potentially visionary or spiritual dimension of "dreaming" (3.1.34) is weighed down by the dross or gross matter of the body as it is envisaged as the mere effluvia of digestion. The Friar-Duke emphasizes only the misery and uncertainty of this world while leaving the next world up to the imagination. In this abstract, indeterminate notion of the afterlife, we might see the Duke anticipating something like a modern secular mentality; however, it is important to note that in the context of an effort to amend a penitent sinner's spiritual state, this seeming secularity is a mark of the failure of the Duke's government, not its success.

Claudio's capacity for a quite vivid imagination of this next world is underscored by his counterspeech to Isabella later in 3.1, after she denies his hope for pardon: "Ay, but to die, and go we know not where . . ." (3.1.118). Claudio envisions this "where" in myriad forms, from "fiery floods" to "thick-ribbèd ice" (3.1.122–23). One explanation for Claudio's rampant imagination and turbulent affective state is that he has been given insufficient direction and solace from the supposed Friar who has just advised him. The deficiency is evident even earlier, immediately after the Friar-Duke has spoken; it is Claudio himself who fills in the scriptural and eschatological gap left in the Duke's discourse. Claudio's response to his supposed confessor's lengthy exhortation--"To sue to live, I find I seek to die, / And seeking death, find life" (3.1.42–43)--paraphrases Matthew 16:25: "For whosoever will save his life, shall lose it: and whosoever shall lose his life for my sake, shall find it."[44] That the sheep (Claudio), in the absence of meaningful guidance from his pastor, must himself provide a hint of saving grace in an allusion to the Gospel is perhaps the most damning index of the Friar-Duke's pastoral failure, his inability to provide apt direction. In Foucault's terms, the Friar-Duke has failed "to conduct" Claudio appropriately toward a Christian end. This failure crystallizes a broader indictment of the Friar-Duke's governmentality in the play.

The Duke's most spectacular pastoral failure occurs in the scenes involving the hapless Barnardine in act 4. Barnardine vividly demonstrates how the Duke fails as both a pastoral and a political governor. It is Barnardine, above all other characters in the play, who makes visible how pastoral power can reinforce political power (and vice versa) without necessarily achieving a coherent semblance of secularization. Barnardine concentrates all the challenges to pastoral government in the play; in particular, the oxymoronically ascetic quality of his debauchery reinforces the sense of a governmentality under pressure from competing versions of spiritual government. In previous criticism, Barnardine has been most commonly discussed as an inveterate "reprobate," and others have associated him with the "figure of the unconverted Jew." Barnardine has also been read in the context of Saint Bernard and other figures from the monastic tradition who sublimate sexual desire into spiritual liberty, as well as a kind of *homo sacer* who persists in a biopolitical state of exception.[45] Alongside these earlier suggestions, in the context of my focus on the problem of pastoral governmentality I want to add that Barnardine acts as a figure of carnivalesque counter-conduct, who marks a more profound limit to the Duke's pastoral government than any other figure in the play.

In this account of the larger economy of pastoral government in the play, it is perhaps less helpful to think of Barnardine as a reprobate and instead to consider whether his behavior might correlate in some way with the motif of counter-conduct and resistance to pastoral power that runs throughout the play. Although Barnardine is not evidently ascetic, he is not entirely irreligious. In some ways, his resistance to the pastoral posture of the Friar-Duke resonates with what Foucault describes as the "hierarchical reversal" characterizing some counter-conduct communities in the sixteenth century:

> [W]e find many other ways of asserting schemas of obedience in these communities, but in a way that is completely different from the pastoral schema . . . the most ignorant or poorest

> person, or someone with the lowest reputation or honor, the most debauched . . . was chosen as leader of the group . . . Somewhat as asceticism had this aspect of almost ironic exaggeration in relation to the pure and simple rule of obedience, we could say that in some of these communities there was a counter-society aspect, a carnival aspect, overturning social relations and hierarchy.[46]

Foucault draws attention to the way in which counter-conduct, while driven by a spiritual imperative to seek alternatives to pastoral government, may also prove disruptive to larger social or political norms. He also emphasizes the diverse ways in which counter-conduct activities can emerge; while asceticism may be the most obvious form of spiritual counter-conduct, exalting extreme debauchery may also incorporate a counter-conduct aspect. Both asceticism and its opposite partake of extremes, which interfere with normal modes of governmentality.

Barnardine paradoxically displays both ascetic and antiascetic qualities redolent of counter-conduct; he also illustrates how resistance to pastoral government may possess broader social and political overtones. The Provost highlights the curiously ascetic debauchery of Barnardine in his initial description of the character: "A man that apprehends death no more dreadfully but as / a drunken sleep; careless, reckless, and fearless of what's past, / present, or to come; insensible of mortality, and desperately / mortal" (4.2.132–35). On the one hand, the Provost underscores the gross embodiedness of Barnardine, whose "drunken sleep" culminates in "desperate" mortality and thereby recalls the Friar-Duke's materialistic cautions to Claudio in act 3. On the other hand, the fact that Barnardine is "insensible of mortality" appears to defy the state of mortal being, as though he reaches the stance and attitude of the ascetic through an absolute "drunken" immersion in mortal things, rather than a denial of them. From this perspective, Barnardine combines the disregard of the body of the ascetic with the disconnection from ordinary temporality of the ecstatic mystic ("fearless of what's past, present, or to come"). Barnardine's debauchery extends beyond mere misconduct; it is seemingly mixed with elements of counter-conduct, making it hard to dismiss him as a simple reprobate or ordinary criminal. This sense of Barnardine as an exceptional quasi-ascetic character continues through the Provost's description of Barnardine's life in prison: "He hath evermore had the liberty / of the prison" without making an effort to escape (4.2.136–37), and he has no reaction to any "seeming warrant" for his execution: "it hath not moved him at all" (4.2.141). In this apparent indifference to the fate of his body, Barnardine demonstrates his affinity with ascetic counter-conduct movements and his capacity to move beyond the realm of pastoral government as ordinarily constituted.

These qualities are on full display once Barnardine actually appears onstage, continuing to resist all efforts at governing his actions, most significantly those of the Friar-Duke. When the Friar-Duke, hoping to persuade Barnardine to accept his execution (so his head can be substituted for Claudio's), yet again adopts the pose of a "ghostly father" (4.3.42), Barnardine remains unmoved. He insists he is "not fitted" for death because he has been "drinking all night" (4.3.36–37), an assertion that strikingly contradicts the Provost's portrayal of a "careless" and "fearless" reprobate. While the carnivalesque debauchery of Barnardine is foregrounded in this initial response, his subsequent face-to-face rejoinder to the "Friar" reinforces the underlying sense of Barnardine as a counter-conduct figure: "Friar, not I. I have been drinking hard all night, / and I will have more time to prepare me, or they shall beat out / my brains with billets. I will not consent to die this day, that's / certain" (4.3.46–49). On the one hand, Barnardine emphasizes his "desperately mortal" condition by reasserting his hungover state; on the other, he does recognize the need for "more time to prepare me" to move into an afterlife, countering the common assumption that he has no spiritual apprehension. He insists on his own right to decide how he will be governed toward this afterlife, however, even to the point of courting violence to maintain this integrity ("beat out my brains with billets"). He articulates this resistance directly in the face of the purported pastoral authority who seeks to govern him in other terms. This resistance is an absurd mixture of spiritual and material considerations; the political stakes become evident, however, in Barnardine's final insistence that he "will not consent" to a present execution. As he recognizes the need for "preparation," he does not altogether deny the validity of the sphere in which the pastorate claims to govern; he does, however, deny its hierarchical demand upon his person. Instead, he seeks to recast the pastorate as a community to which one does or does not give "consent"; in this way, he insists on being governed otherwise, by consent rather than command or coercion. Barnardine's evocation of "consent" crystallizes the way in which he represents a resistance to government that has both pastoral and political implications. In accord with classic instances of counter-conduct, he refuses pastoral "advice" in language with a political register that conveys a spiritual aspiration to be governed in other terms.

The Friar-Duke acknowledges the force of Barnardine's resistance when he abandons his effort to prepare him for death. The Friar-Duke admits that Barnardine is a "creature unprepared, unmeet for death; /

And to transport him in the mind he is / Were damnable" (4.3.59–61). While a bit later, the Provost refers to Barnardine as "[t]his reprobate" (4.3.66), the Friar-Duke's earlier capitulation, particularly the expressed possibility of damnation at executing the "unmeet" man, suggests Barnardine's argument has carried some unlikely spiritual force. The challenge of his "stubborn soul" (5.1.474) is, however, decorously obscured in the pageant of governmentality that takes place in act 5, as Vincentio exchanges the role of pastor for sovereign. In this guise, the Duke pardons Barnardine for his "earthly faults" (5.1.477) while nonetheless striking a note of pastoral concern: "Pray thee take this mercy to provide / For better times to come" (5.1.478–79). Interestingly, however, the Duke passes any further effort to govern Barnardine in actual pastoral terms to a true member of the pastorate: "Friar, advise him. / I leave him to your hand" (5.1.479–80). Thus Barnardine becomes the occasion, again, for the Duke to acknowledge the limitations of his experiment in pastoral government; his pardon makes visible a continuing split between pastoral and political fields of government. As Barnardine is assigned no lines in this scene, we cannot fully assess how he receives the Duke's final effort to govern him through pardon and referral to further pastoral care.[47]

Most readings of *Measure for Measure* that identify a strain of Foucauldian power politics or an emergent secular order in the play argue that the Duke ultimately succeeds in securing a new form of political or biopolitical state government in the final act of the play. Robert Watson reflects this common position when he asserts that at the end of the play the Duke's "version of redemption serves to defend, not faith or moral purity, but the public procreative order of Vienna."[48] In this formulation, a new political form of government is substituted for an older ecclesiastical dispensation. However, the tensions that linger around Barnardine and Isabella suggest, to the contrary, that when the Duke fails as a pastor he also fundamentally fails to establish any meaningful government, whether pastoral or political. The Duke's pastoral failures signify a more profound crisis provoked by the challenge of counter-conduct, an imaginative void in the forms of government that the Duke can never entirely fill. To suggest that the Duke does succeed in introducing a biopolitical form of government to manage the population of Vienna at the end of the play is to overdetermine a factor that is actually underdetermined in Shakespeare's text. It is an intriguing and attractive reading, but it proceeds too quickly to its conclusion. This overdetermined reading is also a premature secularization of the world of the play, which inhibits a reading of the dimension of counter-conduct, particularly asceticism, as a motivating pressure. Under this pressure, the Duke does not succeed in secularization in the sense of either disenchanting the sacred or transferring its values to secular forms of government. Instead, he can only experiment, with uncertain success. The play ends with a proliferation of governmental occasions (in the form of hasty, largely forced marriages and dubious pardons) that do not necessarily coalesce into a recognizable scheme of secular governmentality. Projecting our own experience of a secular state back into Shakespeare's dramatic world forecloses the multiplicity of governmentalities in the political imaginary of *Measure for Measure*.

Notes

1. See Stephen Greenblatt, Walter Cohen, Jean E. Howard, Katherine Eisaman Maus, eds., *The Norton Shakespeare: Later Plays*, vol. 2, 2nd ed, (New York: W. W. Norton & Company, 2008), *Measure for Measure*, 1.1.9, 314n1. All quotations are taken from this edition, unless otherwise noted.

2. Richard Wilson associates the Duke's speech with Foucault's analysis of "governmentality"; see "Prince of Darkness: Foucault's Shakespeare," in *Shakespeare in French Theory: King of Shadows* (New York: Routledge, 2007), 91–94. This association is pursued in a different vein in this essay. Wilson's reading examines governmentality in the play primarily in terms of biopolitics, while I focus more on how Foucault's account of the *longue durée* of governmentality, particularly pastoral government and counter-conduct, illuminates crucial aspects of the play. In the present argument, I consider the full scope of the development of governmentality in Foucault's lectures of 1977–78, published in English as *Security, Territory, Population: Lectures at the Collège de France, 1977–1978*, trans. Graham Burchell (New York: Picador, 2009).

3. Prominent examples include Jonathan Goldberg, *James I and the Politics of the Literature: Jonson, Shakespeare, Donne, and Their Contemporaries* (Baltimore: Johns Hopkins University Press, 1983), 231–39; Jonathan Dollimore, "Transgression and Surveillance in *Measure for Measure*," in *Political Shakespeare: New Essays in Cultural Materialism*, ed. Jonathan Dollimore and Alan Sinfield (Ithaca, N.Y.: Cornell University Press, 1985), 72–87; Steven Mullaney, *The Place of the Stage: License, Play, and Power in Renaissance England* (Ann Arbor: University of Michigan Press, 1995), 88–115; and Leonard Tennenhouse, *Power on Display: The Politics of Shakespeare's Genres* (London: Methuen, 1986), 154–71. Wilson's "Prince of Darkness," 75–122, offers a fine synthesis of the 1980s reception of Foucault. On "biopower" in *Measure for Measure*, see Robert N. Watson, "False Immortality in *Measure for Measure*: Comic Means, Tragic Ends," *Shakespeare Quarterly* 41, no. 4 (Winter 1990): 411–32, and Daniel Cadman, "'The Very Nerves of State': Biopolitics and Sovereignty in Shakespeare's Vienna," in *Lectures de "Measure for Measure" de William Shakespeare*, ed. Delphine Lemonnier-Texier and Guillaume Winter, Mondes Anglophones (Rennes: Presses Universitaires de Rennes, 2012), 159–72. Both Dollimore and Wilson cite Richard Hooker's criticism of Machiavellian religion as a "mere politic device" as if it were also the standard position on this topic in both Shakespeare's play and Foucault's theory (Dollimore, "Transgression and Surveillance," 81; Wilson, "Prince of Darkness,"

101). For his part, Hooker coins the phrase to characterize a Machiavellian position to which he opposes the supposed right government of the English Church; see Hooker, *Of the Laws of Ecclesiastical Polity*, vol. 2, bk. 5, introduction by Christopher Morris (London: Dent, 1964), 19. On the Duke's "omniscience," see Dollimore, "Transgression and Surveillance," 83, and Mullaney, *Place of the Stage*, 114. Goldberg more subtly emphasizes the "presence-in-absence" of the Duke's power but nonetheless underscores his "absolutism" (*James I*, 255). All these accounts highlight surveillance as a salient condition in Shakespeare's Vienna.

4. The critical tradition emphasizing Christian allegory or divine right in the play includes Roy Battenhouse, "*Measure for Measure* and the Christian Doctrine of Atonement," *PMLA* 61, no. 4 (December 1946): 1029–59; G. Wilson Knight, *The Wheel of Fire: Essays in Interpretation of Shakespeare's Sombre Tragedies* (London: Oxford University Press, 1930); Louise Schleiner, "Providential Improvisation in *Measure for Measure*," *PMLA* 97, no. 2 (March 1982): 227–36; and Debora Kuller Shuger, *Political Theologies in Shakespeare's England: The Sacred and the State in "Measure for Measure"* (New York: Palgrave, 2001). On the concept of a "King James Version" of *Measure for Measure*, see Richard Levin, "The King James Version of *Measure for Measure*," *Clio* 3, no. 2 (1974): 129–63. Levin's critique has not discouraged the still-common habit of identifying Shakespeare's Duke with James I and the ideology of divine right rule. More sophisticated variants of the argument include Shuger, *Political Theologies*; Goldberg, *James I*; Andrew Barnaby and Joan Wry, "Authorized Versions: *Measure for Measure* and the Politics of Biblical Translation," *Renaissance Quarterly* 51, no. 4 (1989): 1225–54; and Thomas Fulton, "Shakespeare's *Everyman*: *Measure for Measure* and English Fundamentalism," *Journal of Medieval and Early Modern Studies* 40, no. 1 (Winter 2010): 119–47.

5. The "disenchantment" claim derives from Weber's lecture "Science as a Vocation" (1918); see *From Max Weber: Essays in Sociology*, trans. and ed. H. H. Gerth and C. Wright Mills (New York: Oxford University Press, 1958), 129–56. On Weberian disenchantment, see Brian Cummings, *Mortal Thoughts: Religion, Secularity and Identity in Shakespeare and Early Modern Culture* (Oxford: Oxford University Press, 2013), 1–18. Schmitt's hypothesis appears in *Political Theology: Four Chapters on the Concept of Sovereignty*, trans. George Schwab (Chicago: University of Chicago Press, 2005), 36: "All significant concepts of the modern theory of the state are secularized theological concepts not only because of their historical development—in which they were transferred from theology to the theory of the state . . . but also because of their systematic structure."

6. Giorgio Agamben, *The Kingdom and the Glory: For a Theological Genealogy of Economy and Government*, trans. Lorenzo Chiesa with Matteo Mandarini (Stanford, Calif.: Stanford University Press, 2011), 4–5.

7. Governmentality studies have so far proved most influential among scholars of postcolonial literature; see John Marx, "Literature and Governmentality," *Literature Compass* 8, no. 1 (January 2011): 66–79. For treatments in early modern literary studies, see Mary Polito, *Governmental Arts in Early Tudor England* (Aldershot: Ashgate Publishing, 2005), and David Glimp, *Increase and Multiply: Governing Cultural Reproduction in Early Modern England* (Minneapolis: University of Minnesota Press, 2003). Both studies predate the wider availability of Foucault's full lectures in English.

8. Foucault, *Security, Territory, Population*, 149.

9. For Foucault's full introduction to the concept of "governmentality" and its genealogy, see *Security, Territory, Population*, 108–10. While Foucault usually speaks of governmentality as something modern, with pastoral government as an extensive "prelude" (184), the concepts are so closely intertwined that I refer to "pastoral governmentality" in this context, although that is not Foucault's usual procedure. This section of the present essay recasts some material previously published in a different form in "Forms of Governmentality in *The Alchemist*," *Studies in English Literature* 58, no. 1 (Winter 2018): 95–121.

10. Foucault, *Security, Territory, Population*,108, 192–93.

11. Foucault, *Security, Territory, Population*, 99.

12. Foucault, *Security, Territory, Population*, 191–92.

13. "minister, v.," *OED Online*, December 2018, Oxford University Press, http://www.oed.com/view/Entry/118878.

14. "administer, v.," *OED Online*, December 2018, Oxford University Press, http://www.oed.com/view/Entry/2531.

15. Michel Foucault, *Discipline and Punish: The Birth of the Prison*, trans. Alan Sheridan (New York: Vintage Books, 1979), 28.

16. Foucault, *Discipline and Punish*, 29.

17. See Arnold Davidson's remarks on the "double dimension" of conduct in his introduction to *Security, Territory, Population*, xix–xx, and in "In Praise of Counter-Conduct," *History of the Human Sciences* 24, no. 4 (October 2011): 25–41. For Foucault's own definition of conduct, see *Security, Territory, Population*, 193. See also Matthew Chrulew, "Pastoral Counter-Conducts: Religious Resistance in Foucault's Genealogy of Christianity," *Critical Research on Religion* 2, no. 1 (April 2014): 55–65.

18. Foucault addresses this aspect of the pastorate most fully in the lecture of February 22, 1978; see *Security, Territory, Population*, 164–67.

19. Foucault, *Security, Territory, Population*, 204.

20. Foucault, *Security, Territory, Population*, 214.

21. Foucault, *Security, Territory, Population*, 149.

22. Foucault, *Security, Territory, Population*, 230–31. See also 229: "There is not even a massive, comprehensive transfer of pastoral functions from Church to state. What we see in reality is a much more complex phenomenon." However, by the end of the eighteenth century, Foucault claims, "we see revolts of conduct arising less from the religious institution and much more from political institutions. Conflicts of conduct will occur on the borders and edge of the political institution" (197–98).

23. Michel Foucault, "From *The History of Sexuality, Volume I, An Introduction*," in *The Norton Anthology of Theory and Criticism*, 2nd ed., ed. Vincent B. Leitch (New York: Norton, 2010), 1513.

24. Foucault, *Security, Territory, Population*, 204–5.

25. Foucault, *Security, Territory, Population*, 205.

26. Foucault, *Security, Territory, Population*, 207. For further analysis of asceticism and monasticism, see Foucault, *On the Government of the Living: Lectures at the Collège de France, 1979–1980*, trans. Graham Burchell (New York: Picador, 2014), lecture of March 26, 1980.

27. Gary Kuchar suggested the examples in this paragraph in comments on an earlier draft at the 2015 meeting of the Shakespeare Association of America in Vancouver, Canada (in the seminar "Shakespeare and Transcendence").

28. John C. Olin, ed., *The Autobiography of St. Ignatius Loyola*, trans. Joseph J. O'Callaghan (New York: Fordham University Press, 1992), 34.

29. Marjorie Boyle connects Loyola's experience to a larger tradition of "competitive" asceticism and its corrections within medieval monastic literature in *Loyola's Acts: The Rhetoric of the Self* (Berkeley: University of California Press, 1997), 75–82.

30. Richard Hooker, *Of the Laws of Ecclesiastical Polity*, ed. Arthur Steven McGrade (Cambridge: Cambridge University Press, 1998).

31. Hooker develops this case explicitly in chapter 8 of the preface to the *Laws*, entitled "How just cause there is to fear the manifold dangerous events likely to ensue upon this intended reformation, if it did take place" (35–49).

32. My reading of the political significance of the monastic elements in the play thus differs from that of Marc Shell, who has analyzed, in psychoanalytic terms, the conjunction of the play's monastic and political elements under the sign of incest, as cultural signifiers of family romance; see *The End of Kinship: "Measure for Measure," Incest, and the Ideal of Universal Siblinghood* (Stanford, Calif.: Stanford University Press, 1988).

33. Julia Reinhard Lupton, *Afterlives of the Saints: Hagiography, Typology, and Renaissance Literature* (Stanford, Calif.: Stanford University Press, 1996), 110.

34. In this sense, my argument dovetails with Peter Lake's account of *Measure for Measure* as an anti-Puritan dramatization of the pitfalls of godly rule in *The Antichrist's Lewd Hat: Protestants, Papists and Players in Post-Reformation England* (New Haven, Conn.: Yale University Press, 2003). To Lake's reading, I add a consideration of how the play deploys monasticism and pastoral governmentality as a counterpoint to Angelo's figure of godly government.

35. Darryl J. Gless makes this distinction in *Measure for Measure, the Law and the Convent* (Princeton, N.J.: Princeton University Press, 1979), 97. However, Gless's insistence on reading the play as antimonastic satire turns the drama into an obsessive correction of Isabella's theological errors, while Angelo's atrocities are relatively unexplored.

36. On monasticism and form of life, see Giorgio Agamben, *The Highest Poverty: Monastic Rules and Form-of-Life*, trans. Adam Kotsko (Stanford, Calif.: Stanford University Press, 2013). Agamben develops some implications of Foucault's concept of governmentality, but he does not address the difference between friars and monks within the larger cenobitic tradition.

37. For an argument that Shakespeare's friars are "surprisingly sympathetic" and positively associated with players in "performing a similar kind of spiritual work," see Jeffrey Knapp, *Shakespeare's Tribe: Church, Nation, and Theater in Renaissance England* (Chicago: University of Chicago Press, 2002), 52–53. For a more skeptical appraisal of the friar figure in *Measure for Measure* as continuous with some elements of English anti-Catholicism, see Gillian Woods, *Shakespeare's Unreformed Fictions* (Oxford: Oxford University Press, 2013), 114–19. Sarah Beckwith claims that the Friar-Duke in *Measure for Measure* is actually

an "inversion of anti-Catholic theater" that criticizes the royal supremacy in the Church of England. Beckwith's claim that the Friar-Duke transforms the sacrament of confession into "a coercive external apparatus of the state" echoes earlier Foucault-inspired arguments about the play (*Shakespeare and the Grammar of Forgiveness* [Ithaca, N.Y.: Cornell University Press, 2011], 75, 78).

38. For the range of surveillance readings, see Goldberg, *James I*; Dollimore, "Transgression and Surveillance"; Mullaney, *Place of the Stage*; Tennenhouse, *Power on Display*; and Beckwith, *Grammar of Forgiveness*. Shuger, *Political Theologies*, offers one of the most positive estimations of the Duke's ability to manage both political and divine roles at the same time.

39. Harry Berger Jr. presents a detailed analysis of the Duke's inadequacies as both a pastor and a governor in an extended essay that overlaps with some points pursued here; see "What Does the Duke Know and When Does He Know It? Carrying the Torch in *Measure for Measure*," in *Making Trifles of Terrors: Redistributing Complicities in Shakespeare*, ed. Peter Erickson (Stanford, Calif.: Stanford University Press, 1997), 335–426. While I share Berger's skepticism about the effectiveness of the Duke's tactics, I do insist on framing his problems in a larger social, political, and religious context, an approach that Berger explicitly rejects in favor of a character study of the Duke as a case of "anxiety about self-representation" (338), resulting in a "psychomachian split within Vincentio between the 'Friar' and the Duke" (400).

40. David Scott Kastan reads Juliet as diffident, "replying ambiguously" to the Duke's remonstrations, in *A Will to Believe: Shakespeare and Religion* (Oxford: Oxford University Press, 2014), 69. Kastan also suggests that this is a less-than-persuasive scene of pastoral care, although he overlooks the subsequent destruction of Juliet's spiritual comfort. Stephen Greenblatt does observe that the Duke ultimately heightens Juliet's "anxiety," but he tends to interpret this increased anxiety in secularizing terms: Juliet's anxiety "simply brushes aside the theological categories the duke had taken it upon himself to instill in her" (*Shakespearean Negotiations: The Circulation of Social Energy in Renaissance England* [Berkeley: University of California Press, 1988], 141).

41. Johnson comments on the Duke's assurance that "thy best of rest is sleep . . . yet grossly fear'st / Thy death which is no more. . . ." (3.1.19): "I cannot without indignation find Shakespeare saying that *death is only sleep*, lengthening out his exhortation by a sentence which in the Friar is impious, in the reasoner is foolish, and in the poet trite and vulgar" (*The Plays of Shakespeare from the Text of Dr. S. Johnson*, vol. 1, part 2 [Dublin: Thomas Ewing, 1771], 25).

42. J. W. Lever, "Introduction," in *Measure for Measure*, The Arden Shakespeare, 2nd ser. (London: Methuen, 1965), lxxxvii; compare Watson, "False Immortality in *Measure for Measure*," 421.

43. On the possible Epicurean allusion, see Lever, ed., *Measure for Measure*, 68n, on 3.1.20–21. See also Alexander Leggatt on the Duke's "Stoic" discourse in this scene: "Substitution in *Measure for Measure*," *Shakespeare Quarterly* 39, no. 3 (Autumn 1988): 357.

44. *The Geneva Bible: A Facsimile of the 1560 Edition*, introduction by Lloyd E. Berry (Madison: University of Wisconsin Press, 1969), spelling modernized. Claudio's lines more persuasively echo the Gospels than the sole scriptural resonance sometimes identified in the Duke's consolation, at 3.1.25 ("If thou art

rich, thou'rt poor"); *The Norton Shakespeare: Later Plays*, vol. 2, 2nd ed., suggests an allusion to Revelation 3:17 (338n3), but this seems remote.

45. For Barnardine as "reprobate," see Lake, *The Antichrist's Lewd Hat*, 685, and Musa Gurnis, "'Most Ignorant of What He's Most Assured': The Hermeneutics of Predestination in *Measure for Measure*," *Shakespeare Studies* 42 (2014): 141–69. On Barnardine as a resistant Judaic figure ("the distant cousin of *Barabbas*, the criminal in the Gospels"), see Lupton, *Afterlives of the Saints*, 138–39. Marc Shell raises the possible monastic associations in *The End of Kinship*, 58–61. On Barnardine as *homo sacer*, see Cadman, "'The Very Nerves of State,'" 170–71. See also Jacques Lezra's account of Barnardine's deconstructive effect on the economy of substitution and representation in the play in *Unspeakable Subjects: The Genealogy of the Event in Early Modern Europe* (Stanford, Calif.: Stanford University Press, 1997), 256–94.

46. Foucault, *Security, Territory, Population*, 211–12. Lake also associates Barnardine with the "carnivalesque": "The intransigence and intractability of the carnivalesque body, in the face of forces of control and reform" (*The Antichrist's Lewd Hat*, 685). However, this "carnivalesque" quality can be understood not simply as reprobation but rather as a seeking after alternative forms of spiritual government.

47. Kaori Ashizu discusses the significance of Barnardine's silence in the context of the series of other moments of "open silence" in act 5 (many of which indicate a potentially critical view of the Duke) in "'Pardon Me?' Judging Barnardine's Judge," *English Studies* 78, no. 5 (1997): 417–29. We can sense in this resistant silence an affinity between Barnardine and the ascetic character who seems utterly unlike him in every other way: Isabella. While the Duke's government would seem to triumph over Isabella's insistent asceticism—exemplified by his final marriage proposals at 5.1.486 and 5.1.528–30—Isabella's stubborn silence in the face of these proposals at the end of act 5 introduces a note of uncertainty into the resolution, suggesting that she—like Barnardine—potentially maintains a form of counter-conduct resistance beyond the frame of the play's concluding governmental scheme.

48. Watson, "False Immortality in *Measure for Measure*," 431.

Toward a Coherent Ideology of Protoracism in the Renaissance, or, The Anachronism of Would-Be Secular Modern Racism

Robert Hornback

The two most oft-repeated and widely accepted "truisms" anyone who considers European understandings of race(s) prior to the modern period encounters are that (1) there was no *ideology* or, at least, no *coherent* ideology of race before modern racism and (2) that speaking about any form of racism preceding the late nineteenth or early twentieth century is therefore *anachronistic*.[1] As George Fredrickson puts it, "What was missing—and why I think such ethnic discrimination should not be labeled racist—was an ideology or worldview that would persuasively justify such practices."[2] Likewise, Kim Hall initially qualified her arguments about early modern English culture not being "race-neutral," conceding "the absence of a term for race in the Renaissance and of a distinct and coherent racial ideology."[3] But more recently, pushing back against this "opposition to early modern race studies," Hall and Peter Erickson point out in a 2016 special issue of *Shakespeare Quarterly* focused on race that such dismissals have been "encapsulated in the single word 'anachronism' and informally deployed as a scare tactic and conversation stopper."[4] Together, reflexive invocations of a coherent-ideology standard and of critical embarrassment attending assumed naive anachronism have checked arguments about the existence of premodern racism. But should they?

Typically, so-called (but misnamed) scientific racism and (would-be) biological determinism are said to constitute the gold standard of a "coherent ideology," but in fact modern racism is not even remotely truly scientific, only pseudoscientific. As such, as Shankar Raman has noted, unwarrantedly condescending skepticism about discussions of premodern race is "reductive and misleading" in that it invariably makes comparisons "by referring to the mirage of 'true' biological racism."[5] Nor can we even say that the conclusions modern racism draws—the specific damning stereotypes it assigns to each race—are original; they are instead received, swallowed whole, from prior racial ideologies developed in the age of Shakespeare. Because its conclusions are neither based in nor supported/supportable via science, the truth is that it is *modern* racism that is not a coherent (i.e., logically consistent, connected, cohesive) ideology. By contrast, as this essay demonstrates, the protoracism[6] or earliest, metaphysically oriented racism of Renaissance Europe that first appeared and then spread between the fifteenth century and the mid-seventeenth century was once only too coherent, consistent, unified, and persuasive in justifying its prejudices, which resulted in atrocities like colonialism, the transatlantic slave and sugar trades, ethnic cleansing, and genocide. And because all of modern racism's stereotypical conclusions finally prove, to borrow from standard dictionary definitions of the word "anachronistic," "something that belongs to the past rather than the present," being "appropriate to an earlier period . . . so as to seem conspicuously old-fashioned," we must acknowledge that it is finally modern racism, not the prior protoracism, that is glaringly anachronistic.

That is so because the ostensibly "scientific," hence presumably "secular," rhetoric of modern racism masks the fact that all its specific assumptions about each race are actually those of premodern "race-*belief*" based partly in Judeo-Christian-Islamic hermeneutics and partly in ancient metaphysical philosophy—alike in a metaphysical orientation.[7] At best, then, modern racism exhibits a contradictory, superficially pseudoscientific, empty rhetoric that obscures its logical incoherence, its incohesive chop logic, and its utter inconsistency in being derived from decidedly premodern beliefs/ideology of race. As such, the mistaken assertion of coherence now, but not in the Renaissance, prevents us from understanding racism in either the past or today. With racism, we are dealing with an exceptionally potent combination of religious and "secular" classical metaphysical conceptions that, once compounded, set off transactions of the so-called sacred and secular with profoundly toxic consequences for the world. The main thing preventing recognition of such significant religio-secular transactions and, consequently, of overlooked but unmistakable affinities in racism across premodern and modern race-belief is blind faith in a triumphal narrative of secularization upholding "Scientism." Fredrickson again illustrates the problem when he finds a "supernaturalist racism" in the "late medieval and early modern periods" to be lacking in that it was "primarily religious rather than naturalistic or scientific."[8] Here, the "supernaturalist" (i.e., metaphysical) orientation of racist ideology is explicitly treated as a primitive anachronism at odds with the triumph of supposed rational secularization.[9]

This essay demonstrates that although its assumptions about race were indebted to ancient and medieval racial discourses, the protoracist ideology articulated in Renaissance Europe was innovative and distinct in sometimes rejecting one or the other antecedent by turns while successfully synthesizing the remainder to define a substantially new racial ideology, one consistent in being doubly grounded on or compounded of complementary metaphysical assumptions or race-beliefs. Ultimately, the resulting ideology of race in this period was thus much more coherent than, yet also far more like, modern racism than we have been told. At least, it prefigured uncannily anachronistic assumptions and rationalizations mistakenly believed to have originated in modern racism about the specific damning stereotypical traits supposed to be inherent in Jews and Africans, consistent with what Fredrickson identifies as the two "principal form[s] of modern racism," "racial antisemitism" and "the color-coded white-over-black variety."[10] Along with exploring historical context and theological and philosophical discourse, this essay points to examples from Shakespearean and other literary texts to demonstrate the emergence of protoracism in the Renaissance while thereby showing that this ideology also has implications for how we understand Shakespeare.

On another level, this essay seeks to illustrate that a continuing history of racism from at least the fifteenth century to today offers another compelling instance of Brian Cummings's finding that "both in the past and in our society, the secular and religious, far from being incommensurate, intersect in creative and profound ways."[11] The surprisingly superficial distinction of the modern ideology of race is the addition of Scientism, a facile application of science and pseudoscience in unwarranted situations according to a modern view that only scientific claims are meaningful and truthful. Science is thus venerated like a religion, as itself a source of blind faith, becoming the substitute for metaphysical and theological authorities. Ultimately, then, the reflex assumption that a turn to the secular undeniably occurred in the early modern period and that modern racism is inherently more rational and coherent than previous religious ideology of race has obscured the persistent indebtedness of supposed modern ideology of race to more pervasive and cohesive premodern race-*belief*. Because the "secularization narrative" has underwritten misunderstanding of overwhelming, undeniable continuities between premodern protoracism and modern racism, the critical "turn to religion" in Renaissance studies is a particularly necessary development in understanding racism—as well as representations of race in Shakespeare.

Monstrous Plinian and Biblical Races as Early Antecedents for Protoracist Beliefs

Among the influences on ancient and medieval conceptions of race that shaped the protoracism of Renaissance Europeans was the enduring authority granted to Roman historian, natural philosopher, geographer, ethnographer, encyclopedist, and rampant xenophobe Pliny the Elder (23–79) in his accounts of remote "monstrous races" that were almost but not quite human, written up in his *Naturalis Historia*, or *Natural History*. For the ethnocentric Roman Pliny, "The one race [*gens*] of outstanding eminence in virtue among all the races in the whole world is undoubtedly the Roman."[12] The monstrous races—the Cynocephali (Dog-Heads), the hairy and mouthless Astomi, who lived on scents alone, the headless Anthropophagi, Ethiopians, African Troglodytes, and so on—were freakish because they diverged from Western norms. As John Friedman argues, Greek and Roman ancients "believed that many natural phenomena were signs revealing the gods' attitudes and intentions toward men,"[13] a belief that prepared the way for similar Christian thought about race.

The Bible and its interpreters also offered accounts of accursed, monstrous races/lineages that, whether through disobedience, pride, or other disfavor before God, altered the original proper bounds of kind and nation. Most famously, addressing the problem of all races being descended from Adam, medieval rabbinic tradition offered accounts of "a suitably evil lineage for Cain."[14] For example, the Zohar, a thirteenth-century collection of midrashim, explains that Cain's evil nature was the result of the fact that "the serpent injected his impurity into Eve."[15] Medieval accounts of Cain's exile further emphasize monstrous "changes in his physical appearance as a result of God's curse,"[16] thereby offering ancestral origins for monstrous races, Cain's kin, like "God-cursed Grendel" in *Beowulf*.

Another prominent biblical figure in protoracist theories of origin from the Middle Ages into the seventeenth century was Esau, portrayed in Genesis as hot-tempered, wrathful, rough skinned, hairy, and red (25:25). His marriage to and procreation with foreign Hittite and Canaanite women meant that for Jewish and Christian interpreters, Esau—like the miscegenation in which he disobediently engaged—was associated with wildness. In biblical thought, Alexandra Bergholm explains, wildness was often a moral sign of "a state of accursedness and degeneracy which had resulted because God had withdrawn his blessing from the individual."[17] Thus, *The Supplication of the Blood of the English most lamentably murdered in Ireland, Cryeng out of the earth for revenge* (1598), calls the "wild" Irish the "cursed seed of Esau."[18]

Since the "ancient world believed that many natural phenomena," including "monstrous races," were "signs" of "the gods' . . . intentions," and since Judeo-Christian thought included highly compatible notions, the eventual metaphysical synthesis or fusion of the two was perhaps inevitable.[19] Hayden White has observed, for instance, a "fusion in later Western thought" of "a tendency of Hebrew thought to dissolve physical into moral states" and "the reduction of external attributes to the manifestations of a spiritual condition" with the complementary "Greek tendency" to "objectify, or physicalize . . . internal, spiritual, or psychological states." In Renaissance race-belief, then, we find a distillation of these tendencies resulting in the prejudiced disposition to read perceived/constructed differing physical traits of a race as revelatory of inherent spiritual, moral, and mental predilections.

That is, in the early ideology of race I call protoracism, races were understood as being different from the inside out, though *not* because of would-be biology. On the contrary, races were believed to differ as a consequence of the moral nature/state of the soul. The soul's vehicle, in turn, was understood to be blood, so that, as a result, the soul's condition was made manifest in the body through blood. Therefore, by the sixteenth and seventeenth centuries especially, in Europeans' racial ideology/race-belief, blood took on an even greater role as a carrier of race—now sometimes referred to as a theory of race as blood—than it had had in the Middle Ages as part of a sympathetic metaphysical relationship between soul, body, and mind. Furthermore, geohumoral theory about the relative balance of the four humors (blood, yellow bile, black bile, phlegm) was increasingly "subordinated to a theological interpretation that construed humoral imbalances at times as directly caused by God."[20] Accordingly, "humoral disequilibrium" could be interpreted as "a result of original sin,"[21] the curse on Cain's descendants because of his murder of Abel ("And now art thou cursed from the earth, which hath opened her mouth to receive thy brother's blood from thy hand" [Genesis 4:11][22]), or owing to any number of biblical curses.

A disturbing instance of a supposed accursed race concerns the Old Testament nation of the Amalekites, who are said to be descendants of Amalek, a grandson of the unblessed, wild, reprobate, race-mixing Esau (Genesis 36:2–10, 12). While militant English Puritans had traditionally associated the Amalekites particularly with Turks, Puritan Pilgrims' settling in America appropriated the curse on the Amalekites from 1 Samuel 15:3 ("Now go and smite Amalek, and utterly destroy all that they have, and spare them not; but slay both man and woman, infant and suckling, ox and sheep, camel and ass") toward a more deadly agenda. Among those promoting this agenda was John Winthrop, born during Shakespeare's lifetime (in 1588) and deceased in Boston in 1649 before the end of the Renaissance in England. Delivered shipboard on the journey from England to Massachusetts, Winthrop's ironically titled *A Modell of Christian Charity* speech (1630), most often recalled for its famous reference to the Massachusetts colony as "a city on a hill," also included his ominous comparison of God's supposed commission to the Pilgrims to "when he gave Saul a commission to destroy Amalek." That fact leads John Corrigan and Lynn Neal to consider "the extent to which Puritans, even before landing near Boston, had imagined pursuing a deadly agenda in their relations with American indigenes."[23] Not for the last time, here was an instance of a powerful metaphysically coded Old World protoracist ideology continuing in the New World.[24]

Over the course of the sixteenth and seventeenth centuries especially, there would thus emerge in England and western Europe a coherent, cohesive, and logically consistent racial ideology via a then-persuasive synthesis of ancient Greco-Roman metaphysical natural philosophy about "monstrous races" with biblical hermeneutics about the creation of different kinds/lineages of peoples and the preternatural consequences of mixing them. For centuries, the lineages of biblically cursed peoples/races were thus exploited to advance a coherent protoracist ideology justifying, rationalizing, and sanctioning treating "stranger" ("alien, foreign, not a native of" and "estranged") races as inherently inferior morally, intellectually, culturally, and aesthetically. Often, the most "strange" (foreign/alien) races were constructed as primitives—"wild," irrational, incapable of morality, subhuman, and ugly, thus unworthy of and impervious to humane treatment. In *The Tempest*, then "vild race[s]" (1.2.430) connoted simultaneously "wild" and "vile" or "defiled," those "on whose *nature*," the habitual enslaver Prospero insists, "*Nurture* can never *stick;* on whom . . . pains, / Humanely taken, [are] all, all lost, quite lost" (4.1.212–13).

A Kind of Metaphysical Determinism in Renaissance Protoracism

Metaphysics, that part of philosophy concerned with the basic causes and nature of things, had much to say on the subject of the supposed origins, causes, division, and hierarchy of races. Equally, metaphysical concerns are often at issue in medieval religious drama in moral allegories and miracle-play pageants, as well as in later allusions to such drama and

Christian iconography/symbolism in sixteenth- and seventeenth-century English plays. For example, typically color-coded morality plays are works with intrinsically metaphysical stakes, including the nature and origins of good and evil, states of being, and abstract subjects such as the self and the soul governed by logic that transcends mere physical matter. Furthermore, metaphysics addresses what Aristotle called first principles and causes, abstract concepts such as the "essence" and "nature" of things, including the nature of the soul, the soul's relation to mind and body, and the hierarchy of the universe, analogous to notions of race and nation, "dividing the realm of being into distinct kingdoms."[25] Thus, "for orthodox Aristotelians, there was a Great Chain of Being that ordered an array of different kinds of things (plants, worms, humans, angels) into a hierarchy of increasing metaphysical perfection."[26]

Ancient metaphysical ideology of race and its revival among humanists particularly during the sixteenth and seventeenth centuries can be understood as a kind of spiritual determinism via its assumption of an incarnation of the soul. It was assumed that spirit/soul was expressed equally in terms of bodily/physical features and of moral and intellectual capacity. Therefore, as ancient humoral metaphysics was increasingly subsumed in Judeo-Christian thought, it was understood that one could be cursed as sinful and then one's offspring would be predestined to be inherently accursed, anathema, wicked, foolish, outcast, hated, or enslaved. Alternatively, in strict geohumoralism, extremes in environment, climate, soil, and diet affected the body and its appearance, and these things, in turn, influenced the soul and mind. Soul, body, and mind were thus widely believed to function within mutual and sympathetic relation to one another. As such, external bodily traits were believed to reflect and express one's essential nature and character in intellectual and moral terms (mind and soul). To paraphrase Othello, one's "perfect soul" was believed to "manifest [one] rightly" (1.2.36–37). That meant, in practice, that one was supposed to be able to *read* bodily signs (whether a noble woman's complexion, Richard III's deformity, or an Irishman's, indigenous American's, or African's supposed primitive wildness, a Moor's blackness, or a Jew's appearance) as external expressions of interior states. As a result, real life could be interpreted almost as if it were a moral allegory, since metaphysically inflected hermeneutics of race encouraged physiognomy—the art of discriminating a person's character from appearance, form, shape, and so forth. Yet Shakespeare's plays often ironize or deconstruct such pervasive traditional habits of thought, as in *Othello*, where associations of black and white are reversed and "ocular proof" (3.3.411) means nothing, as symbolically white "virtue [is turned] into pitch" (2.3.380), the Moor Othello's inner "virtue" makes him "far more fair than black" (1.3.330–31), Iago ironically plays the role of a white "demi-devil" (5.2.352) hiding his "blackest sins . . . with heavenly shows" of whiteness/goodness (2.3.371–72), and Othello learns that devils do not always have cloven hooves ("I look down toward his feet; but that's a fable—" [5.2.336]). That is, Shakespeare's tragedy suggests, the real world cannot be interpreted according to allegory or physiognomy—or the protoracism influenced by such interpretive modes.

For the widely assumed visible body-soul-mind correlation, the most authoritative ancient sources were Aristotle and Galen. In *The Soul's Dependence on the Body*, the physician-physiognomist Galen had argued that "the faculties of the soul follow the mixtures of the body."[27] Aristotle makes the connection even clearer: "There never was an animal with the form of one kind and the mental character of another; the soul and body appropriate to the same kind always go together, and this shows that a specific body involves a specific mental character."[28] By promoting assumptions that the same kind of soul, mental character, and body "always go together," metaphysical doctrine inevitably promoted racial stereotypes.

Employing Aristotelian metaphysics, European thinkers like the sixteenth-century Spaniard Juan Huarte could claim that humoral differences produced by climate can be "discerned not only in the countenance and demeanure of the body, but also in the wit of the soule."[29] Frenchman Pierre Charron followed similar logic in his *Of Wisdome* (1612), finding that the tripartite climatic partitions of the world (North, Middle, South) determined the "natures of men," including not simply their wisdom but also "in euery thing, body, soule, religion."[30] Even vaunted empiricist Francis Bacon did not doubt that "every tangible body on earth contains an invisible and intangible spirit; the body envelops and clothes it."[31]

As a further step toward understanding the ideology of a metaphysical and preternatural rather than assumedly biological determinism we need to recognize pervasive metaphysical belief throughout Renaissance Europe about the relationship between blood and spirit. Blood was understood as affecting and being in mutual correlation with spirit, thereby both influencing and being influenced by physical form. As English physician William Harvey explained in *De Motu Cordis*, or *On the Motion of the Heart and Blood* (1628), "the soul as a whole is in the blood, and the soul itself is the blood, as God says."[32] Harvey had in mind several Old Testament quotes to this effect, as had Spanish humanist Michael Servetus in his *Christianismi Restitutio* (1553): "Thereupon it is said that the soul is in the blood and the soul itself is blood . . . as God himself teaches in Genesis 9, Leviticus 17, and Deuteronomy 12."[33]

Through such influences, the soul was widely believed to be incarnate through blood. The character of ancestors and their heirs was interpreted through the metaphysically determined spirit of a family, nation, people, religion, and hence "race." Protoracial ideology assumed certain races, like "the rase of Jesse" or, relative to some "stranger" races, "the Englishe race," to be inherently superior ("chosen," "favored," "blessed," "pure," "noble"), while others like the "wilde Irish" or "the race of Cham [Ham]" were deemed inherently inferior ("cursed," "defiled," "corrupted," "degenerate," "polluted," "blotted," "base"). Whether blessed and pure or accursed and impure, bloodlines were understood as passing on spiritual and complementary intellectual and physical characteristics, including the complexion associated with any race.

The default belief was that if different lineages, bloodlines, or races were pure/blessed and others not, then races ought not to be mixed. Underscoring this tenet were the widely believed consequences of mingling races, chief among them primitive barbarism and degeneracy, with the most infamous example being, among the English in the Renaissance, the Irish. In Edmund Spenser's *A View of the Present State of Ireland* (1596), the Irish possessed the malevolent metaphysical power to cause colonists to "degenerate from their first [English] natures, as to growe wilde." Moreover, mixing of kinds was supposed to be the habitual mode of this mongrelized race, for Spenser writing that the Irish were the product of being "intermingled with many other nations . . . joining unto them." Spenser even singled out so-called Old English settlers who had adjusted to Irish custom by changing their names via the Gaelic prefix "Mac," like the provoked Irishman Captain MacMorris, who reacts combatively to talk about his supposedly degenerate "nation" (race) in *Henry V* (1599):

> FLUELLEN: Captain MacMorris, I think, look you, under your correction, there is not many of your nation—
>
> MACMORRIS: Of my nation? What ish my nation? Ish a villain and a basterd and a knave and a rascal. What ish my nation? Who talks of my nation? (3.2.122–26)

MacMorris responds to the braggart soldier Fluellen's thoughtless remark that there are not many Irishmen fighting on the English side as a racial slur—which it is, whether intended or not. Because "nation" often meant "race," MacMorris confronts Fluellen to see which of the bigoted stereotypes is meant. Is it that the Irish are "basterd[ized]"/degenerate, lowly, and evilly inclined?, he asks. In a sympathetic "What did you just say?"/ fighting-words moment, MacMorris thus passionately confronts the assumption that, owing to his race, an Irishman inherently cannot be a loyal subject or a good man, as MacMorris evidently is.

Above all, the protoracist stereotype of the Irish as wild, brutish, and bestial rendered a brutally subjugated people as subhuman primitives—a "vild race" unworthy of sympathy. Spenser would advocate genocide in *A View*, since the "wilde Irish" were "the most barbarous Nation in Christendome," "a people altogether stubborn and untamed," characterized by "fleshly incontinency, carelesse sloath, and generally all disordered life." The solution such discourse encouraged was the same as that of Conrad's Kurtz in *Heart of Darkness*: "Exterminate all the brutes!" If Homi Bhabha has demonstrated that such stereotypes of arrested cultural progress or somatic development in later usages are consistent with the tropes of "colonial racism,"[34] it is significant that such racism first expanded on a truly global scale alongside Renaissance colonialism.

The Blood Curse on Jews, the Curse of Ham as African Progenitor, and Purity of Blood and Race

The metaphysical race ideology of this period allowed for the paradox of different kinds on the one hand intended by God to be inviolable but also, on the other, subject especially in the biblical past to sudden supernatural change or gradual degeneration from spiritual causes, what I am calling a kind of metaphysical or preternatural determinism. The prime example of Christian antisemitism's rationales for how Jews/Hebrews were once "the Chosen People" and yet later believed to be a base, accursed, tainted, and corrupting race offers a case in point. In the Gospel of Matthew, a Jewish crowd chooses to have Jesus crucified rather than the notorious criminal Barabbas, saying, "His blood be on us and our children" (27:24–25). It is this scripture to which English playwright Christopher Marlowe's *Jew of Malta* (ca. 1589–90) alludes in the rebukes against the titular character of "accurséd Barabas, [a] base Jew" (5.5.114), as in, "If your first curse fall heavy on thy head, / And make thee poor and scorned of all the world, / 'Tis not our fault, but thy *inherent sin*" (1.2.111–13); "For through our sufferance of your hateful lives / Who *stand accursed in the sight of heaven*, / These taxes and afflictions are befall'n" (1.2.66–68).[35] Because of many Christian Europeans' beliefs that Jews were "accursed," Jews were said to have had "inherent sin," the "blood curse" upon them.

The intertwined antisemitic metaphysical conceptions of "race as blood"[36] and of "religion-and/as-race"[37] are found in "Golden Age" Spanish protoracist ideology obsessed with *limpieza de sangre*, or "purity of blood." This obsession requires clarifying that determinism through blood did not in fact equate with a biologism of race, since some modern critics assume just the opposite. To take one example, Jerome Friedman argues that Jewishness was understood to be "not a statement of faith or even a series of ethnic practices but a biological consideration."[38] Amplifying this view, he asserts a conception of "Jewishness as a *biological* fate and infection, both physiologically and spiritually."[39] Yet the notion of Jewishness as fated (and infected) *spiritually*, as well as all the evidence Friedman cites alongside his would-be scientific conclusions, points not to a biological consideration at all but to assumptions of a profoundly metaphysical condition encompassing the preternatural. After all, prior to the preceding quote, he notes, "It was maintained that degenerate Jewish blood was impervious to baptism and grace. If mixed with Christian blood, the Jewish blood would [spiritually] contaminate subsequent generations and would continue to do so indefinitely."[40] Deemed spiritually impervious to conversion, ritual, or spiritual grace, Jews were condemned not naturally/biologically but preternaturally/metaphysically so as to make them both malevolent and beyond mere scientific/natural explanation.

The comparable theory accounting for the blackness of Africans or Moors, the Curse of Ham, was the main justification for the mass enslavement of Africans from the fifteenth through nineteenth centuries, emerging as a rationale for racial slavery among Europeans during the Renaissance (though medieval rabbinic and Islamic scholars had already proposed this interpretation). One proponent was Englishman George Best in *True Discourse of the Three Voyages of Discoverie* (1578). At one point, Best explained coyly how he believed the "blacknesse" of Africans came into being, first suggesting, vaguely, that it "proceedeth of some natural infection of the first inhabitants of that Countrey, and so all the whole progenie of them descended, are still polluted with the same blot of infection." He then explained more certainly that blackness was the result of "the infection of bloud," before declaring its cause as the Curse of Ham.[41]

Best's argument is based in religious and metaphysical thought, not "secular," pseudoscientific theory. Nonetheless, modern critics invariably leap to the familiar ground of biology, pointing to Best's use of "natural infection" as a protoscientific explanation of skin color. Oddly, the assumption is that modern pseudoscientific/sham ideology must be present in accounts of emerging racism, which must resemble modern accounts' faux-scientific quackery. Mary Floyd-Wilson says that "George Best . . . reframed the African's complexion as a scientific mystery" or "scientific problem," giving rise to "scientific skepticism,"[42] and Werner Sollors sees here "an emerging biological view."[43] However, Best had religious and metaphysical causes in mind, explaining that, to punish Ham's disobedience, God willed that his son should be born so that "not only it selfe, but all his posteritie after him, should be so blacke & loathsome, that it might remaine a spectacle of disobedience to all the Worlde. And of this blacke & cursed Chus [Canaan] came all these blacke Moores which are in Africa . . . ," so that "the cause of the Ethiopians blacknesse is the curse and natural infection of the blood."[44] Best thus meant by an "infection" caused by a curse the now archaic sense of "moral contamination; vitiation of character or habits by evil influence" (*OED* 6). When assessing premodern race ideology, particularly that of the Middle Ages and Renaissance, then, words must not be taken out of context as if they were based in a protoscientific naturalism when they most definitely were not. To do so is to overlook the profoundly *preter*natural character of protoracist word usage and race-belief/ideology.[45]

Religious and metaphysical influences on essential character were also inherent in related constructions of "race" and "nation." One of the chief synonyms for "race" in early modern England, "nation" contained "notions of race and common descent [that] predominate[d]" (*OED* 1a) in this period, while echoing biblical/religious senses such as "the heathen nations, the Gentiles" (*OED* 2a). This makes a postcolonial approach to the related formation of race and nation all the more apt. Thus we begin to see more clearly just what was at stake when MacMorris angrily asks, "What ish my nation? Who talks of my nation?" (3.2.126), or when a long-persecuted Shylock objects that Antonio "hates our sacred nation" (1.3.48), or when the bigoted Brabantio says that Desdemona "shunned / The wealthy curlèd darlings of our nation" (1.2.84–85). All these usages involve identification with or objection to assumptions about inherent qualities of a race—and they therefore show Shakespeare interacting with the dominant protoracist ideology of his day, often, it strikes me, skeptically and sympathetically.

Medievalist Robert Bartlett therefore concedes too much when he states, "While the language of race—*gens*, *natio*, 'blood,' 'stock,' etc.—is biological, its medieval reality was almost entirely cultural."[46] Though blood and descent were already key in premodern conceptions of race,[47] neither was conceived or understood biologically or genetically. In fact, none of the words surrounding race were initially biological. Rather, they have *become* so, having been appropriated and reconceived in or as biological terms over time; that is, the language surrounding race involves originally nonbiological words for concepts preceding modern biology that only later came to have biological connotations. Accordingly, anachronism occurs not when we speak of race or racism in the Renaissance but when we read past usages of race-related words from this period as if they already had scientific connotations.

I agree, then, with Janet Adelman's insistence upon a recognition of two languages of race, premodern and modern, which were eventually fused. As she points out, the preacher Foxe's assertion about Jewish unbelief as inherited in the womb employed "a language of (usually immutable) physical differences" that, significantly, "map[s] easily onto what would become the newer language of 'race.'"[48] In the same way, I similarly argue, repeated references to "blood," "nature," and words such as "kind," "lineage," "breed," and the like in contexts of race in the Renaissance easily blurred into what would become the language of would-be biologism of race. After all, it would be these key words especially, with their underlying assumptions of inborn characteristics resulting from disadvantaged or favored ancestors, that would provide the bridge between a protoracist ideology based consistently and explicitly in the synthesis of formerly competing metaphysical determinisms (Aristotelian and Judeo-Christian-Islamic) and the only partial shift toward the pseudoscientific modern rhetoric according to which racists (only sometimes) asserted/assert a basis in so-called biological determinism. In fact, many early usages of even the word "race" listed as examples in the *OED* have religious contexts.[49] What emerges from these early usages of the word are "major divisions" according to "kind" into distinct "set[s]" of "people" or "nation" and "descendants" of "common stock" who share definite tendencies, like "the outward race & stocke of Abraham," "the race of Christ," or "the Race of Satan." In the same way that the language of modern racism is derivative, all the specific assumptions of "modern" antiblack racism are taken, anachronistically, from centuries-old theology and religious iconography.

Renaissance Origins of "Modern" Racist Stereotypes of Blackness

Racial stereotypes of blackness changed radically from ancient, to medieval, to Renaissance ones. Renaissance stereotypes established the so-called modern racist stereotypes of what scholars sometimes refer to as white-over-black (i.e., white supremacist) racism. Because spirit was supposed to correspond with physical form and also to be affected by external, physical traits, it was inevitable that there would be a coinciding metaphysics of skin color or complexion with determinist assumptions about attendant moral character and intellectual capacity. But what paleness/"fairness" versus dark complexion/blackness marked changed among Europeans during the Renaissance.

Among the ancients, geohumoral theory, ascribing bodily and behavioral differences to geography/climate (primarily proximity to the equator and exposure to the sun), had constructed "an interdependent relationship"[50] between climate, body, mind, and soul that deemed the pale-skinned, barbaric white northern Europeans (Celts, Britons, Goths, Gauls, etc.) "temperamentally disadvantaged,"[51] inferior intellectually in binary opposition to the dark-complexioned southerner: "If the southerner is . . . wise, the northerner must be . . . witless."[52] Such color-coded geohumoral logic was revived by some Renaissance humanists and consequently lingered anachronistically in scholarly works before being subsumed fully by color-coded Christianized iconographic associations. For example, consider *The Description of England* (1577), where the defensive Englishman William Harrison, speaking of those "blacker in colour, and some so black in deed as any crow or raven," bitterly concedes, "So I grant, that in pregnancy of wit . . . , they generally exceed us."[53] Similarly, the *Oxford English Dictionary* includes, under one definition of "wit" as "good or great mental capacity; intellectual ability . . ." (*OED* 5a), the following example: "1630 *R. Johnson's Kingd. & Commw.* The weake constitutions of the Southerne Nations are supplied by the extraordinarie gifts of the minde: terme them what you please, either wit, or subtiltie." As fifteenth-century Italian philosopher Marsilio Ficino (d. 1499) put it, Egyptians were "particularly favored" in being "exceptionally intelligent and wise."[54] That is, the stereotype of a dark complexion derived from ancient geohumoralism was diametrically opposite that which became increasingly dominant among western Europeans in the Renaissance beginning in the mid-fifteenth century and which persists in white supremacist racism today.

The stunning change occurred with surprising rapidity because there were such ruthlessly selfish motives behind it: the formerly overwhelmingly white slave trade was cut off by the Ottoman conquest beginning with the fall of Constantinople in 1453; the transatlantic trade in Africans launched by the Portuguese on the West Coast of Africa in 1441 rapidly expanded;[55] more labor was needed in the colonies because of the decimation of indigenous populations in the Americas from epidemics such as smallpox; and the burgeoning transatlantic sugar trade required more labor still. Inevitably for a period whose racial ideology was overwhelmingly defined by a metaphysical determinism chiefly justified religiously, all these things were furthered by papal bulls/decrees such as *Dum Diversas* (1452), *Romanus Pontifex* (1455), and *Sublimis Deus* (1537), which, respectively, granted Portugal the authority to subjugate and enslave these "pagans,"[56] ceded Portuguese conquest and monopoly over the entirety of Atlantic Africa,[57] and recognized "Indians" as "truly men," rational enough to be converted and saved, thereby sanctioning the belief that Africans were not truly human, hence not redeemable, thus fit for inhumane servitude.[58] In consequence, between 1492 and 1580, a quarter of all those brought to the New World were abducted Africans.[59] The centuries-old stereotype of dark-complexioned southerners as wise and rational in comparison with pale and ignorant northerners needed to be reversed in order to rationalize the massive increase in exploitive human trafficking, and so it was.

An inchoate stereotyping against darker-skinned people was found in medieval romances written in the wake of the Crusades. Northern European medieval romances assigned negative, monstrous, villainous characteristics to the "Saracens," who were often (but not always) black. In the wake of relatively limited contact with blackness in the twelfth-century Crusades came negative representations of blackness, but not yet, significantly, ones that resembled the later, most racist association of blackness with inherent stupidity, irrationality, and ignorance. In the Middle Ages, Christianized depictions of blackness simply, in Geraldine Heng's words, "accrued a slate of negative significations that yoked the 'abstraction' of blackness . . . to sin, . . . as well as—more perniciously and unforgivingly—to the devil, the demonic, the infernal, and the damned."[60] In the romances inspired by the Crusades, black Saracens were therefore, above all, evil/villainous enemies, generic antagonists or bogeymen appearing as the mirror image of European culture with their own knights, ladies, courtly love, chivalry, and the like, only more ruthless, treacherous, and lustful. They are further depicted, damningly, as "infidels"—that is, unbelievers. We also find "hybrid bestial-human Saracen giants in romance after romance"—Alagolafre, Estragote, and Barrok in *The Sultan of Babylon*, Gulgafor in *Sir Ferumbras*, Ascopart in *Bevis of Hampton*, Amiraunt in *Guy of Warwick*, Baliagog in *Sir Tristrem*, and Vernagu in *Roland and Vernagu*—with giant wives and babies. Heng notes that the emphasis on family and reproduction is suggestive of a monstrous infidel race rather than mere unusual births.[61] And since in biblical thought giantism was associated with wildness,[62] such depictions established a vague antecedent to later stereotypes of Africans.

By contrast, in accordance with the expanding transatlantic trade in Africans during the fifteenth through seventeenth centuries, racial stereotypes soon veered to emphasize a very different—and equally fabricated—set of characteristics. Specifically, Europeans began to believe in the "insidious stereotype" of black people as "carefree because too stupid to understand the misery of his or her situation"[63]—basically, the antebellum minstrel type of Sambo. Or as Anu Korhonen explains, "black Africans were thought of as foolish or lacking understanding."[64] The stereotype of the black man as a sort of stupid "innocent" or "natural fool," in early modern English parlance, became dominant because it proved useful to Europeans' desire to promote an African slave trade. A popular sixteenth-century proverb, "To wash an Ethiope is a labor in vain," was applied to one who "teacheth a naturall foole wisdom," meaning that foolishness was deemed as immutable a trait as blackness. So commonplace was the racist ideology surrounding blackness that most of the popular English synonyms for "fool" in this period were associated with black or black-headed birds, including the "noddy," "gull" (both the black-headed and the laughing gull), "loon," "booby," and "jackdaw."[65] Such undeniably racist stereotyping preceding modern racism was rationalized, inevitably, by a religious hermeneutics that went beyond the primary medieval associations with blackness connoting sin or evil alone. It was used, moreover, to justify thoroughly secular economic and social desires.

Early modern racism redeployed other Christian allegorical types, iconographic thinking, and color-coded visual symbolic logic, drawn from the moral allegory of religious drama and other religious iconography. For example, consider psalter iconography of the *insipiens*, or "fool," from Vulgate Psalm 52: "Dixit insipiens in corde suo: non est Deus" (The fool said in his heart, "There is no God"). As the archetypal *insipiens*, the devil, depicted as black, was understood to be a fool. Augustine's *Enarrationes in Psalmos* clarified the logic here by explaining that those who rejected the Christian faith were infidel sects, Jews, and pagans.[66] The *insipiens* was therefore often depicted as foreign and black, as was the leaping and shirtless black man wearing a spotted pointed cap and Turkish pants in the ninth-century Stuttgart Psalter.

Contesting Neoplatonists, Augustine further explained that fallen angels had their rational powers impaired in consequence of their fall.[67] In opposing the good angels to fallen ones in terms of rationality versus irrationality and beauty/fairness versus ugliness/darkness in *The City of God against the Pagans*, Augustine compared the *colore nigro* that can improve a beautiful painting to the demons whose existence paradoxically results in good in the world. Augustine thereby suggested that the fallen angels, whose "ugliness is a disfiguring blemish [*deformitas turpet*],"[68] are not merely disfigured and ugly but also so "deprived of . . . light," so dark, as to be black.

Augustine focused above all on the limited rational capabilities of these dark devils. He noted, for instance, how "their minds" are "tossed upon [the] swelling waves of passion."[69] Augustine thus determined that demons were in fact not "in possession of the wisdom [*sapientiae*]" necessary to find God's favor. Indeed, Augustine's devils think and feel "after the usual fashion of stupid minds [*stultarum mentium*]."[70] It followed that demons "resemble foolish [*stultis*] . . . men."[71] The *stultus* was the Romans' stupid fool; it is no surprise, then, that Augustine argued that "the devil" became "a fit subject for the angels to make fun of," having been "consigned to this punishment after his sin."[72] Augustine's black devils therefore ended up being laughable fools.

In subsequent Christian theater throughout Europe, medieval dramatic depictions of Genesis drew above all upon Augustine's particular metaphysical logic and iconography of dark folly. What followed in the drama was, logically enough, not merely the association of devils with blackness but also an emphasis on foolishly tempestuous passions diminishing their rational capacity. Each of the famed English cycle pageants depicting the fall of Lucifer illustrates Augustine's deterministic metaphysical logic. All this is established pithily, for instance, in the Towneley mystery pageant's *The Creation, and the Fall of Lucifer* (ca. 1460), when after their fall, the blackened devils lament, "Alas, alas and welewo! . . . / We, that were angels so fare, / and sat so hie aboue the ayere, / Now ar we waxen blak as any coyll [coal] / and vgly, tatyrd as a foyll [i.e., *fool*]."[73] These fallen angels are at once foolish and no longer light and fair but black as coal and ugly. Likewise, in the York pageant of *The Fall of Lucifer* (ca. 1460), finding himself "brent," or burnt (l. 107), "lorn" of "light" (l. 108), and no longer "stable of thought" (l. 62), Second Devil passionately laments, "Out, out! I go wood [mad] for woe, my wit is all went now!" (l. 105).[74] Such devil lore and such damning implications of blackfaced fools and color-coded metaphysical determinism reconstructed blackness as an assumed sign of irrationality.

Thus, Christian iconographic and allegorical types preceded racial stereotypes of blackness. These ideas were further developed in sixteenth-century Tudor morality plays, particularly Wit marriage interludes like John Redford's *Play of Wit and Science* (ca. 1534), Sebastian Wescott's *The Marriage of Wit and Science* (ca. 1569–70), and Francis Merbury's *The Marriage between Wit and Wisdom* (1579), the last of which became a byword in the repertory of the itinerant professional playing troupes through the 1580s. In each of these moralities, the Everyman character

"Wit" ignores the council of "Reason" and falls under the influence of a Vice, "Idleness," who lulls Wit to sleep, blackens his face, and leaves him to be discovered a fool. In each version, Wit must be restored to his essential "whiteness" and set on a path to redemption, ascent, and marriage with either Science or Wisdom. In the first of these plays, the Henrician humanist Redford's *Wit and Science*, the Vice, Idleness (likely black), sings the all too trusting Wyt to sleep, proclaiming, "whyle he sleepeth in Idlenes lappe / Idlenes marke on hym shall I clappe." After then "mark[ing]" Wyt with some version of blacking up and then dressing him in the "fooles cote" (l. 598) of her attendant "Ingnorance" [*sic*] (who is black), Idleness observes how "[he] beguneth to looke lyke a noddye" (l. 587). Here of course she uses an aforementioned common synonym for a fool, "noddy," which is also the name of a black bird, so the "marke" Idleness "clap[s]" on Wyt to make him look like a noddy is blackface. The allegorical personification Science (simply meaning "Knowledge") discriminates between Wyt's "fayer" (l. 795) portrait and his "fowle . . . & vglye" (l. 796) black visage. After being encouraged to examine his reflection in his "glas of reson" (l. 824), Wyt further connects his blackened face with folly as he exclaims, "[G]ogs sowle a foole[,] [I am] a foole by the mas . . . / & as for this face[, it] is abhominable / as black as the devyll" (ll. 826, 839–40).

Soon, the very words ("wit," "ignorance," "reason") used in morality plays featuring blackfaced allegorical personification were being applied in real life as some Englishmen superimposed metaphysically derived iconography about blackness upon real African people. An allegorical-stereotypical connection between blackness and an assumed witless irrationality thus appears with disturbing frequency in English travel narratives and chorographic literature of the sixteenth through the seventeenth centuries. Robert Baker's account of his voyages to the West African coast in 1562 and 1563, published in Hakluyt's *Principall Navigations, Voiages and Discoveries of the English Nation* (London, 1589), describes black African inhabitants

> Whose likenesse seem'd men to be, but all as blacke as coles.
> Their Captaine comes to me as naked as my naile,
> Not having witte or honestie to cover once his tale.

This portrayal rendered Africans so lacking in "witte" as to only *seem* human and indeed as so irrational as to be animalistic (as implied in the use of "tale" [tail]). The "Second Voyage of John Hawkins, 1564–1565," also in Hakluyt, includes a reference to West Africans as "the ignorant people" who "knewe not" about guns and so were easily shot. Their pain was treated as humorous: "[They] used a marveilous crying in their flight with leaping and turning their tayles, that it was strange to see, and gave us great pleasure to behold them."[75] By the seventeenth century, Peter Heylyn could claim in his *Little Description of the Great World* (1631) that the sub-Saharan African lacked "the use of Reason which is peculiar unto man; [he is] of little Wit." Such application of allegorical types in the protoracist stereotype helps to explain the otherwise curious name Reasonable Blackman, alias Reasonable Blakemore and Resonablackmore (i.e., Reason a blackamoor), a free black Elizabethan silk weaver living in the London theater suburb of Southwerk. While his surname stressed his race, his first name, Reasonable/Reason, emphasized his evidently atypical degree of rationality. His name thus marked an unexpected contradiction in terms that rendered him a walking oxymoron, a prodigy. Reasonable's/Reason's allegorical name reflects the norm of real-life racist discrimination in which black people were "read" according to moral allegories. Emilia resorts to these allegorized racist slurs not only when she calls Othello "the blacker devil" (5.2.161) but also in declaring, "Gull! . . . dolt! As ignorant as dirt" (5.2.20–21), "coxcomb," and "such a fool" (5.2.278). Interestingly, at the very moment in which she discovers that she herself has been totally duped by her husband and that her thoughtless theft of the handkerchief and subsequent callous lie to Desdemona had prompted jealousy, misunderstanding, and tragedy, instead of admitting any complicity or responsibility in the tragedy, blind to her own faults/sins, Emilia resorts to scapegoating racist stereotypes—drawn from Christian iconography and moral allegory—according to which the black character alone is a fool. There is palpable irony, then, when she complacently and sadistically taunts the grieving man in less than truly Christian fashion with a vehement racism inflected by zealous, hypocritical, self-righteous religiosity in her final words: "Moor, she was chaste. She loved thee, cruel Moor. / So come my soul to bliss, as I speak true. / So speaking as I think, alas, I die" (5.2.299–301).

Belief in metaphysical/preternatural determinism lingers on today. After all, of the very word "racism," the *OED* finds that since it was first used circa 1910, it has referred to a *belief*, as in, "The belief that all members of each race possess characteristics, abilities, or qualities specific to that race, especially so as to distinguish it as inferior or superior to another race or races. Hence: prejudice and antagonism towards people of other races." Alden Vaughan likewise defines racism as "a belief that races exist and that members of one or more races are innately inferior in certain characteristics, usually in intelligence."[76] Racism, far from being grounded in any objective or "secular" realities, is always at root about belief—what we may most accurately call *race-belief*.

If medieval and Renaissance racisms rested upon metaphysical and religious airy nothings, modern or so-called scientific racism today, equally, rests upon the same superstitious, magical thinking. But whereas the logic of the dominant race ideology across western Europe for at least two centuries (between the mid-fifteenth and mid-seventeenth centuries), the protoracism defined here, with its nuanced synthesis of ancient and medieval race-beliefs, was at least a remarkably potent, predictable, coherent, and consistent ideology in its believed metaphysical causes and assumed preternatural effects, modern so-called scientific racism illogically appropriated the same specific, metaphysically derived, "supernaturalist" conclusions about each race from the earlier ideology while only partially supplementing these beliefs through what we must recognize at last as a pathetic series of temporary—hence, remarkably inconsistent and incoherent—pseudoscientific explanations using quack forms of "science," each of which was soon discredited, like the entire ideology itself has been, in less than a century. It's therefore increasingly hard to see this iteration of racism as a remotely coherent ideology. At least, being so derivative and anachronistic, modern racism—as an *ideology*—does not possess the primacy, innovation, or supposed rational superiority and greater degree of coherence that have all curiously been granted to it.

Although Christianity in Europe, broadly defined, offered a more cohesive ideology or set of beliefs and a more coherent system of ideas, opinions, and beliefs about race than exist in our own increasingly secular age, modern critics nonetheless object, oddly, that religiously inflected racial ideology was not yet coherent or consistent in the Renaissance. Notably, skeptical critics selectively impose unattainable uniformity as a criterion for granting the existence of medieval and Renaissance racisms. For instance, Fredrickson argues that because "at least some blacks" (i.e., the exception of converted, so-called white-souled Ethiopes and rare black saints) were treated in "favorable" terms, and because the color black in daily life did not "always [have] unfavorable connotations," as in some religious orders and in fashion,[77] premodern racism did not rise to the level of coherence and consistency of modern racism. Of course, uniformity and absolute consistency of ideology and associations with a color across an entire population have never been, and are not now, a criterion for the existence of racism. There have always been competing beliefs, then and now. Though majority opinion, much less uniformity, is thus not necessary to prove the existence of racism in any period, it is nonetheless only all too clearly the case, based on the pervasive stereotypes and practices demonstrated in this essay, that metaphysically oriented antiblack and antisemitic racism became dominant race ideologies during the Renaissance.

Nor can we, with Fredrickson, dismiss premodern "supernaturalist racism" as not truly rising to the level of racism because it was "primarily religious rather than naturalistic or scientific."[78] Such a fallacy fails to account for not only centuries of racism that has never been truly naturalistic/scientific and in which proponents have explicitly or tacitly employed religious beliefs but also the existence of non- and even antiscientific racism in America today. Studies have found that "strongly religious Americans tend to be the worst racists" and, further, that "the more religious a person is, the more likely he or she is going to be racist."[79] Meanwhile, a May 2017 Gallup poll found that 38 percent of Americans are creationists who do not accept evolution,[80] so that the most religious, who "tend to be the worst racists," do not accept science, meaning that their racism is still essentially based on religion and, at best, sketchy metaphysical generalizations. That is another way of saying that protoracism is the original form of racism, that modern racism is an anachronistic throwback to the metaphysical ideology defined during the Renaissance drawn in part from religion, and that late-coming and now largely defunct and utterly unpersuasive pseudoscientific rationales for racism may have been merely a historical blip, a temporary (twentieth-century) adaptation of the original form of racism.

Sophistic dismissals of the original form of religiously oriented racism further fail in their lack of awareness of the emphatic embrace of Christendom—though often not actual faith in Christianity—among racist white nationalists across the Western world today. For them, Christian "tradition" and "culture" were/are coterminous with European identitarian notions of whiteness that must be defended. As Kelly J. Baker explains, for white nationalists, "Christendom helped unify Europe, leading to the creation of their cherished white European identity."[81] It is indeed significant that, by Fredrickson's definition and chief criterion, the most toxic racism of our own time would not count as racism at all, lacking *any*, let alone a "primarily . . . naturalistic or scientific" basis.

Nowhere, then, does the reductive secularization narrative of early modern and modern "disenchantment"—that is, of a supposed shaking off of faith, belief, superstitions, curses, blessings, souls, and divine favor and authority—need to be challenged more than in discussions of racism. After all, the damning allegorical-stereotypical beliefs underlying the supposedly "secular" ideology of modern racism are wholly derivative of previous racial ideology describing cursed and damned races with deficient souls and predetermined moral, mental, and physical characteristics, carried forward via spiritually defiled blood. Modern belief in racism exhibits such superstitiously anachronistic magical thinking as to be analogous to a delayed belief in the power of ancient pagan gods, of the most implausible Pardoner's relics' miraculous ability to cure, and of the malevolent magic of seventeenth-century witches in England or Salem, Massachusetts. Whereas Fredrickson believes that "racism had to be emancipated from Christian[ity]" and from the "primarily religious," "supernaturalist racism"[82] of the Middle Ages and the Renaissance, racism was in truth never so "emancipated." Racism may best be understood, then, as only a would-be, partially secularized version of what was originally—and still is—a metaphysical, chiefly theological ideology.

Notes

1. Via standard usages such as those in *Merriam-Webster* online, the *Cambridge Dictionary* online, and Dictionary.com, here the word "ideology" denotes "a theory or set of beliefs," "a systematic body of concepts," and "a manner or the content of thinking characteristic of . . . [a] culture." I argue that, beginning in the mid-fifteenth century, the Renaissance certainly developed a coherent ideology of race that persuasively justified its racial discrimination. And by "coherent," I presume that arguments dismissing premodern racism mean standard usages including "logical and consistent," "logically connected, consistent," and "having the quality of holding together, cohesive."

2. George M. Fredrickson, *Racism: A Short History* (Princeton, N.J.: Princeton University Press, 2015), 24.

3. Kim F. Hall, *Things of Darkness: Economies of Race and Gender in Early Modern England* (Ithaca, N.Y.: Cornell University Press, 1995), 261.

4. Peter Erickson and Kim F. Hall, "'A New Scholarly Song': Rereading Early Modern Race," *Shakespeare Quarterly* 67, no. 1 (2016): 4.

5. Shankar Raman, *Renaissance Literature and Postcolonial Studies* (Edinburgh: Edinburgh University Press, 2011), 46.

6. Throughout this essay the term "protoracism" refers not to a failed prototype of so-called scientific racism but rather uses the prefix "proto" first to distinguish the earliest observable form of racism, a coherent ideology of race established in the European Renaissance, based on theological and philosophical authorities according to which the notion of racial determinism was thus metaphysical rather than would-be biological. Second, although protoracism is full-blown racism in the sense of being fully racist in the dangerous effects of its racial prejudice, I use the term to clarify that the reader must not fall back into assuming scientific rationales or the primacy or superiority of modern racism when considering the earlier ideology. Third, the term "protoracism" is also used to distinguish this particular ideology as originating the quite specific damning stereotypical assumptions about races still widely believed in modern racism, a fact that makes the earlier ideology more coherent than the late-coming, derivative modern iteration.

7. In the unconventional and therefore arresting compound coinage "race-belief," I aim here both to convey and to uncover an essential concept about race, something akin to the disturbing sense conveyed in the German word *Rassenseele*, often translated in English (hyphenated) as "race-soul," where foremost Nazi ideologue Alfred Rosenburg explained Nazism's racist belief that "Soul means race viewed from within. And, vice-versa, race is the externalization of a soul," so that "race and soul are merely different designations for the same entity" (David Patterson, *Anti-Semitism and Its Metaphysical Origins* [Cambridge: Cambridge University Press, 2015], 147). In much the same way (and even often while making the identical assumptions about race and soul), in premodern ideology, there was no mystification of the fact that race and belief were inseparable to such an extent that perception of "race" was (as indeed it still is) an externalization of belief. Here, then, the hyphenated compound, race-belief, is intended to designate this very meaning.

8. Fredrickson, *Racism*, 46.

9. Here the extreme Fredrickson has most in mind is presumably what Geraldine Heng calls race-as-religion and religion-as-race (*Empire of Magic: Medieval Romance and the Politics of Cultural Fantasy* [New York: Columbia University Press, 2003], 237).

10. Fredrickson, *Racism*, 26.

11. Brian Cummings, *Mortal Thoughts: Religion, Secularity and Identity in Shakespeare and Early Modern Culture* (Oxford: Oxford University Press, 2013), 4–5.

12. Pliny, *Natural History*, Vol. II, Books 307, trans. H. Rackham (Loeb Classical Library online), 7.40.130: https://www.loebclassics.com/abstract/pliny_elder-natural_history/1938/pb_LCL352.593.xml?rskey=Y0BBVH&result=3&mainRsKey=EgetHl; DOI: 10.4159/DLCL.pliny_elder-natural_history.1938.

13. John Block Friedman, *The Monstrous Races in Medieval Art and Thought* (1981; repr., Syracuse, N.Y.: Syracuse University Press, 2000), 108.

14. Friedman, *Monstrous Races*, 95.

15. Friedman, *Monstrous Races*, 95.

16. Friedman, *Monstrous Races*, 96.

17. Alexandra Bergholm, "'Betwixt and Between': Theorizing Liminality and Sacredness in *Buile Suibhne*," in *Approaches to Religion and Mythology in Celtic Studies*, ed. Katja Ritari and Alexandra Bergholm (Newcastle, Engl.: Cambridge Scholars Publishing, 2008), 250.

18. Jean E. Feerick, *Strangers in Blood: Relocating Race in the Renaissance* (Toronto: University of Toronto Press, 2010), 98.

19. Hayden White, "The Forms of Wildness: Archaeology of an Idea," in *Tropics of Discourse: Essays in Cultural Criticism* (Baltimore: Johns Hopkins University Press, 1978), 157.

20. Allen Thiher, *Revels in Madness: Insanity in Medicine and Literature* (Ann Arbor: University of Michigan Press, 2000), 46.

21. Thiher, *Revels in Madness*, 47.

22. Unless otherwise noted, for biblical quotes, I cite *The Bible: Authorized King James Version*, Oxford World Classics edition, ed. Robert Carroll and Stephen Prickett (Oxford: Oxford University Press, 1997).

23. John Corrigan and Lynn S. Neal, eds., *Religious Intolerance in America: A Documentary History* (Chapel Hill: University of North Carolina Press, 2010), 30.

24. Likewise, as Ibram X. Kendi has demonstrated, "some Puritans . . . carried across [from the Old World] racist ideas—racist ideas that preceded American slavery, because the need to justify African slavery preceded colonial America" (*Stamped from the Beginning: The Definitive History of Racist Ideas in America* [New York: Nation Books, 2016], 19).

25. Michael Witmore, *Shakespearean Metaphysics* (New York: Continuum, 2008), 15.

26. Witmore, *Shakespearean Metaphysics*, 25.

27. Mariska Leunissen, "Signs of Physiognomy in Aristotle," *Center for Hellenic Studies Research Bulletin*, November 30, 2010, http://www.chs-fellows.org/2010/11/30/signs-of-physiognomy-in-aristotle/.

28. Leunissen, "Signs of Physiognomy."

29. Juan Huarte, *Examen de ingenios: The Examination of mens Wits. In whicch, by discouering the varietie of natures, is shewed for what profession each one is apt, and how far he shall profit therein* (London: Adam Flip, 1594), 186.

30. Pierre Charron, *Of Wisdome* (London, 1612), 164.

31. Francis Bacon, *The New Organon*, ed. Lisa Jardine and Michael Silverthorne (Cambridge: Cambridge University Press, 2000), 173.

32. William Pagel, *William Harvey's Biological Ideas: Selected Aspects and Historical Background* (Basel: Karger, 1967), 144.

33. Michael Zank, trans., *Leo Strauss: The Early Writings, 1921–32* (Albany: State University of New York Press, 2002), 192n5. The relevant scriptures are as follows: Genesis 9:4; Leviticus 17:14; and Deuteronomy 12:23.

34. Homi Bhabha, *The Location of Culture* (London: Routledge, 1994), 86.

35. Emphases added.

36. See Feerick, *Strangers in Blood*.

37. Heng, *Empire of Magic*, 388n6.

38. Friedman, *Monstrous Races*, 16.

39. Friedman, *Monstrous Races*, 27. Emphasis added.

40. Friedman, *Monstrous Races*, 16.

41. Richard Hakluyt, *The Principal Voyages of the English Nation*, 7 vols. (London: Dent, 1926), 7:261–62.

42. Mary Floyd-Wilson, *English Ethnicity and Race in Early Modern Drama* (Cambridge: Cambridge University Press, 2003), 10.

43. Werner Sollors, *Neither Black nor White yet Both: Thematic Explorations of Interracial Literature* (Cambridge, Mass.: Harvard University Press, 1999), 94.

44. Peter Fryer, *Staying Power: The History of Black People in Britain* (London: Pluto Press, 1984), 143.

45. Recent work on "a system of race as blood" has misread early conceptions of race in other ways too. In *Strangers in Blood*, Feerick assumes, for instance, that "to be of 'base race' was an oxymoron; baseness precluded membership in a race" (3). Unfortunately, that is simply mistaken.

46. Robert Bartlett, *The Making of Europe: Conquest, Colonization, and Cultural Change, 950–1350* (New York: Penguin Books, 1993), 197.

47. Robert Bartlett, "Medieval and Modern Concepts of Race and Ethnicity," *Journal of Medieval and Early Modern Studies* 31, no. 1 (Winter 2001): 39–56.

48. Janet Adelman, *Blood Relations: Christian and Jew in "The Merchant of Venice"* (Chicago: University of Chicago, 2008), 77.

49. Consider the following sampling from the *OED*: (1. b.) A tribe, nation, or people, regarded as of common stock. In early use freq. with modifying adjective, as *British race*, *Roman race*, etc. . . . 1667 Milton *Paradise Lost* i. 780 That Pigmean Race Beyond the Indian Mount . . . ; (2. a.) Chiefly *poet.* The offspring or posterity *of* a person; a set of children or descendants . . . 1549 J. Hooper *Lesson Incarnation Christe* sig. A.viii^v, There shall come forthe of the rase of Jesse a braunche . . . 1570 J. Foxe *Actes & Monumentes* (rev. ed.) II. 1841/1 Thus was the outward race & stocke of Abraham after flesh refused. 1593 R. Hooker *Of Lawes Eccl. Politie* iv. v. 178 Such, as either wee must acknowledge for our owne forefathers or els disdaine the race of Christ . . . 1667 Milton *Paradise Lost* x. 385 High proof ye now have giv'n to be the Race Of Satan . . . ; (3.) Any of the major divisions into which living creatures may be separated . . . (a.) A class, kind, or species of beings other than humans or animals. 1549 T. Chaloner tr. Erasmus *Praise of Folie* sig. Aiii^v, Nor any other of that olde and rustie race of Gods . . . (b.) The class of humans; mankind. Formerly freq. with *the human race*: . . . *c*1580 Sir P. Sidney tr. *Psalmes David* xxi. x, From among the humane race [thou shalt] Roote out their generation.

50. Floyd-Wilson, *English Ethnicity*, 3.

51. Cynthia Marshall, "Cosmology and the Body," in *A Concise Companion to English Renaissance Literature*, ed. Donna B. Hamilton (Malden, Mass.: Blackwell Publishing, 2006), 225.

52. Floyd-Wilson, *English Ethnicity*, 3.

53. Ania Loomba and Jonathan Burton, eds., *Race in Early Modern England: A Documentary Companion* (New York: Palgrave Macmillan, 2007), 104.

54. Floyd-Wilson, *English Ethnicity*, 71.

55. James H. Sweet, "The Iberian Roots of American Racist Thought," *William and Mary Quarterly* 54, no. 1 (January 1997): 157.

56. Sweet, "Iberian Roots," 157.

57. A. Saunders, *A Social History of Black Slaves and Freedmen in Portugal, 1441–1555* (Cambridge: Cambridge University Press, 1982), 5.

58. Elizabeth Abbott, *Sugar: A Bittersweet History* (London: Duckworth Overlook, 2009), 33, 35. For an excellent account of such matters relating to the long history of antiblack racism and the origins of slavery exploiting Africans, see the early chapters of Kendi, *Stamped from the Beginning*.

59. David Eltis, *The Rise of African Slavery in the Americas* (Cambridge: Cambridge University Press, 2000), 11.

60. Geraldine Heng, *The Invention of Race in the European Middle Ages* (Cambridge: Cambridge University Press, 2018), 186.

61. Geraldine Heng, "Jews, Saracens, 'Black Men,' Tartars: England in a World of Racial Difference," in *A Companion to Medieval English Literature and Culture, c. 1350–c. 1500*, ed. Peter Brown (Oxford: Wiley, 2009), 260.

62. Hayden White, "The Forms of Wildness: Archaeology of an Idea," in *The Wild Man Within: An Image in Western Thought from the Renaissance to Romanticism*, ed. Edward Dudley and Maximillian E. Novak (Pittsburgh: University of Pittsburgh Press, 1972), 161.

63. Kate Lowe, "The Stereotyping of Black Africans in Renaissance Europe," in *Black Africans in Renaissance Europe*, ed. T. F. Earle and K. J. P. Lowe (Cambridge: Cambridge University Press, 2005), 25–26.

64. Anu Korhonen, "Washing the Ethiopian White: Conceptualising Black Skin in Renaissance England," in Earle and Lowe, *Black Africans*, 106.

65. Robert Hornback, "Blackfaced Fools, Black-Headed Birds, Fool Synonyms, and Shakespearean Allusions to Renaissance Blackface Folly," *Notes and Queries* 55, no. 2 (June 2008): 215–19.

66. Ahuva Belkin, "Antichrist as the Embodiment of the *Insipiens* in Thirteenth-Century French Psalters," *Florilegium* 10 (1988–91): 71–72.

67. Jeffrey Burton Russell, *Satan: The Early Christian Tradition* (Ithaca, N.Y.: Cornell University Press, 1981), 213.

68. Saint Augustine, *The City of God against the Pagans*, trans. David S. Wiesen, Loeb Classical Library (Cambridge, Mass.: Harvard University Press, 1968), 3:516–17.

69. Augustine, *City of God*, 172–73.

70. Augustine, *City of God*, 154–55.

71. Augustine, *City of God*, 156–57.

72. Augustine, *City of God*, 487n4.

73. Martin Stevens and Arthur C. Cawley, ed., *The Towneley Plays*, 2 vols. (Oxford: Oxford University Press, 1994), ll. 132–36.

74. Robert Hornback, *The English Clown Tradition from the Middle Ages to Shakespeare* (Woodbridge, Suffolk: D. S. Brewer, 2009), 30.

75. Elizabeth Donnan, *Documents Illustrative of the History of the Slave Trade to America*, 4 vols. (New York: Octagon Books, 1965), 1:48.

76. Alden T. Vaughan, *Roots of American Racism: Essays on the Colonial Experience* (New York: Oxford University Press, 1995), ix.

77. Fredrickson, *Racism*, 27.

78. Fredrickson, *Racism*, 46.

79. Phil Zuckerman, "Secularism, Religion, and Racism," *Psychology Today*, August 20, 2014: https://www.psychologytoday.com/us/blog/the-secular-life/201408/secularism-religion-and-racism.

80. http://news.gallup.com/poll/210956/belief-creationist-view-humans-new-low.aspx.

81. Kelly J. Baker, "The New White Nationalists?," *Religion & Politics*, October 20, 2016, http://religionandpolitics.org/2016/10/20/the-new-white-nationalists/.

82. Fredrickson, *Racism*, 46, 47.

Part Three

Spaces of the Secular

"Into the Chapel": Unmodern Interiority and Quintilian Inwardness in *Hamlet*

Jeanne H. McCarthy

> "Go seek him out—speak fair—and bring the body / Into the chapel." (4.1.36–37)
>
> "What, are they children? Who maintains 'em?" (Folio, 1623, 2.2.320)

Child players who famously performed in household chapels in Elizabeth's palaces, in the environs of St. Paul's Cathedral, and on surrendered monastic grounds of the Blackfriars receive a cursory acknowledgment in the brief exchange between Hamlet and Rosencrantz and Guildenstern about the cause of the players' travels in 2.2 of *Hamlet*.[1] The extended reference in the Folio edition of the play (F 1623) to an early modern performance practice associated with one or both of the prominent children's indoor playing troupes that were, even after their revival in 1599, maintaining a relationship with the residual religious and medieval institutions of the household chapel and grammar school recalls an alternative, traditionally religiously affiliated, book-centered performance practice and mode of interpretation. In so doing, the reference to children invites a rethinking of the play's "turn" to or from religion. While the seemingly merely topical nature of the allusion to child players and Hamlet's surprise at their popularity have often been cited as an excuse for dismissing them, their importance in the theatrical culture is far more relevant to modern understandings of Shakespeare's stage and stagecraft, particularly in this play, than is often allowed. Their introduction also challenges the argument that rational interpretive strategies credited to secularization and science (or what Stephen Greenblatt posits is the "swerve" to modernity, away from his curiously characterized benightedness of the Middle Ages)[2] were uniquely shaping Shakespeare's notions of interiority. Rather, not only does *Hamlet* eloquently express ambivalence about the turn to secularization or the reform-inspired abandonment of a fluid exchange between sacred and profane space long associated with medieval thought but also the play's casual reference to a performance practice associated with child playing acknowledges how fully Shakespeare, in his staging of interiority, has assimilated its aesthetics and what Kathy Eden defines elsewhere as a reader-centered "rhetoric and hermeneutics of intimacy"[3] via an engagement with classicism.

Hamlet has long been used as a source text informing critical interpretations of early modern performance and performance space. It is thought to adumbrate modernity and modern subjects' supposed discovery of introspection as well as post-Copernican spatial understandings. In her analysis of theatrical "supernatural environments," for instance, Kristen Poole has emphasized the significance of Shakespeare's invocation of the archaic symbolic architecture of the stage at the Globe to the cosmological crisis underpinning Hamlet's "sense of being entrapped by spatial and ontological paradoxes."[4] She argues that the tradition-bound "wooden fixity" of the Globe's stage, with its painted heavens above and its trapdoor leading to hell below, would have offered audiences, players, and playwrights a comforting "illusion of geographical and eschatological certitude" regarding their cosmos that would have subsequently been challenged by the play's confrontation with what Poole describes as a more accurate Newtonian sense of space.[5] For Poole, Shakespeare's primitive Globe appears to be poorly suited to the culture's emerging, more modern, secularized understanding of reality.

Poole's argument qualifies the narrative offered by E. K. Chambers, who nonetheless similarly plotted the rise of early modern "secular" drama in spatial terms when he hailed the drama's happy escape from the church and churchyard. Rather than embracing Chambers's dating of the emergence of a full-blown secular drama with such a shift, however, Poole sides with those who detect in Shakespeare's depiction of Hamlet an imperfect liberation from the dictates and symbols of an outworn religious faith unsuited to a new *saeculum*, "age," or "world." To the extent that Poole's observation about the importance of stage architecture to Hamlet's musings on the cosmos rings true, it does so, as with Chambers's thesis about the escape from the churchyard, without incorporating findings that a sense of "fixity" and an established performance practice freed of religious traditions did not yet exist, even at the Globe. Indeed, the opposite is true. By the end of the sixteenth century, when a variety of now obsolete performance spaces and related practices persisted, neither Shakespeare's audience's nor his company's conception of how one performs on the public stage was as secular as is conventionally assumed. Indeed, many in the audience would have continued to experience theatrical events beyond the confines of purpose-built public theaters like the Globe, and for them the play's depiction of a world in which competing senses of space and time persisted would not have seemed strange.[6] The play does not thoroughly surrender to modern secular understandings of experience but rather, ironically enough, its protagonist's school-informed interpretation of the changing boundaries between sacred and secular space resists, if not defies, emerging distinctions associated with scientific modernist understandings.

Moreover, Shakespeare's audiences did not yet possess a modern preference for a uniformity or fixity in performance *style* onstage and, more specifically, the approach to characterization required to perform Hamlet's introspective speeches. Even within the play proper, as when the plot momentarily deflects attention in act 2 to the players' arrival, early modern performance practice is defined as diverse. Introduced into the court by Hamlet's "kinde Schoole-fellowes" (Q1, 1603, E2v) Rosencrantz and Guildenstern, the visiting playing troupe engages in at least two dramatic modes that differ stylistically from those evident in the play proper. Though momentarily under threat by a new fad for "humours" or satires, the troupe appears to have achieved popular success by mastering the art, one in which Hamlet once took much "delight," suited to the presentation of allegorical types. This style, like the troupe itself, is associated with the city, not the university, or school. Hamlet believes its popular, more pageantlike aesthetics would similarly suit a learned court audience and thus asks them to perform before it a stock piece in a players' repertory, entitled by Hamlet *The Murder of Gonzago* in act 2 but later informally renamed *The Mousetrap* in act 3. The story is itself drawn from a popular, or at least readily available extant, narrative and is so loosely scripted as to be easily adapted to accommodate the patron's request for a few additional lines or for an abbreviated prologue. In the portrayal of two-dimensional, melodramatic types like a dutiful lady, an ailing ruler (duke or king), and a villainous usurper in both the plot and the performance's spectacular pageantlike dumb show, the players deploy a gestural acting style. As Hamlet's impatience with one player's mugging suggests—"Begin murderer: leave thy damnable faces and begin" (3.2.245–46)—the troupe's style, in fact, is perilously vulnerable to the critique Hamlet offers of more exaggerated contemporaries: "O, there be players that I have . . . heard others praise . . . and that highly (not to speak it profanely), that neither having th' accent of Christians, nor the gait of Christian, pagan, nor man, have so strutted and bellowed that

I have thought some of Nature's journeymen had made men, and not made them well, they imitated humanity so abominably" (3.2.27–33). The troupe appears to have mastered a then-current mode of performance that presented conventional stereotypes in "extant" plots capable of being recombined with other bits or being trimmed for different occasions, a kind of aesthetics that Walter Ong aligns with orality.

But this is not all they can do. Their range is suggested when Hamlet prompts one of the players to recite a speech, that of "Aeneas' [tale] to Dido," from a not very well-acclaimed or frequently staged play. This virtuosic demonstration suggests that at least one of the players had mastered a less-popular, less-pageantlike, and more learned style of performance. That learned style resembles, but is not quite the same as, the one that Polonius recalls when he boasts of having performed the part of Brutus "once i' th' university" (clearly some decades ago), where he was "accounted a good actor" (3.2.95–97), for Polonius critiques the player's vocabulary and, presumably, the extent or quality of his learning. The universities' use of occasional drama that, as records of the queen's visit to the universities in 1564 and 1566 suggest, was designed to demonstrate a mastery of audacity, voice, and rhetorical skills in order to prepare the young men for the kind of public office Polonius now holds but that neither aimed toward, nor was entirely capable of, producing proficient actors. Anecdotes about the uneven performance of university men in their plays even relatively late in the era indicate, as the critic Christopher Marlow concludes, that student-authored plays "fulfill[ed] a social rather than a literary function."[7] Patrons like the Earl of Leicester so distinguished university performance from that of common players that his statutes forbade college students from seeing "common stage players" perform.[8] Polonius's condescension here gives voice to that distinction. The players' unpopular play is also distinguished from another learned mode when the players' style is contrasted with the competing aesthetics of child players.

Shakespeare's company's relationship to these various modes is complex. The acting "companies" emerging in the records in the 1570s were a new kind of acting troupe that was, like the child players, similarly displacing the old-fashioned troupes in cultural importance and preference. Some were associated with the "bellowing" and "strutting" roles of Edward Alleyn, but a role like Hamlet required a skill set, including an ability to arouse empathy in its audiences through subtlety and an attention to inwardness via the careful examination of texts and scripted speeches for motives, that was then being taught not in the university but in the prominent chapel and grammar schools. Indeed, though Hamlet himself appears to be surprised by news of the rise in popularity of children's troupes or their turn to satires, and thus their capacity to challenge the preeminence of his preferred Tragedians, the child players, or "little eyases" (F 1623), aligned in the exchange between Hamlet and Rosencrantz with popularity rather than "caviary," were more likely to perform a learned, literary speech like the one "Aeneas' tale to Dido" (2.2.434–35), which Hamlet prefers. The classically informed acting style of the player and the play that "was not caviary to the general" is actually consistent with the learned children's classical repertory, exemplified in Christopher Marlowe's lone children's company play, *Dido, Queen of Carthage* (dated 1585 to 1588), and John Lyly's tragicomedies of the 1580s, in which children performed the written word in spaces that were also sacred, though understood as transformable and fluid. It was a dramaturgy that even in its comedies drew upon and encouraged a training steeped in a classical study of authors such as Terence, Plautus, and Quintilian.

The affinity of the stagecraft informing Shakespeare's *Hamlet* with such a learned tradition can be detected in his play's imperfect affinity with the style of the traveling players' play. Though Shakespeare's company was similarly popular and city identified, Shakespeare's plays resemble less the reliance on a presentational, pageantlike style of *The Mousetrap* than on classical drama, and particularly the comedies of Terence, which drew fine distinctions between sons, brothers, and fathers. Plays like *Hamlet* take otherwise conventional types like a scheming villain, lovely queen, loyal sons, and a dutiful counselor and convert them to more complicated, unconventional, richly drawn, particularized, and distinctive characters. Even so, *Hamlet* does not entirely abandon the appeal of the pageant or dumb show. The roles in *Hamlet* differ in their requirements. Thus, in the midst of their court pageantry, the lady Gertrude and villain Claudius express a somewhat superficial impatience with Hamlet's tendency toward introspection or distinguishing himself by making such a common thing as death "so particular to thee" (1.2.75). Polonius believes he can detect the source of Hamlet's unhappiness by deciphering his behavior as one would the actions of actors in a dumb show. As a result, even as Hamlet rejects an idea of public performance as one in which outward forms and behavior can be understood to "denote . . . truly" (1.2.83), he is surrounded by other characters who function well within such a hermeneutics or interpretive framework. This play is thus imperfectly positioned in a narrative of an easy, even natural, transition to professional secular drama. Shakespeare incorporates into his popular stagecraft not only a conventional allegorical tradition but also a classically informed performance mode that developed alongside popular or profane theater and, as in *Hamlet*, synthesized classical and sacred understandings of character and space into something new, a different hermeneutics of performance. The play proper's power in performance rests in this synthesis of alternative performance practices in which actors performing in the same play comment upon differing uses of playing space.

Both in the play within the play and the play proper, a variety of secular and sacred playing traditions and practices introduce different kinds or modes of interpretation. When Hamlet seeks, for instance, to "catch the conscience of the king" and to interpret Claudius's "seeming," he requests a typological example of interfamilial murder drawn from the traveling players' more demonstrative, popular practice. During its brief performance, Hamlet adapts to its aesthetics, even taking on the roles of improvising collaborative author and "chorus" to the play (3.2.238). His hope is to use this play, as he has heard plays being used in the past, to force a villain to expose his guilt: "I'll observe his looks . . . If 'a do blench, / I know my course" (2.2.582–83). Of course, though it appears to prompt Claudius into revealing some level of guilt, this style of performance nonetheless lacks the power to reveal motive or affect its audience. Ophelia is puzzled by its plot and Gertrude's superficial response that "the lady doth protest too much, methinks" (3.2.222) hints that confusion rather than identification may have been the extent of the effect of the players' unnatural histrionics on its audience. After all, Hamlet's application of his interpretation of "looks" leaves him still uncertain about the villain's soul and to conclude, wrongly, that Claudius is efficaciously penitent when he observes him kneeling in 3.3. This impact differs markedly from that of the lead player's earlier speech about Hecuba on Hamlet, who finds himself, in comparison, "a peasant slave," and even on Polonius, who finds it so emotionally wrought that he asks the player to stop: "Prithee no more" (2.2.485, 458).

The alternative mode that Hamlet seeks to master as the play continues, one in which actors would have aimed to feel and incite deeper sympathy, would have required some contact with a contemporary Renaissance humanist pedagogy centered on the first-century Roman scholar Quintilian.[9] T. W. Baldwin, who ranked Quintilian "along with Cicero" as of highest importance in the Renaissance curriculum's "new learning," calling him "*the Rhetorician*, at the pinnacle of the grammar school," observed that "it was clearly Quintilian who shaped Hamlet's thought" on players and performance.[10]

Quintilian's "rule" informed the schoolroom interpretation and performance of Terence and Plautus and later English imitations of their comedies. Embraced by the first grammar school master of St. Paul's (home to Paul's Boys), William Lily, Quintilian's teaching also informed the works of such other prominent Renaissance English schoolmasters of the age as Robert Whittinton, Thomas Elyot, Nicholas Udall, Thomas Wilson, Richard Mulcaster, and Charles Hoole. Before being appointed as schoolmaster at St. Paul's in 1596, Mulcaster, who had studied under the schoolmaster-playwright Udall at Eton and had served as the first schoolmaster and famed producer of plays at the Merchant Taylor's School (where he taught dramatist Thomas Kyd) from 1560 to 1586, would claim that "Quintilian's rule is the best."[11]

G. H. Mair praised Wilson's *The Arte of Rhetorique* (1560), elsewhere described as one of the "most successful sixteenth-century books of its kind in England" and one that Gabriel Harvey noted was the "daily bread of our common pleaders and discoursers,"[12] for offering a "judicious compilation of Quintilian."[13] Even when the debt is not obvious, Quintilian's influence appears; the recent editors of George Puttenham's *The Art of English Poesy*, Frank Whigham and Wayne Rebhorn, note that "Puttenham's reorganization works to disguise his dependence on the classical material," and specifically, Quintilian.[14] Puttenham himself recorded finding the lord keeper, Sir Nicholas Bacon, "sitting in his gallery alone with the works of Quintilian before him."[15] Martin Luther, too, had embraced the work and had "declared he preferred Quintilian to almost all other authorities on education, 'for while he teaches he gives us a model of eloquence. He teaches by a happy combination of theory and practice.'"[16] The playwright Ben Jonson, schooled at Westminster under the schoolmaster William Camden, recommended Quintilian to Drummond in his *Discoveries*, noting that Quintilian's "bookes" were "not only to be read but altogether digested."[17]

The technique elevated the status of the text and an interpretive approach focused on words. The training taught not only how to persuade but also, significantly, how to read; humanist schoolmasters applied explorations of motives and distinguishing habits of characters when teaching how to read classical literature and history. Indeed, an emphasis on interiority and introspection, which often appear to modern critics to be so coincident with a Protestant spirituality and a turn to secularity and modern individualism, is more specifically coincident, at least in *Hamlet*, with performance studies in the ancient methods of Quintilian. Quintilian promoted especially the use of *visiones*, or "private images," to elicit an emotional response from hearers. Of utmost significance to the consideration of how a Quintilian-inspired pedagogy in the performance of characters that were more than mere types on the contemporary stage affected Shakespeare—and *Hamlet*—was Quintilian's related coaching on empathy and affect. Baldwin notes that Erasmus had recommended Quintilian "as the best treatment of the affects"[18] and referred schoolmasters to the passages where the pedagogue encouraged a student or orator to *empathize* with the causes for which he advocates. Those encountering Quintilian would find such instruction as, "We must identify ourselves with the persons of whom we complain that they have suffered grievous, unmerited, and bitter fortune . . . and for a brief space feel their suffering as though it were our own."[19] Indeed, "the chief requisite, then, for moving the feelings of others is, as far as I can judge, that we ourselves be moved; for the assumption of grief, and anger, and indignation, will be often ridiculous, if we adapt merely our words and looks, and not our minds to those passions" (11.26.427). Promising that the techniques would allow the legal advocate in a trial to "shake the theatre" (1.53.420), Quintilian throughout uses terms that are apt for the actor: "In delivering . . . whatever we wish to appear like truth, let us assimilate . . . the feelings of those who are truly affected, and let our language proceed from such a temper of mind as we would wish to excite in the judge. Will he grieve, let me ask, who shall hear me . . . speak . . . without concern? Will he be angry, if the orator . . . shows no like feeling? Will he shed tears at the words of one who pleads with dry eyes?" (11.27.427). When pleading a murder case, the student is reminded to imagine the event in vivid terms that conjure Hamlet's dilemma: "I make a complaint that a man has been murdered; shall I not bring before my eyes everything that is likely to have happened when the murder occurred? Shall not the assassin suddenly sally forth? Shall not the other tremble, cry out, supplicate or flee? Shall I not behold the one striking, the other falling? Shall not the blood, and paleness, and last gasp of the expiring victim, present itself fully to my mental view?" (11.29.431). The method also included a focus on what Hamlet calls "motive and the cue for passion" (2.2.545). For instance, Quintilian prompted pupils to wonder about Orestes's motives or "the motive . . . that induced fifty kings to sail for Troy": "'Whether the[se kings] were obliged by their oath, or impelled by example? Or . . . [by] respect to the family of Atreus?'" (7.2.3).

Quintilian had, of course, long been a part of the medieval curriculum, but his method and application to drama gained prominence in the Renaissance schoolroom following the rediscovery of the full text of his *Institutio Oratoria* (*Education of an Orator in Twelve Books*) at the beginning of the fifteenth century and the promotion of performance in the new charters drafted for St. Paul's.[20] Similarly reform-minded educators embracing the Renaissance humanist curriculum likewise began using the pedagogic method known as Quintilian's rule in their own reintroduction of a text-centered performance practice. While many schoolboys exposed to this curriculum were taught some of its techniques, the two most prominent Elizabethan children's troupes practicing this learned profane aesthetics and actor training associated with Quintilian were the Children of Her Majesty's Chapel and the Children of Paul's. Both were, by virtue of their proximity to the court and its humanist circle, evidence suggests, the most public practitioners and earliest proponents of this new method and new style of acting. Shakespeare's synthesis of such a classically informed actor's training into oral or traditional practices onstage yielded a new kind of secular theater that borrowed cleverly from Quintilian.

In application, this style of classical performance, as Hamlet notes in his assessment of the player's speech, struck many as a rarified delicacy, or "caviary" (2.2.425–26). Indeed, the appropriateness of incorporating such classical understandings of self into a popular English stagecraft was being challenged in the late sixteenth and early seventeenth centuries even by the so-called University Wits. Thomas Nashe utterly rejected playwrights who overtly drew upon classicism in writing for the popular stage as "this kind of men that repose eternitie in the mouth of a Player," concluding that the "hybridized public stage" was ill-suited to present true "poetic discourse."[21] Despite Luther's embrace, the introduction of classical learning to the culture at large was also stymied by mainstream Protestants engaging in a "Counter-Renaissance" who privileged inspiration over learning.[22] One Puritan, Arthur Dent, thus claimed "the knowledge of the elect" was superior to classical or heathen study as well as "to the knowledge which a mathematicall geographer hath of the earth."[23] And yet this alternative, bookish aesthetics was, as the news of the rising popularity of child players suggests, nonetheless slowly gaining in popularity even among unlearned audiences. The increasingly favorable reception may have been a result of its use in the schoolroom, which was hardly "a sealed and separate place" or a "hermetic world," as John Astington has concluded, but rather so much a commonplace in rural and urban life that it was capable of generating popular familiarity.[24]

Hamlet's response to the player's empathetic narration of Hecuba's response to the brutal slaughter of Priam after the fall of Troy seemingly recalls him to his own grammar-school training in Quintilian, and his introspections, as well as his oft-quoted professions of classical stoicism, will thereafter reflect a conscious resort to pagan or classical teaching in analyzing character and motive.

His interactions with other characters also afford Shakespeare opportunities to establish contrasts between this training and alternative hermeneutic strategies. Hamlet's use of books or texts thus sometimes offers an ironic commentary upon more modern, and even Protestant, hermeneutics and their impact on reading and interpretation. As Charlotte Scott observes, while the "encouragement of private reading" of sacred texts and the iconoclastic elevation of the word over the image throughout the Reformation has been linked to the "impetus to interiority" in the era,[25] that evolution is hard to detect in the play, where, initially, reading is neither particularly private nor revelatory. Instead, while it may be true that "under the auspices of Protestantism, 'privacy' moves away from its medieval associations of suspiciousness and duplicity, and achieves a respectable status as a condition of deeply personal introspection, self-awareness and integrity,"[26] Scott observes, for instance, that the use of books in *Hamlet* is often "complicit in the world of 'seems' " (1.2.76).[27] Polonius uses a book and feigned reading to excuse Ophelia's supposedly accidental encounter with Hamlet, and Hamlet increasingly uses his books defensively to fend off attempts by Polonius or Claudius to sound the depths of his melancholy or unveil his knowledge of his father's murder. In an exchange with Polonius that begins, "What do you read my lord?" (2.2.187–88), for example, Hamlet mockingly denies the referential "truth" or utility of the book's innocuous depiction of the physical decay of old men: "I hold it not honesty to have it thus set down" (2.2.100–101). In refusing to grant such seemingly harmless conventional judgments authority, and in the related mocking of the kind of conventional wisdom that informs Polonius's cultural truisms, Hamlet also refuses to allow "shared lines of meaning" between him and Polonius to develop.[28] Hamlet's differing from Polonius's more literal reading habits is but one of the ways in which the play appears to be resisting the critical tendency to align his character with emerging secularism or Protestantism. Private reading was, after all, similarly associated with evolving Catholic practice. Eamon Duffy has demonstrated the "inward-looking, meditative, and affective dimension" of pre-Reformation piety and the statuary and iconography that worked to inspire it.[29] One of the major critical debates of recent decades, then, has been not only whether the end of the sixteenth century witnessed a greater emphasis on inwardness or interiority but also to what extent such a development can be considered a turn from medieval religious practice to a more secular rationality.[30] One must overlook many details to find support for such a turn in *Hamlet*.

The use of theatrical space to represent inwardness and privacy in *Hamlet* is, after all, less secular than we often assume. The prominent, humanist-trained children's troupes, which in the early years of Elizabeth's reign appeared more frequently at court than any other company, performed in transformable sacred spaces. The Children of Paul's appear to have rehearsed and performed "either in the Cathedral . . . or in the small church built next to it, St. Gregory's, where the singing school had been housed since the twelfth century."[31] As for the Children of Her Majesty's Chapel troupe, a Puritan's complaint of 1569 charges that this troupe was also performing plays "even in her maiesties chappel." Moreover, "these pretty vpstart youthes" were offending reformers by "profane[ing] the Lordes day by the lascivious writhing of their tender limbs, and gorgeous decking of their apparell, in feigning bawdie fables gathered from the idolatrous heathen poets."[32] The chapel children were "feigning," or performing, "fables gathered from the idolatrous heathen poets" (i.e., classically/humanist-inspired profane drama involving characters like Aeneas and Dido) within the royal chapels before they moved into the previously holy grounds of the First and Second Blackfriars in 1576 and again in 1599. The children were not the only ones comfortable with such supposed profanations, however. Indeed, disproving Chambers's thesis that Renaissance drama was the product of a move out of church space to wholly secular environs, the use of sacred spaces for nonreligious, "profane" entertainments by all kinds of entertainers continued throughout the era. According to John M. Wasson, "It is arguable that far more than half of all vernacular plays of the English Middle Ages and Renaissance were in fact performed" in religious sites.[33] Even professional troupes used such space; as he notes, "the last professional performance in a church seems to have been in 1625–1626, the earliest in 1339,"[34] and, as Paul W. White observed, the church seems to have been "the normal playing space" for performances by local and traveling players.[35] Indeed, White has argued that not only were churches still "a popular venue for Reformation dramatic performances"[36] but also in many villages the *preferred* site for evangelical drama—contra Chambers's thesis—remained the local church. Against a long-standing critical narrative, Reformation-era performance records therefore often defy the long-held notion that there was a "steadily evolving progress from the sacred to the secular in sixteenth century English theatre,"[37] for they indicate that sacred spaces were being used for secular performance before, during, and after the period of professionalization that made playing in theaters in London commonplace. Even secular, professional performance remained tied to sacred space.

Similarly, the interior spaces (including the chapel referenced in 3.2) and exterior spaces are imagined in *Hamlet* as connected to and part of a royal household in which post-Reformation notions of a separation between the sacred and the profane are at best under construction but do not yet hold. Indeed, Claudius's desire to erect or impose boundaries of various kinds is resisted as soon as it begins. The invading Fortinbras is on the march. Hamlet is having "bad dreams." Claudius's brother's ghost refuses to stay dead and Purgatory refuses to disappear. Old Hamlet manifests and then laments that he was given "no reckoning" nor the final sacrament before his death and, far from endorsing his brother's "remembering" only the living and the present, urges his son to "remember me" (1.5.91). Moreover, assertions of control over uncontained emotional response similarly do not hold. Though Claudius wishes to impose a pragmatic, would-be rational order that might seemingly allow one to forget and escape a primitive past or one's conscience, the household enables a movement of characters in and out of the castle's indoor rooms and walls and interactions that prevent such forgetting or exclusions. This inherited or "residual" sense of architectural space imposes itself on daily life and refuses to maintain a secure boundary between public and private places, memories and present experiences, or sacred and secular understandings. The household space in the tragedy thus contributes to a dramaturgy in which the stage fails to uphold a purely modern idea of secular purpose.

In such a context as well as in terms of the theme of secularization, the allusions to a chapel in *Hamlet* are particularly significant. References to this space offer another intervention in the play's staging of pre- and post-Reformation understandings of the secular self. In performance, the chapel, more than other rooms in the play, may be a purely imaginary space: the actors need never reveal the actual room (unless Claudius has gone there to pray and be seen by Hamlet when he bows his "stubborn knees" [3.2.70]), and so for actors, audiences, and readers alike, it exists as imagined space, a place somewhere beyond the entrances and exits of the stage itself. It is conjured when, after Polonius's death, Claudius uses the chapel as a means of deflecting public outrage from his murder. When he learns, for instance, that Hamlet has dragged the body of Polonius from Gertrude's "closet" to the stairs to the "lobby," where he can be "nosed out," he orders his servants to "Go seek him out—speak fair—and bring the body / Into the chapel" (4.1.36–37). At first, Claudius's insistence on the body's removal to a sacred space seems to reflect his respect for the dead and heightens the shocking impact of Hamlet's desecration, but consistent with Claudius's behavior elsewhere, it even more clearly points to his compartmentalized idea of the sacred; here, he intends to use it to prevent discovery of actions he wishes to contain and conceal, an attempt that fails.

If Claudius endeavors to impose a simple pragmatic secularism on his castle, using the chapel instrumentally to tamp down anticipated outrage over Polonius's death, the household's thin boundary between the sacred and the profane, as between the living and the dead, nonetheless persists. Despite all the obstacles to public exposure Claudius's new reign demands, Denmark's permeable court spaces enable easy and fluid movement—and not only by the Ghost or the armies of Fortinbras. After beginning out of doors with a spectral visitation on the walls of the castle and in the night air, the action moves seamlessly indoors to a diplomatic ceremony that has presumably been well advertised since, as the sun rises, Marcellus assures Horatio that he knows where Hamlet may be found "this morning" (1.1.175). Subsequent events of the play transpire in any number of rooms and spaces in the household: on stairs leading to a lobby or public meeting space, in Gertrude's and Ophelia's closets, within the apartments of Polonius and his family or the chapel to which Polonius's body is supposedly carried and where, perhaps, earlier marriages and funerals were conducted, and in a hall where Hamlet agrees to meet Laertes for the final fencing challenge and where the players' play might have been performed (if not in the chapel). Again, somewhere in the household, Claudius kneels to pray and Ophelia walks with what is "presumably a prayer book."[38] Bodies (whether alive or dead) moving through the castle walls, garden, burial grounds around churchyards or churches, into the castle's lobby, chapel, closets, and hall may be unsafe, but their access to such locations is unrestricted.

To the extent that Shakespeare might imagine a performance space as conveying "fixity," as it does for Poole, that notion is only one possible understanding of space available in this period in which the separation between sacred and secular, in terms of space and ritual, had not yet emerged. As Suzanne Westfall's study of the early modern household suggests, a significant feature of medieval and sixteenth-century household architecture was the way it enabled clear overlap and connections between what moderns would regard as distinct sacred and secular spaces and functions. A fluid interconnectedness between the rooms of the pre-Reformation royal, noble, or monastic site prevailed, so much so that fluidity is a defining feature of early modern ideas of space. So, too, is the use of space and ceremony to convey public identity. The same space could and did serve sacred and secular functions. For example, the size and grandeur of the Tudor-era chapel at the Percy family's Wressle, whose chapel rooms included a Nether Chapel, a High Chapel, and a Rood Loft and whose dimensions "rivaled . . . the Great Hall," suggest its usefulness to displays of the noble family's wealth and power.[39] Fiona Kisby has argued that the "pre-Reformation Henrician chapel" similarly played a "'preeminent'" role in the "display of royal power."[40] Royal chapels were thus typically adorned with heraldic glass displaying shields of arms, badges, mottoes, and scrolls, incorporating images of worldly kings and queens along with those of saints.[41] According to articles in the household ordinances reflecting the practices of Henry VII and Henry VIII, "the holy days when both kings went to chapel services were the '*festa ferienda*' of the household," accompanied by lavish banquets and the keeping of "'open house'" at court.[42] The king's journey to the chapel, moreover, "was a highly formal ceremonial procession . . . The route he processed went through the Privy Chamber, into the Presence Chamber, past the Great Chamber through a gallery and into the chapel."[43] The sacred space was itself treated as both transformable and adaptable for different kinds of sacred and secular uses, a performance space in its own right.[44] Westfall observes that "at family occasions such as christenings and weddings, the entire property could be theatre space, as ceremonial processions progressed throughout the space from chapel, to antechamber, to great hall, to bedchamber, and outdoors for hunting and dancing."[45] The expenses paid for adapting chapels for christenings or weddings further attest to the blending of sacred and secular political ritual and a theatricality that was true of household revelry generally—that is, its "blur[ring] the distinction between communal and personal space, public and private experiences, liturgical and secular activities."[46] That lack of distinction was also true of space as portrayed in *Hamlet*, where most of the drama appears to be set in the similarly fluid environs of the royal household.

Interestingly, until fairly late in the early modern period, the chapel was given a prominent position in early noble and royal households. The physician Andrew Boorde (d. 1549) recommended, for instance, "that as many of the rooms that looked into the court as possible should have a view of the chapel."[47] The chapel was a "gathering and performing place" that was connected by entryways and passageways on all floors to halls and private rooms, enabling members of the household to move freely and easily between them.[48] Interior doors were a typical feature. At the Northumberland household at Wressle, Westfall observes, "a lobby and stair connecting the chapel . . . to the hall . . . [offer] a clear indication that movement between these two locations was frequent and necessary" in the earlier period.[49] The entrances into and out of Wressle's two-story chapel allowed personnel and household members ease of access to it during daily household activities. The chapel's centrality in the early Tudor household and its entertainments contrasts markedly with its later isolation from the manor's interior rooms, when the walling off of the household chapel from the domestic space was a significant, late development encouraged by much later Protestant reformers. Westfall notes, for example, that the seemingly anomalous lack of interior entrances to the chapel of Haddon House reflects alterations to the chapel completed prior to 1782 but certainly well after the sixteenth century.[50] That is, the architectural and conceptual distinction between sacred and secular was a post-Renaissance, late-Protestant development—yet another reason such distinctions quite evidently do not obtain in *Hamlet.*

Hamlet concludes with a final, violent spectacle in a public space that, like the players' play, does not speak for itself but requires an explanation of unseen motives and emotions. And so Hamlet requests that the classically minded Horatio revise a classical martial custom of dutiful self-sacrifice and instead redeem his wounded name and what he can of the "dismal sight" by "tell[ing his] story" (5.2.333, 338). That is, Hamlet asks for a Quintilian-inspired explanation of interior motive and affect—of his "motive and the cue for passion" (2.2.545). In keeping with his emphasis on "that within which passeth show" (1.2.85), Hamlet's demand for a fuller laying out of the truth recalls Old Hamlet's aggrieved appeal to his son. Death is not, then, final, since memory is not, and remembering itself becomes a concern more profound than Laertes's horror at the breach of convention achieved by the "maimèd rites" that had been enjoined for Polonius's and Ophelia's burials, or Claudius's dismissive disregard for anything but the most pragmatic, temporal, and worldly matters: "So much for him. / Now for ourself" (1.2.25–26). Horatio's account will keep the past from being subsumed into the mere historical or political show that Fortinbras's promise of a heraldic soldier's funeral for Hamlet portends.

As many have found, the abbreviation of the rites of burial used for Old Hamlet, Polonius, and Ophelia, which proved so emotionally unsatisfying for the survivors, recalls the changes to the old religion's burial rituals advocated by Luther.[51] Luther's promotion of extramural burial—that is, the burying of bodies outside the churchyard in order to rationalize and disenchant the treatment of death and the dead—reflected a desire to have the living behave in accord with the belief that the dead had already entered a better age or *saeculum*. However, in practice, as in the play, such reformist ideals had little persuasive appeal to many or even most believers. The representation of the shattered emotional impact of abandoned burial rites is but one instance of what David Loewenstein and Michael Witmore have characterized as Shakespeare's entry into the "fault-lines of sectarian debates" and his incorporation of "diverse religious traditions" into his plays.[52] Shakespeare's response—voiced when Horatio, having alluded to the classical Roman ritual, also sounds a call for "flights of angels" that appear to be part of his interpretation of the final "dismal" "sight" (5.2.356)—appears to challenge the imposition of a rationalized boundary between the practical and the emotional, the dead and the living. The theatrical stage is defined, like the medieval and Renaissance household, as advancing a hermeneutical method that exceeds the literalism and modernism that Claudius's narrowly defined secularism and empty prayers embraced, one that invites a rereading that makes the past—and the mystery of death—if not a concern "forever and ever," then at least a lingering presence in a continuous present age.

Notes

The chapter epigraphs and all quotes from *Hamlet* in this chapter are from William Shakespeare, *Hamlet*, ed. Ann Thompson and Neil Taylor, The Arden Shakespeare, 3rd ser. (London: Arden Shakespeare, 2006).

1. The 1623 Folio edition's reference to the children's troupes as the cause of the players' travels differs in the three texts of *Hamlet*; it is reductively attributed to a fad for the "humours of children" in the first published quarto edition (Q1, 1603) and veiled in the second published quarto version (Q2, 1605), where the explanation is simply the "late innovation." See Thompson's and Taylor's comments on 2.2.295 and appendix 1 in *Hamlet*. Though the exchange is typically regarded as containing merely "topical" or theatrical trivia, I argue in this essay that an engagement with the children's tradition is far more organically integrated into the play. For an argument that disputes the particular strands of theater history long thought to be contained in the allusions, see Roslyn Lander Knutson, *Playing Companies and Commerce in Shakespeare's Time* (Cambridge: Cambridge University Press, 2001).

2. Stephen Greenblatt, *The Swerve: How the World Became Modern* (New York: Norton, 2011), 10.

3. Kathy Eden, *The Renaissance Rediscovery of Intimacy* (Chicago: University of Chicago Press, 2012), 122.

4. Kristen Poole, *Supernatural Environments in Shakespeare's England: Spaces of Demonism, Divinity, and Drama* (Cambridge: Cambridge University Press, 2011), 16.

5. Poole, *Supernatural Environments*, 4, 8.

6. For alternative interpretations of these tensions, see Stephen Greenblatt, *Hamlet in Purgatory* (2001; repr., Princeton, N.J.: Princeton University Press, 2013); Roland Mushat Frye, *The Renaissance Hamlet: Issues and Responses in 1600* (Princeton, N.J.: Princeton University Press, 1984). For an emphasis on secularization, see Richard Southern, *The Staging of Plays before Shakespeare* (London: Faber and Faber, 1973), 20; Hardin Craig, *English Religious Drama of the Middle Ages* (Oxford: Clarendon Press, 1955); O. B. Hardison Jr., *Christian Rite and Christian Drama in the Middle Ages: Essays in the Origin and Early History of Modern Drama* (Baltimore: Johns Hopkins University Press, 1965), 16, 19. Hardison cites E. K. Chambers, *The Mediaeval Stage*, 2 vols. (Oxford: Clarendon Press, 1903), 2:18.

7. See Christopher Marlow, *Performing Masculinity in English University Drama, 1598–1636* (Farnham, Surrey: Ashgate Publishing, 2013), 40–44.

8. Marlow, *Performing Masculinity*, 139.

9. Harold F. Harding, *Quintilian's Witnesses*, reprint from speech monographs, v. 1, no. 1, September, 1934. For an alternative reading of the school's influence upon Shakespeare, see Lynn Enterline, *Shakespeare's Schoolroom: Rhetoric, Discipline, Emotion* (Philadelphia: University of Pennsylvania Press, 2011).

10. See T. W. Baldwin, *William Shakspere's Small Latine & Lesse Greeke*, 2 vols. (Urbana: University of Illinois Press, 1944), 2:197, 205; emphasis in original. An online version is available at http://franklin.press.uillinois.edu/baldwin/, accessed 15 Jan. 2019.

11. Cited in R. Mulcaster, *The Educational Writings of Richard Mulcaster (1532–1611)*, ed. James Oliphant (Glasgow: James Maclehose, 1903; digitized, University of Michigan, 2006), 112.

12. Cited in Peter Medine, ed., *Art of Rhetoric* (University Park: Pennsylvania State University Press, 1994), n.p.

13. G. H. Mair, ed., *Arte of Rhetorique*, by Thomas Wilson (Oxford: At the Clarendon Press, 1909).

14. George Puttenham, *The Art of English Poesy: A Critical Edition*, ed. Frank Whigham and Wayne A. Rebhorn (Ithaca, N.Y.: Cornell University Press, 2007), 55. First published in 1589.

15. S. L. Lee, "Bacon, Sir Nicholas (1509–1579)," in *Dictionary of National Biography*, 1st ed., 63 vols. (London: Smith Elder, and Co., 1885), 2:370.

16. Cited in James Jerome Murphy, ed., *Quintilian on the Teaching of Speaking and Writing: Translations from Books One, Two, and Ten of the "Institutio Oratoria"* (Carbondale: Southern Illinois University Press, 1987), xii.

17. Ben Jonson, *Conversations of Ben Jonson with William Drummond of Hawthornden*, ed. Philip Sidney (London: Gay and Bird, 1900), 20; Drummond's manuscript record of the conversations is dated January 1619; cited in Sean McEvoy, *Ben Jonson, Renaissance Dramatist* (Edinburgh: Edinburgh University Press, 2008), 9.

18. Erasmus, *De Escribendis Epistolis*, *Works*, 1.386, cited in Baldwin, *Small Latine and Lesse Greeke*, 2:206.

19. See Quintilian, *The Institutio Oratoria* (1538), p. 88r, as translated in Baldwin, *Small Latine & Lesse Greek*, 2:204n29. See also Baldwin's discussion of the relevance of a larger portion of this passage to *Hamlet* in *Small Latine & Lesse Greeke*, 2:204.

20. His influence in the English curriculum had nonetheless survived through the medieval period as evidenced by such medieval fragments as the fourteenth-century *Interludium de Clerico et Puella* (*The Interlude of the Student and the Girl*). As James Jerome Murphy notes, prior to 1416, "copies of . . . *Institutio oratoria* were extremely rare . . . the only version known at all to medieval writers was the so-called *textus mutilatus*, which had huge gaps and could not easily be understood as a coherent whole"; see his *Latin Rhetoric and Education in the Middle Ages and Renaissance, Volume 1* (Aldershot: Ashgate Publishing, 2005), 176.

21. Steven Mentz, "'A Note Beyond Your Reach': Prose Romance's Rivalry with Elizabethan Drama," in *Staging Early Modern Romance: Prose Fiction,*

Dramatic Romance, and Shakespeare, ed. Mary Ellen Lamb and Valerie Wayne (New York: Routledge, 2009), 79.

22. John Morgan, *Godly Learning: Puritan Attitudes towards Reason, Learning and Education, 1560–1640* (Cambridge: Cambridge University Press, 1986), 62; see also Robert Hornback, *The English Clown Tradition from the Middle Ages to Shakespeare* (Cambridge: D.S. Brewer, 2009), 115–17.

23. Quoted in Hornback, *English Clown Tradition*, 117.

24. John H. Astington, *Actors and Acting in Shakespeare's Time: The Art of Stage Playing* (Cambridge: Cambridge University Press, 2010), 39; Andrew Pettegree, *The Book in the Renaissance* (New Haven: Yale University Press, 2010), 199.

25. Charlotte Scott, *Shakespeare and the Idea of the Book* (Oxford: Oxford University Press, 2007), 138.

26. Scott, *Shakespeare*, 138.

27. Scott, *Shakespeare*, 139.

28. Scott, *Shakespeare*, 138.

29. Eamon Duffy, *The Stripping of the Altars: Traditional Religion in England, c. 1400–c. 1580* (New Haven: Yale University Press, 1992), 39. See also Jeanine Curvers, "Burial Rituals and the Reformations in Early Modern England: A Comparative Study," Master's Thesis, Utrecht University, 2010, pp. 3–4, https://dspace.library.uu.nl/handle/1874/198630. See also Craig M. Koslofsky, *The Reformation of the Dead: Death and Ritual in Early Modern Germany, 1450–1700* (London: Macmillan, 2000), 5–10; Margo Todd, "England after 1558," in *The Reformation World*, ed. Andrew W. Pettegree (London: Routledge, 2000), 365; Christopher Haigh, *English Reformations: Religion, Politics, and Society under the Tudors* (New York: Oxford University Press, 1993), 15–21; and Clare Gittings, *Death, Burial and the Individual in Early Modern England* (London: Croom Helm, 1984), 53–55.

30. See the summary of critical arguments in Katherine Eisaman Maus, *Inwardness and Theater in the English Renaissance* (Chicago: University of Chicago Press, 1995), 1–34; for influential entries into the debate, see Margreta de Grazia, "Teleology, Delay, and the 'Old Mole,' " *Shakespeare Quarterly* 50, no. 3 (Autumn 1999): 251–67, and Margreta de Grazia, "The Motive for Interiority: Shakespeare's *Sonnets* and *Hamlet*," *Style* 23, no. 3 (Fall 1989): 430–44. See also the collection of essays in *Selfhood on the Early Modern English Stage*, ed. Pauline Blanc (Newcastle: Cambridge Scholars Publishing, 2008). For a reassessment of the debate surrounding interiority and Maus's argument, see David Schalkwyk, *Speech and Performance in Shakespeare's Sonnets and Plays* (Cambridge: Cambridge University Press, 2002), 102–49. For an application to the Strange's Men's repertory, see Lawrence Manley and Sally-Beth MacLean, *Lord Strange's Men and Their Plays* (New Haven: Yale University Press, 2014).

31. Paul Whitfield White, *Theatre and Reformation: Protestantism, Patronage and Playing in Tudor England* (Cambridge: Cambridge University Press, 1993), 138. See also Michael Shapiro, "Patronage and the Companies of Boy Actors," in *Shakespeare and Theatrical Patronage in Early Modern England*, ed. Paul Whitfield White and Suzanne R. Westfall (Cambridge: Cambridge University Press, 2002), 281, and M. C. Bradbrook, *The Rise of the Common Player: A Study of Actor and Society in Shakespeare's England* (London: Chatto and Windus, 1962), 217, 227.

32. *The Children of the Chapel Stript and Whipt* (1569). All that remains of the pamphlet is the following passage: "Plaies will never be supprest, while her maiesties unfledged minions flaunt it in silkes and sattens. They had as well be at their Popish service, in the deuil's garments . . . Even in her maiesties chappel do these pretty vpstart youthes profane the Lordes day by the lascivious writhing of their tender limbs, and gorgeous decking of their apparell, in feigning bawdie fables gathered from the idolatrous heathen poets"; this version is excerpted in E. K. Chambers, *The Elizabethan Stage*, 4 vols. (Oxford: Clarendon Press, 1923), 2:34.

33. John M. Wasson, "The English Church as Theatrical Space," in *A New History of Early English Drama*, ed. John D. Cox and David Scott Kastan (New York: Columbia University Press, 1997), 25.

34. Wasson, "The English Church," 35.

35. White, *Theatre and Reformation*, 134; see also Peter H. Greenfield, "Drama outside London after 1540," in *The Cambridge History of British Theatre: Volume 1, Origins to 1600*, ed. Jane Milling and Peter Thomson (Cambridge: Cambridge University Press, 2004), 178–99. Greenfield cites Rosalind Conklin Hays's discovery that both church houses and churches themselves were used as playing spaces at "Sherborne, Dorset, and . . . in Doncaster" (194); see Rosalind Conklin Hays, "Dorset Church Houses in the Drama," *Research Opportunities in Renaissance Drama* 31 (1992): 13–23.

36. White, *Theatre and Reformation*, 131; as evidence of the extent of such a movement, White cites John Bale's scriptural dramas, typically written for three to four players; a professional-troupe-performed *Mary Magdalene*; the learned school drama *Jacob and Esau*; and Nicholas Udall's university play based on a biblical episode popular with Protestant iconoclasts, *Ezechias*.

37. Paul Whitfield White, "The Bible as Play in Reformation England," in Milling and Thomson, *Cambridge History*, 88.

38. See the note to 3.1.43 in *Hamlet*, 282.

39. Suzanne R. Westfall, *Patrons and Performance: Early Tudor Household Revels* (Oxford: Clarendon Press, 1990), 22.

40. Fiona Kisby, "'When the King Goeth a Procession': Chapel Ceremonies and Services, the Ritual Year, and Religious Reforms at the Early Tudor Court, 1485–1547," *Journal of British Studies* 40, no. 1 (January 2001): 75.

41. Hilary Waymen, "Stained Glass in Henry VIII's Palaces," in *Henry VIII: A European Court in England*, ed. David Starkey (London: Collins and Brown, 1991), 28–31.

42. Kisby, "'When the King Goeth,'" 53, citing a letter sent to Charles V of Spain from his ambassador to the Henrician court, Eustace Chapuys, *Letters and Papers, Henry VIII*, no. 826, 315.

43. Kisby, "'When the King Goeth,'" 53.

44. Edwardian reforms suspended the opulent Royal Chapel's use as a site for political ceremony. In the Edwardian era, Cambridge and Oxford Universities were thus both encouraged to "follow Chapel Royal liturgical practice" in forbidding processions and ceremonial movements, the recitation of the rosary, and "the burning of candles in front of . . . the rood," which was "one of the few exceptions for devotional lights which Henry VIII had allowed"; see Diarmaid MacCulloch, *The Boy King: Edward VI and the Protestant Reformation* (Berkeley: University of California Press, 1999), 70–71, 81–82.

45. Suzanne R. Westfall, "'An Example of Courtesy and Liberality': Great Households and Performance," in Milling and Thomson, *Cambridge History*, 206.

46. Westfall, "'An Example,'" 206.

47. Maurice Howard, *The Early Tudor Country House: Architecture and Politics, 1490–1550* (London: G. Philip, 1987), 114.

48. Westfall, *Patrons and Performance*, 222.

49. Westfall, *Patrons and Performance*, 24.

50. Westfall, *Patrons and Performance*, 23, 233.

51. Duane J. Corpis, "Mapping the Boundaries of Confession Space and Urban Religious Life in the Diocese of Augsburg, 1648–1750," in *Sacred Space in Early Modern Europe*, ed. Will Coster and Andrew Spicer (Cambridge: Cambridge University Press, 2005), 322. For an alternative reading of the play's ending, see David Scott Kastan, *A Will to Believe: Shakespeare and Religion* (Oxford: Oxford University Press, 2014), 142.

52. David Loewenstein and Michael Witmore, eds., *Shakespeare and Early Modern Religion* (Cambridge: Cambridge University Press, 2015), 10.

Leaving the Place of Conscience in *All Is True*

Rachael Deagman

The language of conscience saturates William Shakespeare and John Fletcher's *All Is True* (*Henry VIII*), where the word "conscience" itself appears twenty-four times—nearly twice as often as in any other Shakespeare play.[1] Frequently, we think of conscience as being an intellectual act that, aided by emotion and practical experience, helps us differentiate right from wrong. Yet in the famous divorce-trial scene at Blackfriars, Henry VIII invokes conscience to escape his marriage with Katherine of Aragon: "But conscience, conscience! / O, 'tis a tender place, and I must leave her" (2.2.142–43).[2] Henry refers to conscience not just as an act but also as a "place"—a place he wishes to leave, perhaps by privileging emotion over ethics in order to divorce his wife. Henry VIII's figuration of conscience as a place merits further reflection because the model he uses to describe conscience reimagines the intellectual act to be an interpretive space for ethical reflection. Moreover, Henry's model for thinking about conscience signals a changing penitential discourse in the wake of the English Reformation—a change that also necessitates our reappraisal of both ritual and space as they pertain to secularity. This essay pursues Henry's figuration of conscience as a place in order to show how the play uses spaces both sacred and secular as a hermeneutical paradigm through which to represent the changing nature of penitential discourse across the Reformation.

All Is True is not the first English play to employ spatial metaphors to describe penitential theologies. In order to shape such a reading of space, conscience, and secularization in Shakespeare and Fletcher's play, I begin with a late fifteenth-century morality play, *The Castle of Perseverance*. The *Castle* was likely written in the Lincoln area of northern England around 1425.[3] It is one of several morality plays that blend elements of professional secular drama with both liturgical tropes and theological tenets.

Such plays were performed by traveling troupes of actors who relied on public support for their sustenance. *The Castle of Perseverance* sets aside traditional images of conscience (figured conventionally as gnawing, pricking, or as a worm that never dies) and synderesis (figured as a murmur back against sin) and authors a new iconography of conscience by way of architectural space. When Henry VIII refers to conscience as a "tender place," I argue, he recalls this earlier dramatic usage. Thus Shakespeare and Fletcher's *All Is True*—a presumably secular drama written for a secular commercial playhouse—explores the matter of conscience precisely by looking back to its representation in both medieval theology and drama.

The "interpretative density" that emerges when Shakespeare and Fletcher intertwine the secular and sacred in *All Is True* is not unique to their work. As Katherine Steele Brokaw and Jay Zysk remind us in the introduction to this volume, Shakespeare sits in a long tradition of theater in which the sacred and secular intersect, whether in a city street, on a pageant wagon, in a churchyard, or in the public theater. Moreover, Helga Duncan's essay in this volume shows us that a sizable body of post-Reformation writing stressed recuperation rather than the destruction of places where the holy might be encountered: "The writers of these tracts thus addressed not only the crossing of boundaries marked by traditional sacred architecture but also the need for spiritual dwelling, the making of a home in a secular world of profound religious and political upheaval." In both cases, whether we're looking back from Shakespeare's perspective to a medieval past or forward to post-Reformation writers, we see a constantly transforming model of the medieval that eventually seeks a new vocabulary for the relationship between Church and world. My essay focuses on Shakespeare and Fletcher's representation of that critical moment—Henry VIII's break from the medieval Church—upon which many of the pages in this volume hinge. I argue that Henry's departure from the Catholic Church, and indeed from the notion of conscience as a place, leaves the play lingering between two vocabularies of penance, because Henry attempts to create, though he does not ultimately achieve, a secular vocabulary for thinking about conscience.[4]

Figurations of Conscience on the Post-Reformation Stage

Shakespeare and Fletcher use the word "conscience" in several ways: to talk about the King's struggles with marrying his brother's wife, to describe Henry's attraction to Anne Boleyn, and to explain Wolsey's role as confessor. For example, the Lord Chamberlain announces that he has left the King full of sad thoughts and troubles: "It seems the marriage with his brother's wife / Has crept too near his conscience"; in a witty reply, the Duke of Suffolk suggests that the King's conscience "has crept too near another lady" (2.2.16–18). The Lord Chamberlain refers here to the historical arrangement made by Henry VII in 1509 to strengthen England's allegiance to Spain by marrying his son Henry VIII to Katherine of Aragon. We know that the historical Henry VIII substantiates his marriage to his deceased brother's widow by resorting to scriptural authority; namely, Deuteronomy 25: "When brethren dwell together and one of them dye and haue no childe, the wyfe of the [dead] shall not be geuen out vnto a straunger: but hir brotherlawe shall goo in vnto her and take her to wife and marie her."[5] The same King later turns to a different scriptural text—the Old Testament book of Leviticus—to justify the divorce of that same union: "Yf a man take his brothers wife, it is an vnclene thinge, he hath vncouered his brothers secrettes, they shalbe childlesse therfore."[6] Henry petitions Rome for a divorce on the grounds that Katherine will be unable to produce a male heir because she has married her deceased husband's brother. Shakespeare and Fletcher's version, of course, moves beyond the Deuteronomy reference to suggest Anne Boleyn as another possible destination for the King's creeping conscience.

While the concept of "conscience" plays a significant role in detailing Henry VIII's troubles with marriage and divorce, its primary signification throughout *All Is True* is penitential. During the consistory scene in 2.4, Henry offers a quasi confession—not a sacramental confession to a priest but a public declaration of his errors. In particular, he thinks of divorcing Katherine during the negotiation of his daughter's dowry because of questions about her legitimacy. "This respite," he says, "shook the bosom of [his] conscience" (2.4.170–83). By beginning with an account of his daughter's marriage, Henry removes the language of conscience from his own life and links it instead to the well-being of his daughter and, because she is his only child, to the prosperity of the realm. He goes on to interpret the deaths of his male children mothered by Katherine as a sign of judgment on him and his domain, a judgment that leads to his severely troubled conscience. "Thus hulling in / the wild sea of my conscience," Henry says, "I did steer / Toward this remedy, whereupon we are / now present here together: that's to say, / I meant to rectify my conscience—which / I then did feel full sick, and yet not well" (2.4.200–205). Henry figures his conscience as a wild sea—a vast, natural, and potentially dangerous place that might leave him adrift. The seasick feeling prompts Henry to "rectify" his conscience; this word combines the nautical language of adjusting a compass to navigate one's way with the penitential language of amendment. Yet this rumination on conscience is not a sacramental confession. Rather than follow the rubric of a *forma confitendi*, Henry rejects a confessor altogether and seeks to rectify *himself*. He examines his own conscience (albeit selectively, glossing over his lust for another woman) and confesses the sins caused by marrying Katherine and possibly fornicating with his brother's wife.

Henry's desire to rectify himself becomes quite striking if we consider how his dominantly secular mode of confession nonetheless partakes of certain aspects of a late medieval penitential model. As many of the essays in this volume suggest, while the early modern stage transformed certain aspects of sacred ceremony, doctrine, and discourse within the secular space of the commercial playhouse, playwrights did not reject the sacred wholesale. *All Is True* illustrates how medieval penitential theology—as shaped in both literary and religious contexts—continues to inform Henry VIII's struggles with conscience on the post-Reformation stage. Shakespeare and Fletcher's Reformation play thus mobilizes, without having to reconcile, sacred and secular vocabularies for thinking about conscience as both a penitential concept and a dramatic device.

According to Catholic penitential theology, the penitent was required to engage in a tripartite process: contrition of heart, confession of mouth, and satisfaction of deed. The audience might expect the wringing of Henry's conscience to involve this ritual, especially after watching him get "a little heated"—an emotional state associated with the deadly sin of lechery—while dancing in the same room as Anne Boleyn (1.4.100). A late medieval penitential manual like *Jacob's Well*, for example, would teach Henry the four degrees of lechery: thought, delight, consent of will, and a burning desire to do lecherous deeds.[7] A Catholic confessor working from the manual might examine Henry's conscience and in hopes of amending his sin encourage him to confess his burning desire for Anne. But conscience works in a very different way in *All Is True*. Not only does Henry attempt to rectify his own conscience but also the Duke of Norfolk raises doubts about Henry's ordained confessor, Cardinal Wolsey. (We should remember that in the world of the play, as in the court of Henry VIII, the King was doctrinally conservative and, in his Six Articles of 1539, defended auricular confession as "expedient and necessary to be retained and continued, used and frequented in the Church of God.")[8] Norfolk claims that Wolsey "dives into the King's soul, and there scatters / dangers, doubts, wringing of the conscience, / Fears, and despairs, and all these for his marriage. / And out of all these to restore the King, / He counsels a divorce, . . ." (2.2.26–30). Instead of providing sacramental absolution or spiritual counsel, Norfolk suggests, Wolsey dispenses bad advice. Unlike a conventional medieval confessor, Cardinal Wolsey does not extract sin from the King's mind by wringing Henry's conscience but instead "scatters" the remorseful conscience (along with danger, doubts, fears, and despair) in the space of Henry's soul. What is more, the Duke's use of the nominal "wringing," as opposed to the verb "wring," to describe the effect of Wolsey's actions on Henry's conscience suggests that the cardinal does not press the moisture from Henry's conscience, leaving the King's "wild sea" (2.4.201) to overtake him as a result.

Henry VIII himself adopts a conventionally medieval image of conscience when he tells Wolsey, "O my Wolsey, / The quiet of my wounded conscience, / Thou art a cure fit for a king" (2.2.73–75). The wound caused by sin, a trope in medieval literature, relies on sacramental gifts as salve.[9] Describing conscience as being wounded by sin and the sacrament of penance as salve draws attention to the medicinal quality of the sacrament but does not go so far as to suggest that confession might be a permanent cure for the injured sinner. Indeed, penance does not provide the salve for Henry's wounded conscience. The King does not clarify whether the quieted conscience or Wolsey himself would be an apt cure. The scene ends as Henry directs Wolsey to deliver the news of the impending divorce to the Queen:

> The most convenient place that I can think of
> For such receipt of learning is Black-Friars;
> There ye shall meet about this weighty business.
> My Wolsey, see it furnish'd. O my lord,
> Would it not grieve an able man to leave
> So sweet a bedfellow? But conscience, conscience!
> O, 'tis a tender place, and I must leave her (2.2.137–43).

The repetition of "place" in this speech yokes the physical place of Blackfriars to the spiritual place of the "tender conscience." The last four lines in Henry's speech in 2.2 remain captivatingly ambiguous. Does Henry associate the "tender place" with his conscience? When he says he must leave her, does he speak of Katherine, his tender bedfellow, or of his (feminine) conscience? Or must he abandon the "tender place" of conscience to quit his wife?

In order to pursue the implications of Henry's attempt to abandon this spatial metaphor, I turn first to an earlier dramatic model of conscience as place in *The Castle of Perseverance*, a morality play that situates Mankind's troubled conscience in relation to architectural space.

Spatializing Conscience in *The Castle of Perseverance*

The Castle of Perseverance, like most morality plays, functions as a memento mori insofar as the play provides the audience with ethical instruction intended to encourage sacramental practice, particularly confession, for the salvation of souls. The plot centers on Humanum Genus (Mankind), who faces temptation by the Seven Deadly Sins before he encounters the sacramental resources of the Church as a gift with which to amend his life. Humanum Genus must choose whether to confess and abide in virtue or to sideline the sacraments and continue to sin. Yet unlike *Wisdom* (another fifteenth-century morality play bound with both *Castle* and *Mankind* in the unique Macro Manuscript [Folger V.a.354]), in which the confession scene takes place offstage, *Castle* puts acts of confession center stage. This is in part, as Sarah Beckwith claims, to introduce the audience to the sacramental rite of penance.[10] Though dramatic representations of confessional acts do not themselves constitute a sacrament, Beckwith notes that actors may be dressed in the costumes of clerics to emphasize the efficacy of penitential ritual. Conversely, the figure of Confession could also be clothed as a layperson, thereby anticipating later reforms to the sacrament, such as Henry VIII's efforts to rectify himself in Shakespeare and Fletcher's play.

The confession scene in *Castle* occurs when Confessio appears at the behest of the Good Angel, who sighs and sobs for the sinful Humanum Genus. Unlike Cardinal Wolsey in *All Is True*, Confessio is represented as an efficacious confessor. Humanum Genus follows a proper confessional formula, known as a *forma confitendi*, which provided both priest and penitent with the script by which to achieve a proper confession and administer an efficacious absolution.[11] In staging the sacrament of penance according to the scripted formula derived from Catholic penitential theology, *Castle* draws from religious works written in response to the fourth Lateran Council's decree issued in 1215 that newly obliged parishioners to make annual confession prior to receiving the Eucharist at Mass.[12] As the demand for pastoral education grew, a corpus of literature was produced to edify the Church. Catechetical manuals circulated to teach the laity the basics of belief and practice and to instruct the clergy to competently attend to the needs of their parishioners. The texts provide the *forma confitendi* that Humanum Genus follows in the *Castle*. For example, he admits committing each of the seven deadly sins (1475), breaking the Ten Commandments (1481), misusing his five wits (1482), and failing to give alms to the poor (1485–86). Finally, and perhaps most importantly, Humanum Genus confesses his inability to use speech properly, suggesting a linguistic lack: "I can nat alle say," he admits, before kneeling to pray for absolution (1489–94). Upon hearing Humanum Genus's confession according to this proper formula, Confession recites the words of absolution, "I þee asoyle" and restores Humanum Genus to harmony with the Church (1523).

While *The Castle of Perseverance* draws from the *forma confitendi* as set out in medieval confessional manuals, the play also introduces an unconventional model of penance by resorting to spatial metaphors that emerge from theological discourses of conscience in the late Middle Ages. In the thirteenth century, for example, conscience consists of two related but distinct processes: *synderesis* and *conscientia*. For Thomas Aquinas, synderesis is a natural habit that serves as the ontological foundation of man's moral life. This natural habit of the intellect is inextinguishable and incapable of error. In this model, human beings hold a common understanding of the good and are capable of following a rightly ordered conscience; they are also capable of sinning, or acting against conscience. *Conscientia* is less a habit than an act, understood as the application of knowledge to an individual case. Aquinas states that this application occurs in three possible ways. In the first, we recognize that we have done or not done something (and so conscience is a witness); in the second, we decide whether or not to do something through conscience (and so conscience either incites or binds action); in the third, conscience decides whether or not something is done well (and so conscience excuses, accuses, or torments) (*ST*.I-I.79.12–13).[13]

Aquinas further develops the question of whether an erring conscience binds and whether or not an erring conscience can excuse.[14] In particular, he wonders if a person is bound to do the wrong thing if he has an erring conscience. Aquinas contends that if a man's erring reason or conscience leads him to lust after another man's wife, the will that abides by that act is evil since this error arises from ignorance of the Divine Law, which every human being is bound to know. But if a man's reason or conscience errs in *mistaking* another wife for his, and if he wishes to consent to her right when she asks for it, his will is excused from being evil; this error arises from ignorance of a circumstance and causes the act to be involuntary (*ST*.I-I.19.6, resp.). The fundamental point for Aquinas is that a person can make a poor judgment or commit a wrong act if he follows an erring conscience. The goal in this case presumably would be to help him to recognize the gap between the "spark of synderesis"—that flashpoint of human contact with the divine—and his own erring *conscientia*.[15]

The Castle of Perseverance dramatizes this very struggle in the character of Humanum Genus, who must recognize and correct an erring conscience. The elaborate allegorical pageant of the conventional deadly sins heightens this struggle (830–1240), after which he assents to sin despite the appeal of the Good Angel's call for mercy and amendment. Even with the dominance of penitential content in the play, the *Castle* writer curiously does not include a character called Conscience. Instead, the matter of conscience is taken up in the play's Banns, or prologue, where the second flag bearer says,

> whanne mans sowle is soylyd with
> synne & with sore,
> þanne þe goode aungyl makyth mykyl mornynge
> þat þe lofly lyknesse of God schulde be lore
> þorwe þe bade aungellis fals entysynge.
> He sendyth to hym concyens, pricked Ful pore
> & clere confescyon, with penauns doynge (40–46).

Such an announcement leads us to anticipate that "He" (likely understood as "God") sends a "pricked Conscience" to Humanum Genus. (Shakespeare and Fletcher's Henry also experiences the prick of conscience, though his version departs from the medieval model). The phrase "prick of conscience" likely refers to the *Pricke of Conscience*, a popular, widely circulated Middle English poem dating to the first half of the fourteenth century that encourages penitential reflection. While the character of Conscience does not actually appear in *Castle*, I contend that the play characterizes Conscience not as a speaking character but as the iconographic space of the castle—a space displayed prominently in the drawing of *Castle*'s stage design contained in the Macro Manuscript, which is still regarded as the oldest surviving illustration of early theatrical staging in England. In turn, Humanum Genus's entry into the architectural space of the castle signals his affirmation to a rightly ordered synderesis.

The drawing in the Macro Manuscript shows a circle surrounded by water with a castle that stands "at the middle of the place," or in the center of the playing space. There are several scaffolds at each of the cardinal points on the compass for the World, the Flesh, the Devil, and God, and one additional scaffold to the northeast for Covetousness. Through this set design, which Catherine Belsey terms the play's emblematic geography, spectators are offered an image of their own human condition, to regard themselves as mirror images of Humanum Genus.[16] Belsey places the castle's iconography (and the play in general) within the very secularization narrative that this volume seeks to challenge. She sees *Castle of Perseverance* as a definitive example of "emblematic theater," which she associates with the morality play genre that is dismantled by the time Shakespeare writes for the commercial stage. This shift away from emblematic, medieval theater is, for Belsey, part of the birth of liberal humanism. The advent of Shakespearean drama necessitates the eradication of earlier dramatic forms.

Both positions, as this volume argues, require rethinking. In contrast to Belsey's secularization narrative, I suggest that the famous drawing in *Castle of Perseverance* is far more than a trite example of emblematic (and implicitly premodern) theater; instead, the diagram constitutes a visual iconography by which to map the play's moral economy, an economy in which conscience, and especially synderesis, is located at the center. Understanding the complexity of the drawing allows us to see how space acts hermeneutically to combine sacred and secular as a way of working through the sacrament of penance. What is more, the spatial economy of conscience and synderesis that emerges in the context of a fifteenth-century morality play provides us with a way to reconsider the operations of conscience in the context of Shakespeare and Fletcher's *All Is True*, which is staged after the reformation of sacramental confession in sixteenth-century England.

Having succumbed to the influence of sin, Humanum Genus learns that Christ will bring him to the "bower of bliss" so long as contrition, or sorrow of heart, strikes him with a lance (1421–22). The lance of contrition, much like a prick of conscience, takes Humanum Genus holy to Penance (1426), at which point Confessio hears Mankind's confession and offers absolution (1470–96, 1510–22). In particular, Confessio forgives Mankind for following an erring conscience: "I þee a-soyle, wyth mylde mod / of al þat þou hast ben ful madde, / In forsakynge of þyn aungyl good, / & þi fowle flesche þat þou hast fade, þe werld, þe deuyl þat is so woode, / & folwyd þyne aungyl þat is so badde" (1523–28). Humanum Genus responds by asking Confessio to "putte [him] / In-to sum place of surete," a place defined by both certitude and safety, in order to avoid being harmed by sin (1545–46). Confessio has just the place in mind: "To swyche a place I schal þee kenne, / þer þou mayst dwelle with-outyn dystaunsce; / & al-wey kepe þee fro synne, / In-to þe Castel of Perseueraunce" (1549–52). For Confessio, the Castle of Perseverance is a place in which Mankind shall avoid sin by leading a rightly ordered life oriented toward the good. Lest we miss that Mankind can dwell in the castle "with-outyn dystaunsce," Confession repeats the phrase just four lines later (1554). The line appears to refer to linear space, suggesting that the castle will keep Humanum Genus quite literally out of sin's reach. But the Middle English word "dystaunsce" also refers to the ability to distinguish between good and evil; in this sense, the castle removes Mankind from the discord and strife he experiences living in a world of sinful conflict. Whereas we might expect the sanctuary from sin to be a church in a medieval morality play, in this case it is a castle, an entirely secular space that takes on religious connotations. In particular, the castle actually marries the secular to the sacred: "For [it] is strenger þanne any in Fraunce" and is a precious place "fful of vertu & of grace" (1556, 1559). Humanum Genus assents to the will of the Good Angel, or follows his conscience up to the castle (1601–4).

While we do not hear Humanum Genus describe the interior of the Castle of Perseverance (for the manuscript has a missing leaf), the play suggests nonetheless that to see the stage diagram only emblematically is to flatten out the interiority, or the internal space, of conscience as it was described theologically in late medieval Europe. Seeing the castle only from the outside, moreover, mitigates the hermeneutic work the space performs by joining a secular architecture to a religious understanding of ethics.

Returning now to *Henry VIII*, I want to investigate how Shakespeare and Fletcher adapt *Castle*'s model of using secular space to represent religious concepts, particularly as the archetype relates to the historical space of the Blackfriars priory, which, following the dissolution of the monasteries, was converted into an indoor theater (and one used by Shakespeare's company, at that). The changing space of Blackfriars marks a significant shift from the medieval morality play to early modern drama—a shift from drama performed in a temporary space in the streets of a city or at a theater-in-the-round to a permanent structure within city walls. The priory-turned-theater becomes a place that blends the sacred and the secular—or, put another way, becomes a "convenient place" (2.2.137) through which to consider the troubled conscience of Henry VIII on the post-Reformation stage.

"The Most Convenient Place": The Convergence of Sacred and Secular in Blackfriars

While the idea of conscience-as-space continues to inform Shakespeare and Fletcher's post-Reformation play, *All Is True* at once preserves and abandons the medieval model set forth in *Castle of Perseverance*. Paul Strohm writes that the historical Henry was "caught between older and emergent conceptions" of conscience, though Strohm concludes that Henry embodies the "full development" of a "Reformation conscience."[17]

While Strohm admits that claiming "a *wholly* new view of conscience emerged in the sixteenth century would undervalue the subtlety and diversity of more than a millennium of previous consideration," he nonetheless insists that conscience is regarded "less as a body of ecclesiastical precepts imported from the 'outside in' and more as a set of deeply lodged convictions speaking from the 'inside out.'"[18] Rather than thinking of Henry VIII as speaking his convictions from the "inside out," I suggest that we consider instead how *All Is True* dislodges conscience from the allegorical space of the castle to the historical place of the Blackfriars priory—a place that functions as a shifting signifier at the same time that it indexes the oscillation in ways of thinking about the relation between conscience and secular space more broadly in the sixteenth and seventeenth centuries.

Shakespeare and Fletcher refer to Blackfriars directly when Henry VIII declares to Wolsey the site of the divorce trials for Katharine of Aragon: "The most convenient place that I can think of / For such receipt of learning is Black-Friars; / There ye shall meet about this weighty business" (2.2.137–39). Why might Shakespeare and Fletcher describe Blackfriars as "the most convenient place"? Certainly the splendor of Blackfriars would make it a comfortable place to convene, not to mention that the priory was indeed conveniently located in the heart of London.[19] Moreover, the space proves convenient for the present analysis of how the sacred and secular converge in the play's representation of conscience. Blackfriars is, by the time *All Is True* was performed, an indoor playhouse and thus a secular space; at the same time, Blackfriars retains its former history as a monastic priory—the very priory where the historical divorce trial of Henry VIII and Catherine of Aragon occurred. The historical trial takes places in a chamber within the medieval Dominican priory that, after the Reformation, becomes a playhouse where the trial scene in Shakespeare's *All Is True* is performed.[20] Blackfriars is indeed "the most convenient place" to think through such complicated shifts of the English Reformation, particularly as they impacted the reuse of spaces like the monasteries.

The dual identity of Blackfriars (as ecclesiastical and secular, priory and playing space) is not an invention of the English Reformation, however. Even when the building functioned solely as an ecclesiastical space, Blackfriars was linked to the crown and to Parliament from its early origins, and such a connection persists well into Henry VIII's reign. The Dominicans, also known as Friars Preachers or Blackfriars because of their black garb, served as confessors to the crown for 144 years, until the reign of Richard II.[21] In 1311 the Parliament of the realm held meetings in the priory, and as early as 1322 state records were deposited in the friary.[22] In addition to providing space for courts and the convening of Parliament, the medieval priory also hosted an important ecclesiastical trial, known as the Blackfriars Council or the Earthquake Council, in 1382. The council gathered in 1382 to condemn twenty-four articles set forth by a group of Oxford theologians, drawing from the works of John Wycliffe, as heretical.[23] Moreover, when Charles V of Spain (the nephew of Catherine of Aragon and the head of the Holy Roman Empire) visited London in 1522, Henry VIII chose Blackfriars to house his guest. As Irwin Smith argues, Henry's choice to house Charles V in Blackfriars suggests that the guest accommodations at the priory were likely more magnificent than any palace would have been.[24] Henry VIII possessed space in the priory that existed separately from the church and from the areas used by friars.[25]

We should appreciate, then, how Blackfriars crossed the categories of sacred and secular even when it was a monastic space; such categorical crossovers were equally at play after the dissolution of the monasteries. In other words, though Blackfriars became secularized, it retained its religious significations—significations evoked by Shakespeare and Fletcher in *All Is True*. We know that many open-air playhouses in early modern London were situated outside the official jurisdiction of the city, usually in the liberties located beyond the city walls. Blackfriars, however, was an exception. The building was an interior theater located *inside* the city walls precisely because of its former status as a Dominican priory.[26] What is more, Blackfriars was one of the last priories to be dissolved in London. Although the friars no longer occupied the space, the material fabric of the church remained intact until after the dissolution of the monasteries and the death of the King. When Henry VIII died in 1547, Sir Thomas Cowarden, the master of revels, inherited the space and used it to house theatrical props and costumes. Cowarden left the Parliament Chamber standing but divided the building into residential apartments; later these residences were converted into Blackfriars Theatre.[27] James Burbage first attempted to convert the monastery into a playhouse in 1596, but he encountered protests from neighbors fearing that it might lead to the gathering of vagrants and lewd people that would work mischief under the guise of attending a play. Burbage finally succeeded at reforming the space in 1608.[28] An audience watching *All Is True* performed in Blackfriars—as it was, especially after the Globe burned during a performance of the same play in 1613—would sit in a space that signifies both sacred and secular to watch a play that represents conscience as a shifting signifier that precipitates the changes to the performance space itself.

How, then, do Shakespeare and Fletcher present conscience in such a complicated way, and how do the term's sacred and secular meanings both appropriate and depart from what we see in *Castle of Perseverance*? For as many times as he repeats the word "conscience" in the play, not once does Henry use the term "synderesis." Like Wolsey, Henry VIII sidelines the notion of the shared good described by Thomas Aquinas and instead privileges his own desires. Moreover, Henry leaves the "tender place" of conscience and considers what alternative vocabulary might be available to him once he abandons this older hermeneutical model. He tries to leave the place of conscience, and his wife, in the divorce scene in the transitional place of the Dominican priory.

First and foremost, Shakespeare and Fletcher draw from the chronicle sources to describe Henry's scrupulous conscience. In Holinshed, Henry's knowledge of the possibility of Mary's illegitimacy stirs his conscience when the Bishop of Bayonne raises doubts: "Which words once conceiued within the secret bottome of my conscience, ingendered such a scrupulous doubt, that my conscience was incontinentlie accombred, vexed, and disquieted; whereby I thought my selfe to be greatlie in danger of Gods indignation."[29] By comparison, Cavendish emphasizes the role of the breast in Henry's speech: "These words were so conceived within my scrupulous conscience that it bred a doubtful prick within my breast, which doubt pricked, vexed, and troubled so my mind, and so disquieted me, that I was in great doubt of God's indignation."[30] In both versions, Henry puns on procreation. The bishop's words lead his mind to conceive doubt about Katherine's inability to produce a male heir, thus nodding to the medieval political theology of the King's two bodies. These words, moreover, introduce to the play a key medieval topos—the prick of conscience—that Henry will use to reimagine conscience once he abandons the notion of conscience as a place.

Shakespeare and Fletcher take up the medieval figuration of conscience as a "prick," and in doing so, they feminize and sexualize Henry's conscience. The King states, "My conscience first receiv'd a tenderness, / Scruple, and prick, on certain speeches utter'd / by the Bishop of Bayonne, then French embassador" (2.4.171–72). This prick to the King's conscience does not, however, serve as a nudge for Henry to confess. Rather, the bishop's prick leads to a brief linguistic deferral, a respite, until the King returns to his reflection: "This respite shook / The bosom of my conscience, enter'd me, / Yea, with a spitting power, and made to tremble / The region of my breast, which forc'd such way, / That many maz'd considerings did throng / and press'd in with this caution" (2.4.182–87). Shakespeare and Fletcher's version of Henry's scrupulous, pricked conscience draws from the medieval trope of the prick of conscience but at the same time sexualizes—and secularizes—the language, making the metaphors work to illuminate the specifics of Henry's situation. Henry's conscience receives a tenderness from the bishop's prick; that is, the King's conscience becomes delicate, easy to yield, and more likely to be divided. When the Bishop of Bayonne requires a delay in the divorce proceedings after pricking Henry's conscience, the respite enters the King's body with a sexualized spitting power, making the King's conscience shake and his breast throng. However, he also carefully negates the potential reference to pleasure by referring to force and pressure in violent terms and making himself into the feminized victim of penetration.

Once Henry abandons the notion that his conscience can be described as a place, he tries out various vocabularies, such as the medieval topos of the prick of conscience, but they all break down. But the process by which Henry experiments with these different discourses for conscience, as well as the process by which such terms fail him, is of interest to Shakespeare and Fletcher. For example, once Henry's reliance on the prick of conscience trope unravels, he moves on to another medieval topos: the shipwreck. This trope extends Henry's description of a trembling breast so that the conscience metaphor reaches from an inner, corporeal trembling to the outer world, to the waves of the wild sea: "Thus hulling in / The wild sea of my conscience, I did steer / Toward this remedy, whereupon we are / Now present here together" (2.4.200–203). Here Henry echoes Peter Lombard, the twelfth-century scholastic who describes penance as the "second plank after shipwreck" because "if anyone corrupts by sin the clothing of innocence which he first receives at baptism, he may repair it by the remedy of penance" (dist. XIV, ch. I).[31] For Lombard, only the sacramental resources of the Church—namely, baptism and penance—can remedy the shipwrecked conscience. Henry cleverly invokes the language of the wayfarer and the cleansing effects of the sea. However, his conscience never actually wrecks. As a result, unlike the figures of a dramatic or practical medieval confession of conscience, Henry does not think he needs the planks—the sacramental resources of the Church—to hull the wild sea. Henry steers himself, and his solitary steering, his own ability to rectify his conscience, has the power to draw the community together; the transformative, conscience-clearing power is thus monarchical and worldly rather than divine. The apt water metaphor at once signals the possibility for change and expansion and presents the notion of volatility, unreliability, and danger. Henry's singular conscience seems far removed from the safe space of synderesis, from a shared understanding of the communal good.

When the second trope of the shipwreck collapses, Henry grasps for an alternative vocabulary. As a result, he morphs the shipwreck metaphor into a wound. Not only does Henry's water imagery implode but also his speech ironically becomes muddied with a reference to the sacrament of marriage: "Thus hulling in / The wild sea of my conscience, I did steer / Toward this remedy, whereupon we are / Now present here together: that's to say, / I meant to rectify my conscience—which / I then did feel full sick, and yet not well— / By all the reverend fathers of the land / And doctors learn'd" (2.4.200–207). His drawing of them "present here together" creates an unclear referent as the "we" of the consistory audience blends with the "we" of the play's audience. At the same time, his words also disconcertingly echo the opening words of the matrimonial ceremony: "Dearly beloved friends, we are gathered together here in the sight of God, and in the face of his congregation, to join together this man and this woman in holy matrimony . . ."[32] Henry's confession scene reveals his divided conscience with respect to marriage, a double infidelity that anticipates his divorce from Katherine and his political and religious divorce from the Church.[33] Moreover, Henry's rambling speech shifts from the shipwrecked conscience to the language of the wounded conscience, as he feels his conscience to be "full sick, and yet not well." He means to rectify his conscience with the reverend fathers of the land, but just as his conscience never actually wrecks, he never actually seeks a salve for his ill conscience.

Unlike Humanum Genus, who acknowledges that his faulty language "can nat alle say," Henry pursues an alternative ethical vocabulary as he abandons the place of conscience. He resorts to medieval tropes that repeatedly fail, either because the linguistic ruptures reflect the pressures on sacramental resources in the late medieval Church or because he purposefully fractures the metaphors in hopes of creating a new, secularized model. Albeit Henry never successfully articulates what the new model will be, the play does focus on the process of moving from one hermeneutical platform to another. Henry leaves the place of conscience, and indeed leaves the Church, but does not yet have access to an alternative place to locate or work through these ideas. *All Is True* tries out different models for thinking about conscience—prick, shipwreck, wound—without necessarily turning any of them into something fully secular. The play illustrates a hermeneutics of sacred and secular crossover in action, thereby emphasizing the process of religious reform rather than depicting a wholly intact mechanism for thinking about a secularized conscience. Only in retrospect do we recognize alternative vocabularies for conscience and celebrate at least one alternative place to work through these complex ideas: the secular stage.

Notes

I wish to thank Jay Zysk; Katherine Steele Brokaw; Sarah Beckwith and her Folger "Shakespeare and Sacraments" seminar; and Jay Zysk and Katherine Cleland and their SAA "Ritual Shakespeare" seminar for the invaluable feedback and generative conversations.

1. Paul Strohm, *Conscience: A Very Short Introduction* (Oxford: Oxford University Press, 2011), 28.

2. All references to *All Is True* are to "The Famous History of the Life of King Henry the Eighth," in *The Riverside Shakespeare: Second Edition*, ed. G. Blakemore Evans, 1026–64 (Boston: Houghton Mifflin, 1997). Quotations from the play are cited parenthetically with reference to line number.

3. All references to *The Castle of Perseverance* are from *The Macro Plays: The Castle of Perseverance, Wisdom, Humanum Genus*, ed. Mark Eccles (London: Oxford University Press, 1969). Quotations from the play are cited parenthetically with reference to line number.

4. My understanding of conscience in medieval and early modern England comes from Brian B. Cummings, *Mortal Thoughts: Religion, Secularity and Identity in Shakespeare and Early Modern Culture* (Oxford: Oxford University Press, 2013), 79–90.

5. Translation from Olga L. Valbuena, *Subjects to the King's Divorce: Equivocation, Infidelity, and Resistance in Early Modern England* (Bloomington: Indiana University Press, 2003), 2.

6. Valbuena, *Subjects*, 2.

7. *Jacob's Well, an English Treatise on the Cleansing of Man's Conscience, Part I*, ed. Arthur Brandeis, EETS 115 (London: Kegan Paul, Trench, Trübner, 1900), 163.

8. "The Six Articles (1539)," in *Documents of the Christian Church*, 4th ed., ed. Henry Bettenson and Chris Maunder (Oxford: Oxford University Press, 2011), 249–50. We should be careful to differentiate between the historical Henry and the theatrical Henry. On taking the distinction seriously, see Michael Davies, "Converting Henry: Truth, History, and Historical Faith in *Henry VIII*," in *Shakespeare and Early Modern Religion*, ed. David Lowenstein and Michael Witmore (Cambridge: Cambridge University Press, 2015), 271–73.

9. David Aers, *Salvation and Sin: Augustine, Langland, and Fourteenth-Century Theology* (Notre Dame, Ind.: University of Notre Dame Press, 2009), 100–101. Although this essay focuses on penance, the rich depictions of sacramental practice in *All Is True* should not be ignored. For the Eucharist, baptismal ceremony, and last rites in *Henry VIII*, see Jay Zysk, "Of Ceremonies and *Henry VIII*," in *Stages of Engagement: Drama and Religion in Post-Reformation England*, ed. James D. Mardock and Kathryn R. McPherson (Pittsburgh: Duquesne University Press, 2015), 241–62. For the link between sin and wounds, see Eamon Duffy, *The Stripping of the Altars: Traditional Religion in England, c. 1400–c.1580*, 2nd ed. (New Haven, Conn.: Yale University Press, 2005), 241–48.

10. Sarah Beckwith, *Shakespeare and the Grammar of Forgiveness* (Ithaca: Cornell University Press, 2011), 117–20.

11. Duffy, *Stripping of the Altars*, 54. For an example of the *forma confitendi*, see, John Myrc, *Instructions for Parish Priests*, ed. Edward Peacock (London:

Early English Text Society / Kegan Paul, Trench, Trübner, 1868), pp. 28–29, ll. 923–60.

12. See Canon 21 in *Decrees of the Ecumenical Councils*, ed. Norman P. Tanner, S.J., vol. 1 (London: Sheed and Ward; Washington, D.C.: Georgetown University Press, 1990), 245.

13. Thomas Aquinas, *Summa Theologiae*, trans. Timothy Sutton (London: Blackfriars, 1970).

14. For the language of "binding and loosing" in Thomas Aquinas, see Sheryl Overmyer, "The Wayfarer's Way and Two Guides for the Journey" (Ph.D. diss., Duke University, 2010), 14–15n2.

15. For the intertwined linguistic and theological relationship between synderesis and conscience, and especially for the medieval trope of synderesis as a spark, see Robert A. Greene, "Instinct of Nature: Natural Law, Synderesis, and the Moral Sense," *Journal of the History of Ideas*, 58, no. 2 (April 1997): 173–98. For "scintilla" as a metaphor for "synderesis," see Robert A. Greene, "Synderesis, the Spark of Conscience, in the English Renaissance," *Journal of the History of Ideas*, 52, no. 2 (April–June 1991): 198–99.

16. Catherine Belsey, *The Subject of Tragedy: Identity and Difference in Renaissance Drama* (London: Methuen, 1985), 21.

17. Strohm, *Conscience*, 221.

18. Strohm, *Conscience*, 207–8; emphasis in original.

19. Irwin Smith, *Shakespeare's Blackfriars Playhouse: Its History and Its Design* (New York: New York University Press, 1964), 20.

20. Smith, *Shakespeare's Blackfriars Playhouse*, 20.

21. Smith, *Shakespeare's Blackfriars Playhouse*, 10–11.

22. Smith, *Shakespeare's Blackfriars Playhouse*, 12.

23. Smith, *Shakespeare's Blackfriars Playhouse*, 16.

24. Smith, *Shakespeare's Blackfriars Playhouse*, 13.

25. Smith, *Shakespeare's Blackfriars Playhouse*, 99.

26. Smith, *Shakespeare's Blackfriars Playhouse*, 97. On the liberties, see Steven Mullaney, *The Place of the Stage: License, Play, and Power in Renaissance England* (Chicago: University of Chicago Press, 1988).

27. Smith, *Shakespeare's Blackfriars Playhouse*, 115–22.

28. Also relevant is Thomas Rist, *Revenge Tragedy and the Drama of Commemoration in Reforming England* (Aldershot, Hants, UK: Ashgate Publishing, 2008), 76–81.

29. Raphael Holinshed, *Holinshed's Chronicles of England, Scotland, and Ireland, Volume 3: England* (New York: AMS Press, 1976), 738.

30. References to Cavendish are from *Two Early Tudor Lives*, ed. Richard S. Sylvester and Davis P. Harding (New Haven, Conn.: Yale University Press, 1962), 86–87.

31. Peter Lombard, *The Sentences, Book 4: On the Doctrine of Signs*, trans. Giulio Silano (Toronto: Pontifical Institute of Mediaeval Studies, 2007).

32. *The Book of Common Prayer, 1559: The Elizabethan Prayer Book*, ed. John E. Booty (Charlottesville: University of Virginia Press, 2005), 290.

33. I borrow the concept of double infidelity from Valbuena, *Subjects*, 1–2.

“In This Most Desolate Isle”: *The Tempest* and Its Sacred Spaces

Helga Duncan

> I learned to take my holy spot with me, and I learned with mobility to bring it where I went.
>
> —Judith Herman, *Trauma and Recovery*

The Tempest dramatizes the search for and recovery of sacred space in a world it constructs as ostensibly secular. It is not that the play evacuates the sacred from space in a gesture of Weberian disenchantment; this essay disagrees with notions that the play is about mere theatrical hoax. The play’s “pagan” or “secular” symbolism and its representation of worldly “magic” serve as media through which to examine Christian spatial reaccommodations of the sacred in a post-Reformation world.[1] Indeed, *The Tempest* examines early modern spatial instabilities of the sacred by mediating between an emplaced sacramentalism reminiscent of the old faith and a spatial dislodgment animated by reformed scripturalism (Prospero is equally defined by his robes and his books). In doing so, it presents sacred space as a sanctuary and place of reconciliation that is wrested by cultural labor from a temporal world. As the editors of this volume observe, religious practice is a human enterprise, and the spaces it creates are necessarily of this world and sacred by symbolic association. *The Tempest*’s configurations of space also challenge the notion, central to many narratives of secularization, that the Protestant emphasis on the “Word” necessarily removed sacramentality and other senses of the sacred from lived experience in the world. The spatial operations and contestations in *The Tempest* are proof of a spiritual dynamism and instability that perpetually (re)locates the sacred and thus partakes in an ongoing hermeneutical process that seeks to negotiate the relationship between church and world.

Shakespeare’s play complicates the relationship not only between sacred and secular but also between space and text. Prospero’s relationship to his books shapes his dwelling in space, in the sense that his physical exile from Milan is arguably rooted in his preoccupation with books. At the same time, texts are crucial to the creation of imagined space: Prospero manipulates the spatial perception of sojourners on the island with the help of his books. Based in textual exegesis, Prospero's handling of sacramental poetics focuses intensely on rites of passage and merges ostensibly contradictory paradigms of emplacement and mobility. Shakespeare's play questions the reformed sense of liberation from spatial imprisonment through hermeneutic innovation (i.e., the doctrine of *sola scriptura*) and demonstrates the provisional yet powerfully efficacious nature of consecrated space—space carefully marked out by social gestures to accomplish shifting objectives. In the play, movement and emplacement are mutually constitutive and perpetually contested aspects of Christian religious practice that situate the believer vis-à-vis what they deem holy—in ritual and scriptural reading alike.

Work on secularization has long argued that spatial perceptions of the sacred in Shakespeare's age had shifted as a result of changing modes of worship occasioned by reformers' commitment to scripture and an ensuing antiritualism and antisacramentalism. According to this view, traditional ecclesiastical spaces—considered visible manifestations of church corruption—became targets of iconoclastic defacement and were subject to profound alterations; hallmarks of the old faith's sacramental space-based theology, such as altars, rood screens, and baptismal basins, were moved and changed or disappeared altogether. The departure from traditional Catholic belief was palpably expressed in spatial changes initiated by rapidly altering clerical and lay responsibilities in the conducting of worship.[2] Yet a sizable body of early modern writing on the subject stressed not abandonment or destruction of places where the holy might be encountered but rather recuperation—in newly designed "temples" and entire "cities" situating reformed congregations. The writers of these tracts thus addressed not only the crossing of boundaries marked by traditional sacred architecture but also the need for spiritual dwelling, the making of a home in a secular world of profound religious and political upheaval.[3]

John Sommerville bases his argument about English secularization processes on the spatial transformation occasioned by the Henrician appropriation of monasteries and other church holdings and suggests that this event, above all, erased England's traditional religious topography, yielding an empty, conceptual (and therefore secular) space.[4] He argues that the medieval sense of labyrinthine, emplaced "mystery" gave way to the notion that "God was everywhere, and nowhere" (19). Such a reading relies on older theories of religion rooted in binary conceptions of inherent sacrality and secularity that recent work in the field, focused on position, movement, and relation, has challenged.

The editors of this volume argue in the introduction for a sustained examination of the gulf still separating the medieval from the early modern age in critical discourse, where the former signifies an antiquated, religious worldview and the latter a progressive, secular one. Likewise, I proceed from the assumption that religious reformations neither disconnected the sacred from the secular nor ushered in a protomodern secular age. In my reading of *The Tempest*, I work against the bifurcation of historical periods by turning to Jonathan Z. Smith's conception of "locative" and "utopian" perspectives. The former signifies emplacement, boundedness, and hierarchical social arrangements, while the latter speaks to the move away from spiritual centers and ecclesiastical control.[5] Smith, who suggests that sacred space is generated by human labor, also argues that both locative and utopian orientations, far from denoting "primitive" and "advanced" stages of religious development, are at work concurrently. More recently, Thomas Tweed has suggested in a similar vein that religions, above all, seek to situate the believer in space and in relation to the divine; for Tweed, this process centers on culturally and politically contested enterprises of "dwelling" and "crossing" that render the sacred and secular situational.[6]

The tensions between emplacement and movement, so palpable in early modern attitudes toward spaces for the holy, can also be traced in post-Reformation hermeneutics with its move between literalist, text-anchored reading practices and individual encounters with and sense making of scripture that challenged systematized, clerically mediated ways of reading the Bible. I suggest that hermeneutical shifts in the period are analogous to changes in spatial perception and organization. Literalist leanings in early modern hermeneutic theory—what I would call emplacement by language, grammar, historical context, and especially the object of the text itself—are coupled with a dislodging spiritualism, which holds that scripture is "the product of God's Holy Spirit at work in history" and is accessible only through the Spirit's intervention.[7] In other words, Reformation hermeneutics moved between a locative, syntactical, and historico-grammatical self-authenticating authority of scripture, on the one hand, and, on the other, a utopian eschatological impulse that moves beyond the here and now. Thus the "Word," in Luther's formulation, is "not . . . an exhibition of present things but only testimonies of future things"—it is always already out of reach.[8]

In *The Tempest*, Shakespeare brilliantly dramatizes these tensions between emplacement and movement so deeply emblematic of Christian forms of belief and, according to Michel de Certeau, rooted in conceptual divergences signified especially by the empty tomb, which stands for both presence and absence, for particularity and universality, for orthodoxy and heterodoxy, for stability as well as fragmentation.[9] By doing so, the playwright validates neither a deeply religious nor a thoroughly secular worldview. Instead, these spatial tensions emerge as expressions of hermeneutic transactions through which spiritual matters are shaped by human—and therefore worldly—language and ritual. Moreover, like the other essays in this section, "Spaces of the Secular," I hope to show that the theater was an important site for working through or theorizing the interplay of sacred and secular.

Prospero and Caliban: Spatial Conflict

Through the relationship between Caliban and Prospero, *The Tempest* demonstrates the culturally constructed dimensions of sacred and secular space. Shakespeare juxtaposes Prospero's emplaced textualism against Caliban's locative sense of sacred dwelling connected to the natural world of his island home. Prospero's first reference to his insular exile—he calls it "a full poor cell"—establishes the play's spiritual and spatial contexts as well as outlines the dramatic tension between locative dwelling and utopian crossing.[10] Given the remoteness of the isle, the phrase "full poor cell" conjures up visions of eremitic seclusion that also reiterate Prospero's former spatial isolation in Milan. The isle, where none of the inhabitants (except Caliban) are "honoured with / A human shape" (1.2.285–86), is a wild and lonely place. The term "cell" could simply refer to the smallness and extreme simplicity of Prospero's abode, but the choice of moniker also suggests that this kind of dwelling carries spiritual significance.[11] The exilic "cell" points to Prospero's political as well as his spiritual displacement, which the play ultimately counters with its movement from conflict to reconciliation.

The initial image we have of Prospero is one of purposeful emplacement, for in the character's early speeches Milan is almost exclusively associated with static, self-absorbed dwelling in a secluded chamber. Although Prospero's studies are not overtly coded religious, his project seems to have spiritual rather than political ends: he tells Miranda that he had been "transported / And rapt in secret studies" (1.2.76–77). Prospero pursues a kind of learning not focused on worldly affairs but on personal illumination, a learning that perhaps even sanctifies domestic space through a kind of scriptural reading.[12] At the same time, Prospero's acquisition of knowledge in the secrecy of his closet also suggests the mysteries of priestly ritual, concealed from lay observers. But his insistence on rootedness in place eventually drains away his "verdure" (1.2.87), or life force, while his mobile brother, Antonio, devoted to the secular pursuit of power, takes his place.[13]

After Prospero's forced exilic crossing to the island, thc play stages the mediation between seemingly incompatible spatial perspectives—sacerdotal spatial circumscription, for one, and, for another, a reformed preference for moving beyond the boundaries of ecclesiastical emplacement because, according to Calvin, God's glory renders holy "this most beautiful theater," the world in which we live.[14] It is thus the interplay of Prospero's locative "magic garment" (1.2.24) and his utopian books that initiate the move across the old boundaries of hatred:

> The direful spectacle of the wreck . . .
> I have with such provision in mine art
> So safely ordered, that there is no soul—
> No, not so much perdition as an hair,
> Betid to any creature in the vessel
> Which thou heard'st cry, which thou sawst sink. (1.2.28–32)

Prospero has reason to bring down the ship and some of its passengers, notably his usurping brother, but he has decided to do otherwise. Prospero's (albeit forced) departure from isolationist dwelling in his study provides him with a sacerdotal agency that turns what he considers an inhospitable island into a sanctuary. The baptismal ritual he has created with the aid of books and robe fashions a space for reconciliation by merging disparate spatial paradigms.[15]

For Caliban, however, Prospero's spatial manipulations profane the island's spaces. The newcomer's attempts at integrating the island native into his household by "lodg[ing]" him in his "own cell" (1.2.347) clashes with Caliban's pantheistic paradigm of spatial sanctity that merges emplacement and mobility. Manifested in Caliban's attitudes we observe what Gerardus van der Leeuw termed a profound wonder in the face of a nature deemed sacred that marks a time in human history long past.[16] Although van der Leeuw argues for the inherent sacrality of certain natural sites (rivers, mountains, springs, etc.), he also acknowledges the workings of power in the perception and maintenance of sacred space and maintains that the sacredness of natural space is always subject to human explication and appropriation (210). In their reading of van der Leeuw, David Chidester and Edward Linenthal observe that the sanctity of space "can be directly related to a politics of property" and add that it extends not only to the ownership of land but also to possession of "sacred objects . . . religious symbols, myths, or rituals," all of which can be enlisted in support of certain political or economic projects.[17] The use, meaning, and, mythology (associated with memories of his powerful mother and her god, Setebos) of Caliban's land is powerfully overwritten by European settlers and visitors—a process that the play registers in some detail. With little or no appreciation for the island's indigenous sacred nature, Prospero superimposes his own religious tropes on its topography in a violently proprietary gesture supported by his numinous books. Ironically, these tropes, in contradistinction to Caliban's association with dwelling, center on an aesthetic of movement and flow.

In the play's first exchange between the two antagonistic figures, Caliban speaks of his inviolable dwelling rights on the island and Prospero's contestation that seeks to dislocate the former's worldview:

> This island's mine by Sycorax, my mother,
> Which thou tak'st from me. When thou cam'st first
> Thou strok'st me and made much of me; wouldst give me
> Water with berries in't, and teach me how
> To name the bigger light and how the less
> That burn by day and night. And then I loved thee
> And showed thee all the qualities o'th' isle:
> The fresh springs, brine pits, barren place and fertile. (1.2.332–39)

It is worth noting that Prospero would teach Caliban about the sun and moon in order to expand the latter's purview beyond the narrow boundaries of the isle and change his spatial perception. Prospero's lesson about sublunary and cosmic spaces has scriptural provenance, but Caliban rejects a model that would undervalue the island's numinous natural resources. He is not concerned with Prospero's celestial bodies—in short, with a distant, intellectual sacred; instead he insists on a material and firmly emplaced holy.

In Caliban's mind, newcomers try to erase the island's inherently sacred, nurturing cast by exploiting its natural resources. "Be not afeard. The isle is full of noises, / Sounds, and sweet airs that give delight and hurt not" (3.2.135–36), he tells the Neapolitans Stephano and Trinculo. Caliban's perception of the island's natural blessedness is admirable—none of the other characters in the play share this viewpoint, with the possible exception of Gonzalo in his famous utopian vision. "In dreaming," Caliban says, "the clouds, methought, would open and show riches / Ready to drop upon me" (3.2.140–42). If Prospero's relationship with the island is adversarial, Caliban's is symbiotic and deeply rooted in his consciousness. His spatial perspective, moreover, is mobile and flexible rather than locative and self-involved; he is willing to share the island's blessed bounty with those newly arrived:

> I'll show thee the best springs; I'll pluck thee berries;
> I'll fish for thee, and get thee wood enough.
> . . . .
> I prithee, let me bring thee where crabs grow,
> And with my long nails will dig the pignuts,
> Show thee a jay's nest, and instruct thee how
> To snare the nimble marmoset. I'll bring thee
> Clustering filberts, and sometimes I'll get thee
> Young scamels from the rock. Wilt thou go with me? (2.2.157–58, 164–69)

This speech is important because it confirms Caliban's reverential view of the isle's varied physical features—its topography as well as its flora and fauna. The island's bounty offers itself up and sustains the grateful dweller. The Neapolitans, however, are not concerned with survival, with finding food or shelter in this unfamiliar environment, nor are they interested in the island's beauty and natural wonders; instead they ponder how best to exploit its singularity, represented especially by their native informant Caliban. Trinculo wishes he were in England because there people would gladly "give a piece of silver" (2.2.29) if he put Caliban on display. Caliban addresses immediate bodily concerns in his speech, but Trinculo ponders abstract economic advantage. Although the term "mooncalf," employed by Stephano and Trinculo, conceives of Caliban as a figure of far-flung crossings through his association with an extraterrestrial body,[18] the association between Caliban's otherness and extreme spatial distance confirms his confinement by the island's "colonizers" and signifies his subjugation through a perspective that denies the spatial complexities of Caliban's insular dwelling. The association of Caliban with the distant moon severs the spiritual connection the island native has with his homeland and allows outsiders to take possession of it.

Caliban and Prospero also clash profoundly over the meaning of spiritual dwelling. Caliban's song at the end of the first encounter with the Neapolitans rejects European modes of husbandry and domestic dwelling because they are rooted in hierarchical models rather than autonomous habitation:

No more dams I'll make for fish
Nor fetch in firing at requiring
Nor scrape trenchering, nor wash dish. (2.2.176–78)

Caliban, who celebrates the free access to and liberal circulation of insular sustenance, laments the erection of boundaries (dams containing fish, etc.) that will deny his (social and geographical) mobility. What theologian William Perkins deems the orderly space of the pious home in which master and servant work together for the glory of God, Caliban repudiates, for in his eyes this sort of domestic emplacement is exploitative and profane rather than holy. Prospero, by contrast, insists on his role as divinely instituted "good man or master of the familie . . . in whom resteth the priuate and proper gouernment of the whole household . . . [bestowed upon him] by the ordinance of God."[19] This textually encoded Christian microcosmic emplacement is challenged by Caliban's freewheeling "pagan" materialism and, ironically, his advancement of radical endogamy. Caliban's attempt to "violate" Miranda (1.2.349), his sister of sorts, because he wishes to "people" (1.2.351) the island with Calibans (i.e., with copies of himself), takes domestic emplacement to a logical and extreme conclusion that horrifies Prospero and forms the basis for conflict on the island.

Sacramental Poetics: Spatial Rituals

Prospero's project of reconciliation is based in a sacramental politics, which forges sacred space from an otherwise secular environment through rites of passage. Christianity's key space-sanctifying rite, the Eucharist, moves believers closer to God, while nuptial rites move individuals from the single to the married state, from one family to another, and, in the play, from one land to another. Prospero makes use of both to advance his seemingly secular plan of regaining his dukedom. The harpy banquet and the wedding masque in particular are useful scenes through which to chart Prospero's creating of consecrated space where rituals of mobility become possible and produce political results. Moreover, both map a path toward Prospero's sacred circle that makes reconciliation possible. Despite the classical iconography these scenes employ their spatial sensibilities are decidedly Christian.[20] Shakespeare focuses on the human journey through life events in terms of the crossing of thresholds. Communion in particular becomes a "rite of incorporation" during which individuals move toward one another, if only for the duration of a meal.[21]

The point about incorporation is an important one, especially if considered in relation to the island's purgatorial appearance. Catholic notions of purgatory were deeply rooted in forging connections between the living and the dead: the living were to pray for the souls of the dead, but the deceased might also reach beyond the boundary of death and remind the living to do penance for their sins. In other words, the relationship between living and dead was defined by strong familial and personal ties and especially by movement rather than stasis.[22] In the play the line between death and life is unsettlingly indistinct for most characters. After the shipwreck, half the Neapolitan party is deemed dead by the other half; and the play's villains, Alonzo, Sebastian, and Antonio, believe that Prospero perished long ago. Making full use of the island's topography, Prospero's staging of the banquet as a complex rite of passage aims at establishing communication between enemies and movement across the boundaries of resentment. Spatially, the scene facilitates the characters' entrance into a liminal place on their way to a new position in the societal hierarchy. During the harpy banquet, Prospero and the Neapolitans must negotiate the liminal stage of sacrifice to move toward compromise and appeasement.

In Shakespeare's staging of Eucharistic ritual, the play's three villainous figures are removed from temporal space to a transitional stage in their progress across the island and toward reconciliation. The scene demonstrates the need for and efficaciousness of sacred space generated by bloodless ritual sacrifice. The Counter-Reformation's most significant tract on sacred space, Cardinal Roberto Bellarmino's *Disputationes*, identified sacrifices to God offered in *templa* as the most important practice of spatial sanctification.[23] *The Tempest*'s banquet scene begins with a reference to questions of spatial signification, when Gonzalo terms the island a maze (3.3.2), just before reminding the audience that Alonzo is to be sacrificed to Antonio's and Sebastian's lust for power. With the lines "The next advantage / Will we take thoroughly" (3.3.13–14), the two conspirators announce their intention of carrying out Alonzo's murder, prevented earlier by Ariel. The banqueting ritual that begins immediately following this exchange obscures the line between secular feasting and religious service, with music so ethereal and motions so extraordinary that Alonzo feels compelled to remark on them: "I cannot too much muse / Such shapes, such gesture and such sound" (3.3.36–37).[24] Awed by Prospero's "ministers," the Neapolitans may be unsure as to the spiritual meaning of their ceremonial gestures. Alonzo, for instance, views the victuals left by the spirits with some suspicion, but this food clearly carries significance beyond its profane use as sustenance. Alonzo, as well as the audience, must ask whether the proffered victuals are ritually transformed into the food of redemption or damnation. Ariel, appearing in the guise of a harpy, seems to dispense not grace but punishment to the "three men of sin" (3.3.53) and alludes to "powers" that "pronounce . . . / Ling'ring perdition, worse than any death" (3.3.73, 77). The emergence of purgatorial iconography that suspends Eucharistic sacrifice does not refute but rather confirms the scene's function as an allegory of spatial sanctification because it denotes the passage from sin to redemption.

The banquet scene shows that ritual labor as well as a more passive reception of divine grace (associated with reformed understandings of the sacraments) plays a role in the carving of sacred space from a secular world. In counterdistinction to Bellarmino's notion of the bloodless sacrifice as prime spatial marker, Luther had argued that the Eucharist was a *Wohltat* (a blessing or benefit), and other reformers agreed that it was a gift, a *testamentum*, received and witnessed by a congregation.[25] In the *Lawes*, Richard Hooker comments on the conveyance of grace through the sacraments as "means effectuall whereby God when we take the sacraments delivereth into our hands that grace available unto eternall life, which grace the sacraments represent or signifie."[26] Ariel's ominous reference to "perdition, worse than death" intensifies the psychological terror experienced by the sinner Alonzo at the sight of the harpy banquet. Coupled with his emotional pain over the loss of his son, this unites him with Prospero in redemptive suffering. In a space set apart by ritual, grace is dispensed even to the play's most abject sinners. Prospero's lines to Ariel are instructive: "Bravely the figure of this harpy hast thou / Performed, my Ariel; a grace it had, devouring" (3.3.83–84). These lines speak to the way in which sacrificial ritual sanctifies space. Ariel has played a role not unlike a priest engaged in ceremonial motions reenacting Jesus's gestures at the Last Supper. The term "devouring" alludes to the ingestion of the sacrificial, redemptive meal, but it also means that the ritual (as a metaphor for divine grace) will consume the sins of those witnessing Ariel's consecrating performance. Alonzo and his party may not have partaken of the Eucharist in a literal sense; they have not ingested food, for the harpy takes it away before a morsel enters their mouths. But Alonzo's acceptance of sin sets in motion the process of redemption here, in this space, where the gestures of Ariel and Prospero's "meaner ministers" (3.3.87) invoke the ritual of redemptive sacrifice before a congregation of sorts and thus initiate the crossing over from purgatorial suffering into deliverance—into the territory of salvation.

The second rite of passage, briefly transforming the island from non-spiritual or mundane to Edenic and consecrated space, is the wedding ceremony of Miranda and Ferdinand. For part of his sojourn on the island, Ferdinand resembles a log- (or cross-) bearing pilgrim journeying toward redemption. His fidelity, though, is to Miranda: "The mistress which I serve quickens what's dead, / And makes my labours pleasures" (3.1.6–7). Ferdinand's effort, which has him "remov[ing] some thousands of these logs and pil[ing] them up" (3.1.9–10), appears to be a Petrarchan service of devotion, but it can also be understood as a work of atonement. His pilgrimage helps to counteract his father's wickedness and fall from grace, for Miranda, like the Virgin Mary, turns death into life for Ferdinand.[27] Prospero in his sacerdotal role confirms the trial of faith Ferdinand has undergone, and he speaks of the great spiritual and physical reward he is about to reap:

> . . . All thy vexations
> Were but trials of thy love, and thou
> Hast strangely stood the test. Here, afore heaven,
> I ratify this my rich gift (4.1.5–8)

The love for which Ferdinand bears his cross on the island is not only that which he feels for Miranda. He is also devoted to the memory of his father, and his union with the saintly Miranda comes to signify the reconfirmation of his as well as his father's spiritual deliverance after purgatorial suffering.[28]

The sacramental character of Miranda and Ferdinand's nuptials draws our attention to the spatial accommodation of reconciliation.[29] For a short span of time, the masque renders a portion of the island inviolable through "sanctimonious ceremonies . . . / With full and holy rite" (4.1.16–17). At the same time, Prospero's comment to Ariel makes us keenly aware of the theatrics of sacred space, a theme that the remainder of the play explores in some depth:

> Thou and thy meaner fellows your last service
> Did worthily perform, and I must use you
> In such another trick. Go bring the rabble
> (O'er whom I give the power) here to this place.
> Incite them to quick motion, for I must
> Bestow upon the eyes of this young couple
> Some vanity of mine art. (4.1.35–41)

Prospero alludes to the ritual Ariel presented to Alonzo's party, the ritual that set the Neapolitan king on the path to repentance and redemption.

Prospero's word choice here seemingly derides ritual labor—and by extension the space it is meant to consecrate. Indeed, the term "trick" recalls the language of Protestant ideologues who considered the mass and its attendant rituals nothing more than "popish tricks."[30] Spatially, this sorcery imprisons its practitioners, according to Swiss reformer Pierre Viret, in "labirinthes" (29); indeed, Gonzalo terms the landscape generated by Prospero a "maze." Prospero's choice of words reduces his sacerdotal power to a "vain art," carried out by an indigenous mob under the supervision of the ambivalent Ariel. We might even say that this constitutes a parody of ritual and the spaces it generates, but ultimately it is difficult to deny the spiritual and political efficacy of these spectacular ceremonies, which arguably constitute the play's most important dramatic objective.

Iris, Ceres, and Juno may not be bona fide deities, but the rite of passage over which they preside generates a consecrated space of appeasement, expressed most powerfully in the Edenic landscape their speeches evoke. This paradisiacal topography becomes the imaginative space of spiritual redemption: Ceres's "rich leas" are brimming with fruitfulness, with "wheat, rye, barley, vetches, oats and peas," and her "turfy mountains" are home to "nibbling sheep" (4.1.60–62). Iris's description focuses on important foods the earth produces and forges a connection to the harpy banquet. In the masque setting the promise of bodily sustenance becomes a more palpable catalyst for redemptive action. Moreover, the purpose of the goddesses' descent to earth is the establishment of a reciprocal bond between corporeal and divine domains. Iris tells Ceres she is called to witness the "contract of true love" and to provide "some donation freely to estate / On the blessed lovers" (4.1.84–86). If the Eucharist is a gift, as reformers argued, the play registers the blessings it conveys through images of fecund acreage that sustains the faithful—"Earth's increase, foison plenty . . . Vines with clustering bunches growing, / Plants with goodly burdens bowing" (4.1.110, 112–13)—and thus celebratory emplacement. For Ferdinand the Edenic space of the wedding masque completes the passage from purgatory to salvation: "Let me live here ever! / So rare a wondered father and a wise / Makes this place paradise" (4.1.122–24).

Yet the hallowed space of the wedding masque has palpable limitations. Sacred space is sanctuary space and as such provides temporary refuge from the violence and impiety of the world, but it cannot keep either at bay permanently. Indeed, the holiness of the sanctuary site is generated by the profound contrast with the sinfulness of surrounding secular spaces.[31] The masque ends abruptly with Prospero acknowledging "that foul conspiracy / Of the beast Caliban and his confederates" (4.1.139–40). Prospero's reference to Caliban as "the beast" here indirectly associates him with the devil, with the ruler over hell—a space utterly profane. At the same time, Prospero's speech about the masque as ephemeral performance confirms sanctification as a cultural process by juxtaposing sacred and secular spatial perceptions: "Our revels are now ended. These our actors, / . . . Were all spirits and / Are melted into air, into thin air" (4.1.148–50). Because Juno, Iris, and Ceres were only performers, whatever power they commanded in the masque seems to have utterly disappeared. However, as Lindsay Jones points out, "the sanctification of space is only rarely conceived as a permanent, once-and-for-always project," and "in many cases, the purity and sanctity of a place . . . is perceived as fleeting in the extreme."[32] For critical onlookers, the words and gestures of ritual specialists may seem to be insubstantial hocus-pocus, "a phenomenon," in Jones's words, "that is often more disturbing to outsiders than to the actual ritual participants."[33] On the one hand, the play seems to suggest that religious ritual is ephemeral and has no material impact but provides a "vision" that is nothing but a "baseless fabric" (4.1.151). Yet on the other hand, the play demonstrates the tangible efficacy of performative space (whether ritual or theatrical), for Prospero's spatial histrionics effect political and spiritual change.[34]

Tracing a Circle: Spatial Reconciliation

Prospero's final ritual action reestablishes peace because it revives the dynamic, communal aspect of the sacrament of penance, which had been abolished by Cardinal Borromeo at the Council of Trent when he introduced the "confessional box."[35] Prospero's circle signifies sanctuary space in which moral and spiritual reformation can take place; though it appears rigidly emplaced, it facilitates movement. Alonzo regains his senses and power of reasoning in the consecrated circle and seeks to repair the damage his tyranny and Antonio's treachery have caused: "Thy dukedom I resign and do entreat / Thou pardon me my wrongs" (5.1.115–16, 118–19). Alonzo's confession and his plea for mercy are preceded by Prospero's gesture of humble resignation from his previous position of sacerdotal power. He "abjures" his "rough magic" (5.1.50–51) and promises to "break his staff" (5.1.54) and "drown [his] book" (5.1.57). His words not only draw attention to the provisional character of human interactions with the divine (be they based in scriptural reading, ritual gesture, or spatial accommodation) but also demonstrate that sacramental penance and reconciliation work only in a space where one is willing to make room for, responsively encounter, and accommodate the "other."[36] The circle facilitates communication across the boundaries of hate. The play presents the sacrament of reconciliation in a dramatically literal affirmation of Tertullian's phrase "the second plank [of salvation] after the shipwreck which is the loss of grace."[37] Even if Calvin and other reformers insisted that no scriptural precedent for the sacrament existed and that only God had the power to absolve humans of their sins, there was nonetheless a need for a space in which serious transgressions might be encountered and dealt with. The playwright spatializes this process, always clear-eyed as to the culturally constructed aspect of these maneuvers (confirmed by Prospero's term "subtleties" [5.1.124]) and aware that such actions are provisional and perhaps even rejected by some participants (such as Sebastian and Antonio).

Static as Prospero's numinous circle might seem, it signifies movement, for within its provisionary boundary the play's figures proceed from enmity to alliance and from ignorance to illumination, while Prospero's final act of spatial management reaffirms the island's sacred cast. By his own pronouncement, Prospero landed on the island "to be the lord on't" (5.1.163), and in the process desacralized the island for the native inhabitant Caliban.[38] Now Prospero has undergone a "sea-change" (1.2.400) that causes him to forgive his enemies and leave the island to Caliban and its spirit population. Caliban, who, despite the many references to his physical and ethical defects, shows himself entirely capable of "seek[ing] for grace" (5.1.296), moves from idolatry—"what a thrice-double ass / Was I to take this drunkard for a god, / And worship this dull fool" (5.1.296–98) and hatred of Prospero, "The red plague rid you" (1.2.365)—to a state of illumination and blessing. With Prospero and the Neapolitans leaving the island, we can assume that Caliban will resume his symbiotic, dynamic dwelling on the island. Prospero's newfound understanding of the power of crossing is also palpable in his release of the strikingly mobile Ariel. The spirit's songs celebrate movement and change. There is the famous "Full fathom five thy father lies" early in the play, which revels in the endless cycle of becoming and decaying: "Nothing . . . that doth fade / But doth suffer a sea-change" (1.2.400–401); and then we get the ditty in which Ariel vows to chase summer: "On the bat's back I do fly / After summer merrily" (5.1.91–92). His final service to Prospero is to provide "auspicious gales" that will convey the royal party back to Naples (5.1.315). Ariel's kinetic power benevolently conveys home the interlopers that interfered with a sacred spatial balance on the island. Prospero's last words of the play—excepting the epilogue—are directed to Ariel and encourage the character to take "to the elements" and "be free" (5.1.318–19).

Prospero's lines in which he announces that "every third thought shall be my grave" (5.1.307–12) point to his newfound understanding of the power of crossing. No longer is he committed to rigid emplacement, as he once was in his isolated study or on the island, where, from his "cell," he ruthlessly altered the spaces previously sacred to Caliban (and the spirit inhabitants). Now he thinks of the grave, which signifies a consecrated final resting place but also the mutability of human experience and spatial perception; now Prospero seems to understand that dwelling is always provisional and impermanent. In the epilogue, Shakespeare's protagonist speaks eloquently to the tension between crossing and dwelling and the stage's power to represent and mediate between both. The epilogue has long been considered Prospero's repudiation of magic.[39] Yet the epilogue's spatial imagery takes us back to the play's examination of traditional spatial economies, in particular the spiritual properties of purgatory, a space, I would contend, that itself exemplifies the Christian tension between crossing and dwelling. Prospero asks to be released from "this bare island" by "prayer" (epilogue 8, 16). Prospero's plea for relief may well demonstrate his kinship with other confined characters in the play, from Ariel and Caliban to Ferdinand and the Neapolitans;[40] but it registers his newfound communal, and hence dynamic, spatial perspective. His plea at the end for prayer and "indulgence" (epilogue 20) alludes to ancient spiritual topographies. Rather than delivering "an irreverent pun" with this choice of word,[41] the play endorses a spiritual geography that includes a form of purgatory because it exemplifies spiritual life in terms of dwelling and crossing.

Conscious of spatial power and exploitation in general and the relational, constructed nature of sacred space in particular, the play demonstrates the efficacy of spatial consecration—the marking out of a space that exists briefly beyond the human temporal world—for even if Prospero's ritual gestures and Ariel's machinations deliver a "show," they are effectual in moving the play's characters toward spiritual conciliation and peace. Perhaps *The Tempest* does not constitute Shakespeare's farewell to the stage but an eloquent endorsement of its remarkable power to facilitate a temporary move beyond narrow self-interested mundaneness,[42] in which audiences and actors alike can proceed beyond conflict, even if only for the duration of a performance.[43]

Notes

1. For recent engagement with religion in *The Tempest*, see Kristen Poole, *Supernatural Environments in Shakespeare's England: Spaces of Demonism, Divinity, and Drama* (New York: Cambridge University Press, 2011); Robert L. Reid, "Sacerdotal Vestiges in *The Tempest*," *Comparative Drama* 41, no. 4 (2007): 498; Grace R. W. Hall, *"The Tempest" as Mystery Play: Uncovering*

Religious Sources of Shakespeare's Most Spiritual Work (Jefferson, N.C.: McFarland, 1999), 29; Velma B. Richmond, *Shakespeare, Catholicism, and Romance* (New York: Continuum, 2000), 173; and Mary Frances Williams, "Shakespeare as Catholic Dramatist in *The Tempest*," in *Catholic Theatre and Drama: Critical Essays*, ed. Kevin J. Wetmore Jr. (Jefferson, N.C.: McFarland, 2010), 52.

2. See, for instance, Carlos M. N. Eire, *War Against the Idols: The Reformation of Worship from Erasmus to Calvin* (New York: Cambridge University Press, 1989); Eamon Duffy, *The Stripping of the Altars: Traditional Religion in England, c. 1400–c.1580* (New Haven, Conn.: Yale University Press, 1992); and Michael O'Connell, *The Idolatrous Eye: Iconoclasm and Theater in Early Modern England* (New York: Oxford University Press, 2000).

3. Roberto Bellarmino theorized Catholic sacred space in *Disputationes* (Ingolstadt, 1586–93); Rudolphus Hospinianus developed a Protestant model of sacred space in *De Templis* (Zürich, 1587), reissued in 1603 with a section responding to Bellarmino. See also Catholic and Protestant treatises on urban architecture and sacred space: Jacques Perret, *Des fortifications et artifices* (Paris, 1601); Tommaso Campanella, *The City of the Sun* (Frankfurt, 1623); Johann Valentin Andreae, *Christianopolis* (Strasbourg, 1619). Recent work on the persistence and reemergence of spaces for the sacred includes Will Coster and Andrew Spicer, eds., *Sacred Space in Early Modern Europe* (New York: Cambridge University Press, 2005); Sarah Hamilton and Andrew Spicer, eds., *Defining the Holy: Sacred Space in Medieval and Early Modern Europe* (Aldershot, Hants, UK: Ashgate Publishing, 2005); and Alexandra Walsham, *The Reformation of the Landscape: Religion, Identity, and Memory in Early Modern Britain and Ireland* (New York: Oxford University Press, 2011).

4. C. John Sommerville, *The Secularization of Early Modern England: From Religious Culture to Religious Faith* (New York: Oxford University Press, 1992), 18.

5. Jonathan Z. Smith, *Map Is Not Territory* (Chicago: University of Chicago Press, 1978); Jonathan Z. Smith, *To Take Place: Toward Theory in Ritual* (Chicago: University of Chicago Press, 1987).

6. Thomas Tweed, *Crossing and Dwelling: A Theory of Religion* (Cambridge, Mass.: Harvard University Press, 2006). In this essay, I use the terms employed by Smith (locative and utopian) and Tweed (crossing and dwelling) interchangeably.

7. Martin H. Franzmann, "Seven Theses on Reformation Hermeneutics," *Concordia Theological Monthly* 4, no. 40 (1969): 245. On Reformation hermeneutics, see chapters in Gerald L. Bruns, *Hermeneutics, Ancient and Modern* (New Haven, Conn.: Yale University Press, 1992), and David Jasper, *A Short Introduction to Hermeneutics* (Louisville, Ky.: Westminster John Knox Press, 2004).

8. *Lectures on the Psalms*, cited in Gerhard Ebeling, "The Beginning of Luther's Hermeneutics," *Luther Quarterly* 16 (1993): 319.

9. Michel de Certeau, *The Mystic Fable, Volume One: The Sixteenth and Seventeenth Centuries*, trans. Michael B. Smith (Chicago: University of Chicago Press, 1992).

10. William Shakespeare, *The Tempest*, ed. Virginia Mason Vaughan and Alden T. Vaughan, The Arden Shakespeare, 3rd ser. (London: Arden Shakespeare, 2006), 1.2.20. All references to the play are to this edition, with act, scene, and line information cited parenthetically.

11. In *Romeo and Juliet*, "cell" refers to ecclesiastical space. Friar Laurence's cell is associated with the administering of sacraments, penance and marriage in particular; see 2.3.161–64 and 2.4.67–68. Titus Andronicus refers to the hallowed site of burial as the "sacred receptacle of my joys / Sweet cell of virtue and nobility" (1.1.95–96). See also the entry on "cell" in the *Oxford English Dictionary*, 1a, which lists Shakespeare's use of the term in *Romeo and Juliet* as an example of the term's connotations as spiritual dwelling place.

12. On the home as a site of worship acquiring layers of sanctity, see Alexandra Walsham, "Beads, Books, and Bare Ruined Choirs: Transmutations of Catholic Ritual Life in Protestant England," in *Catholic Communities in Protestant States: Britain and the Netherlands, c. 1570–1720*, ed. Benjamin J. Kaplan et al. (Manchester, UK: Manchester University Press, 2009), 103–22; Benjamin Kaplan, *Divided by Faith: Religious Conflict and the Practice of Toleration in Early Modern Europe* (Cambridge, Mass.: Belknap Press, 2007).

13. Cynthia Lewis notes the inverse relationship between Saint Anthony, the founder of desert monasticism, and Prospero's brother Antonio; *Particular Saints: Shakespeare's Four Antonios, Their Contexts, and Their Plays* (Newark: University of Delaware Press; London: Associated University Presses, 1997), 49.

14. John Calvin, *The Institutes of the Christian Religion*, trans. John T. McNeill and Ford Lewis Battles (Louisville, Ky.: Westminster John Knox Press, 2001), 1.14.20.

15. On *The Tempest* and baptism, see Reid, "Sacerdotal Vestiges," 498; Hall, "*The Tempest*," 29; Richmond, *Shakespeare, Catholicism, and Romance*, 173; and Williams, "Shakespeare as Catholic Dramatist," 52.

16. Gerardus van der Leeuw, *Religion in Essence and Manifestation*, trans. J. E. Turner (1938; repr., Princeton, N.J.: Princeton University Press, 1986), 394–95.

17. David Chidester and Edward T. Linenthal, *American Sacred Space* (Bloomington: Indiana University Press, 1994), 8.

18. Douglas Trevor, "Mapping the Celestial in Shakespeare's *Tempest* and the Writings of John Donne," in *Shakespeare and Donne: Generic Hybrids and the Cultural Imaginary*, ed. Judith H. Anderson and Jennifer C. Vaught (New York: Fordham University Press, 2014). According to Trevor, Caliban, utterly foreign and otherworldly, hopes to escape the narrowly terrestrial Prospero by ascending to the heavens (119).

19. William Perkins, *Christian Oeconomie*, trans. Thomas Pickering (London: Felix Kyngston, 1609), 163–64.

20. On *The Tempest* and the *Aeneid* in the harpy banquet scene, see Virginia Mason Vaughan and Alden T. Vaughan, *Shakespeare's Caliban: A Cultural History* (New York: Cambridge University Press, 1991), 58–60; Robert Reid discusses *The Tempest* as Judeo-Christian mystery play at 497–98.

21. Arnold van Gennep, *The Rites of Passage* (1960; repr., New York: Routledge, 2004), 29.

22. See Eamon Duffy's discussion in *Stripping of the Altars*, 349.

23. The others were praying, associated with *oratoria*; venerating relics, undertaken in *basilicae*; and preaching, accomplished in *ecclesiae*. Roberto Bellarmino's *Disputationes* were based on lectures given at the Collegio Romano in 1576. The work went through numerous editions. For a discussion of Bellarmino's spatial

theory, see also Per Gustav Hamberg, *Temples for Protestants* (Gothenburg, Swed.: Acta Universitatis Gothoburgensis, 2002), 10–15.

24. For Chris Meads the banquet presents a secular "metaphor of court lifestyle, manners, and ritual" (*Banquets Set Forth: Banqueting in English Renaissance Drama* [Manchester: Manchester University Press, 2001], 181). Joseph M. Ortiz acknowledges that in Neoplatonic thought "the inability to be moved by harmonious music is a sign of moral degeneracy" and therefore carries spiritual significance; but he concludes that in the play music's meaning (both Virgilian and Ovidian in nature) is ambiguous rather than clearly religious, and that the banquet as well as the masque scene are performances; *Broken Harmony: Shakespeare and the Politics of Music* (Ithaca, N.Y.: Cornell University Press, 2011), 171, 174. By contrast, I argue that the banquet scene as a whole (music, gesture, and Eucharistic allusion) constitutes a liminal moment during which the sinners glimpse a new path leading toward redemption. The fact that ritual is performative does not invalidate its efficacy.

25. Martin Luther, *Ein Sermon von dem neuen Testament* (Wittenberg, 1520), cited in Hamberg, *Temples for Protestants*, 12.

26. Cited in Lee Palmer Wendell, ed., *A Companion to the Eucharist in the Reformation* (Leiden: Brill, 2014), 151. Grace Tiffany reads grace as a marker of Calvinist theology in the play; "Calvinist Grace in Shakespeare's Romances: Upending Tragedy," *Christianity and Literature* 49, no. 4 (Summer 2000): 421–45. However, for me the play is far more ambivalent in its religious iconography. Indeed, even in reformed congregations ritual labor is required in readying a space where grace can be properly received. In other words, worship space is never "empty" of spiritual meaning—or, to put it differently, secular.

27. On the traditional view of Mary as the sin- and death-defying "antithesis to Eve," see, for example, Marina Warner, *Alone of All Her Sex: The Myth and the Cult of the Virgin Mary* (New York: Vintage Books: 1983), 59–61, and Miri Rubin, *Mother of God: A History of the Virgin Mary* (New Haven, Conn.: Yale University Press, 2009), 37–38. On Marian pilgrimage and the carrying of a penitential cross by pilgrims, see, for instance Joseba Zulaika, *Basque Violence: Metaphor and Sacrament* (Las Vegas: University of Nevada Press, 2000), 272; Jill Dubisch and Michael Vinkelman, eds., *Pilgrimage and Healing* (Tucson: University of Arizona Press, 2005), 61–62. To this day at Altötting in southern Germany, pilgrims carry crosses around the chapel of the Black Madonna; I last observed this practice in the summer of 2012. A frequently reprinted work by the theologian Martin Eisengrein revived Altötting as a major pilgrimage site in the sixteenth century; *Historia Mariae Veteris Oettingensis* (Ingolstadt, 1571).

28. On Miranda as a version of the Virgin Mary, see Peter Milward, *Shakespeare's Religious Background* (Bloomington: Indiana University Press, 1973), 26, 29. See also Reid, "Sacerdotal Vestiges," 500.

29. We could view that marriage through the lens of territorial acquisition, as a good many critics have done, but this perspective fails to address the spiritual cast of the wedding scene. On patriarchalism and colonialism in reference to Miranda, see Ania Loomba, *Gender, Race, Renaissance Drama* (Manchester, UK: Manchester University Press, 1989), 153–55, and Jyotsna G. Singh, "Caliban versus Miranda," in *Feminist Readings of Early Modern Culture: Emerging*

Subjects, eds. Valerie Traub, M. Lindsay Kaplan, and Dympna Callaghan (New York: Cambridge University Press, 1996), 191–207.

30. In the English translation of Pierre Viret's *Les cauteles, canon et ceremonies de la Messe* (Lyon, 1564), the first chapter heading reads, "Howe and in what maner the priest that will say Masses is to prepare himselfe, & what gestures & countenances he must use therein, & likewise, all the cunning devises of legier de main or juggling required thereto." The title of Viret's book insists on the shiftiness of consecrating gestures; *The Cauteles, Canon, and Ceremonies*, trans. Thomas Stocker (London, 1596), 1. The term *cautel* means "crafty device, artifice, stratagem, a trick, sleight of hand, device"; its first appearance is in Wyclif's *Sermons*; *Oxford English Dictionary*, 1a, retrieved August 24, 2015, http://www.oed.com.ezproxy.stonehill.edu/view/Entry/29186?rskey=t2eIlt&result=1&isAdvanced=false#eid.

31. On sanctuary mode, see Lindsay Jones, *The Hermeneutics of Sacred Architecture, Volume 2: Hermeneutical Calisthenics* (Cambridge, Mass.: Harvard University Press, 2000), 264–68.

32. Jones, *Hermeneutics*, 225.

33. Jones, *Hermeneutics*, 225.

34. Andrew Gurr points out that because of the physical limitations of early modern theaters audiences were quite aware of theater as "illusion," and playwrights such as Shakespeare exploited the stage's metatheatrical aspects; *Playgoing in Shakespeare's London*, 2nd ed. (New York: Cambridge University Press, 2002), 105, 108. Yet *The Tempest*'s metatheatrics demonstrate the efficacy of spatial performance.

35. Hamish M. Scott, ed., *The Oxford Handbook of Early Modern History, 1350–1750, Volume 1: People and Places* (New York: Oxford University Press, 2015), 727.

36. Philip Sheldrake, *Spaces for the Sacred: Place, Memory, and Identity* (Baltimore: Johns Hopkins University Press, 2000), 168. See also C. Michael Weldon, *A Struggle for Holy Ground: Reconciliation and the Rites of Parish Closure* (Collegeville, Minn.: Liturgical Press, 2004), 49–80.

37. Tertullian, *De Paenitentia* 4.2, cited in Mark J. Boda and Gordon T. Smith, eds., *Repentance in Christian Theology* (Collegeville, Minn.: Liturgical Press, 2006), 240. On "shipwreck" as a penitential metaphor, see Rachel Deagman's essay in the present volume.

38. See Dympna Callaghan's discussion of Prospero's spatial domination of Caliban in *Shakespeare Without Women: Representing Gender and Race on the Renaissance Stage* (New York: Routledge, 2000), 158.

39. In Keith Thomas's reading it is a turning away from materialist (Catholic) superstition and marks the first step toward a secular world; *Religion and the Decline of Magic* (New York: Oxford University Press, 1971). See also James Kearney's insightful refutation of Thomas's argument in *The Incarnate Text: Imagining the Book in Reformation England* (Philadelphia: University of Pennsylvania Press, 2009), 219–40.

40. William Shakespeare, *The Tempest*, ed. Stephen Orgel (New York: Oxford University Press, 1987), 204.

41. See Vaughan and Vaughan, *Shakespeare's Caliban*, 308n20.

42. See Ralph Yarrow and Frank Chamberlain's statement about theater's capacity to initiate a "performative movement outside the known configuration of self and world" in *Sacred Theatre* (Chicago: Intellect Books, University of Chicago Press, 2007), 18.

43. Henri Lefebvre, *The Production of Space*, trans. Donald Nicholson-Smith (1991; repr., Malden, Mass.: Blackwell Publishing, 2007), 222.

Part Four

Secular Aesthetics

Shakespeare and the Hymnody of State

Angela Heetderks

In two of Shakespeare's history plays, the staging of a medieval hymn, the *Te Deum*, blurs the boundaries between the sacred and the secular. It also bridges the historiographic divide between medieval and early modern, as well as the confessional divide between Catholic and Protestant. In *Henry V*, following the battle of Agincourt, the English king orders that the dead be buried and that the *Te Deum* and the psalm *Non nobis* be sung. In *Henry VIII*, or *All Is True*, a gentleman relates how the choir has sung *Te Deum* at the coronation of Queen Anne. In each play, the *Te Deum* signals the aural dimension of the pageantry by which a monarch enacts his will.[1] At first glance, the kings in these plays appear to use the *Te Deum* to shore up their political authority. Indeed, Holinshed's accounts of the monarchical uses of the *Te Deum* support this interpretation. A closer examination of the hymn's liturgical and musical history reveals that such sung invocations in these scenes do not merely use sacred ceremony to reinforce political pomp. Rather than underwrite political and ecclesiastical power, Shakespeare's hymnody illuminates its instability. In these plays, the performance of sacred art both enacts and questions secular power.

Staged performances of the *Te Deum* and other hymns and psalms refute the too-neat historiographies that, as the editors of this volume summarize, move "from a medieval, superstitious, and thoroughly religious society to a secular modernity."[2] These hymns demand a scholarly accounting that moves as nimbly between medieval and early modern, Catholic and Protestant, sacred and secular motifs as do the plays themselves. In *Henry V*, the *Te Deum* performs doubly as thanksgiving hymn for a political victory and requiem for the men and boys slain in battle. In *Henry VIII*, scenes portraying the physical and political decline of Anne's predecessor, the cast-off Queen Katherine, precede and follow the exaltation of Anne in her coronation, reminding audiences that political glory, even when propped up by ecclesiastical pomp, is fleeting. Both plays ask audiences to reflect on the power of the state as instantiated in princely bodies—in the one, the kingly body; in the other, the two queenly bodies. In both scenes, the sung *Te Deum* is a performance of religious devotion that spans political and ecclesiastical realms.

The *Te Deum*'s long-standing role in western Christian liturgy (of both Catholic and reformed varieties) made it an ideal hymn for a playwright like Shakespeare, who was invested in portraying the always-entangled relationship between sacred and secular power across the Reformation divide.[3] One of the most ancient ecclesiastical texts, the *Te Deum* is first attested in the *Rule of Saint Benedict* in the sixth century, by which point the hymn was probably already a well-known part of the liturgy.[4] Because it was a thousand-year-old hymn by Shakespeare's day, it could serve as a key to reading devotional, aesthetic, and political change across time. That is, it functioned as a *performed*, rather than theoretical, witness to the exercise of sacred and secular power in an early modern playwright's representation of the medieval past. It was a familiar part of English liturgy in Shakespeare's day, having become integral to early Protestant devotional practice when Thomas Cranmer included its English translation as part of the service of Morning Prayer in the *Book of Common Prayer*.[5] The 1549 Act of Uniformity, by which Parliament stipulated that all ministers should perform services "in such order and form as is mentioned" in the *Book of Common Prayer*, specifically mentions "Matins" (Morning Prayer) as one of the key services to follow the new liturgy.[6] Because the 1549 *Book of Common Prayer* required that the *Te Deum* be said throughout the year, except in Lent, the inclusion of the *Te Deum* in the Morning Prayer service made it a quotidian part of the lives of frequent churchgoers.[7] The *Book of Common Prayer*'s accessibility to unlearned churchgoers made it an ideal ecclesiastical tool of a state newly unleashed from the papacy. As Alan Jacobs writes, "The *Book of Common Prayer* came into being as an instrument of social and political control."[8] The prayer book's political genesis was inextricable from efforts to make it the backbone of devotional practice in the English Reformation.

Accordingly, and in contrast with the stately grandeur with which the *Te Deum* is associated in *Henry V* and *Henry VIII*, the hymn's context in the Morning Prayer service is designed to be transparently accessible. The directions for the performance of Morning Prayer emphasize a simple, clear, vernacular aesthetic. In the first (1549) edition of the *Book of Common Prayer*, the instructions following the readings of the lessons from the Bible and preceding the singing of the *Te Deum* say,

> *And (to the ende the people maye the better heare) in suche places where they do synge, there shall the lessons be songe in a plaine tune after the maner of distinct readinge: and likewise the Epystle and gospell.*
>
> *After the firste lesson shall folowe,* Te deum laudamus, *in Englyshe dayly throughe the whole yere.*[9]

Cummings's editorial gloss on the instruction to sing "*in a plaine tune after the maner of distinct readinge*" reminds us that this rubric works aesthetically and theologically, "referring to the argument (expressed explicitly by Cranmer) that musical performance should assist meaning rather than conceal it, by making one syllable correspond to one note."[10] Cranmer, like the continental Reformers, preferred simple—that is, both vernacular and syllabic—musical settings in contradistinction to complex Latin choral polyphony. The liturgical aesthetic dictated by Cranmer via the *Book of Common Prayer* made direct participation in the service attainable by all parishioners, regardless of class, knowledge of Latin, or even literacy. That is, the book that had been created in order to effect *secular* sociopolitical control introduced a participatory, sacred aesthetic into the daily lives of English churchgoers.

The aesthetic enjoined by the *Book of Common Prayer*'s instructions and liturgy was borne out in vernacular musical settings of the *Te Deum* by Thomas Tallis and William Byrd, both composers favored by Queen Elizabeth I. Just as Cranmer set the stage for English Protestant worship by creating a clear vernacular liturgy, Tallis and Byrd created a clear musical aesthetic that was accessible to lay listeners. While both men had composed Latin pieces for Catholic services, their vernacular service music was especially conducive to the aims of English Protestant liturgical reforms. The *Te Deum* from Tallis's *Short ("Dorian") Service* is largely homophonic—that is, the four parts move lockstep in roughly the same rhythm. The rhythmic similarity allows the words to be heard and understood with ease.[11] The *Te Deum* from Byrd's *Great Service*, while more polyphonic, clearly foregrounds the vernacular English text.[12] Both settings begin with a solo intonation of the hymn's opening words, "We prayse thee, O God," followed by a homophonic setting of the next phrase, "We knoweledge thee to be the Lorde." The effect of the solo chant and homophony is to render the text as intelligible as possible to listeners; the subject ("we") and object ("God"/"the Lorde") of praise and knowledge are made aurally clear. Byrd sets the next line of text, "All the earth doth worship thee, the Father everlastynge," more polyphonically, as if to compel listeners to hear the great plurality of voices contained in "all the earth." Still, throughout each of these *Te Deum* settings, both Byrd and Tallis eschew the more intricate, melismatic styles available to sixteenth-century composers, favoring instead clear entrances and syllabic settings of one note per syllable in order to make the English words intelligible to lay listeners' ears. While this clear, accessible aesthetic is not absent from Tallis's and Byrd's Latin-language settings, it lends itself particularly well to their purpose of making the Englished liturgical texts of the *Book of Common Prayer* available to newly Protestant churchgoers.[13]

Would this Protestant aesthetic have been audible in the singing of the *Te Deum* in Shakespeare's *Henry V*, a play that takes place in England's pre-Reformation past but that was first performed for officially Protestant playgoers late in the reign of Elizabeth I? Here, as elsewhere in premodern drama, clues about early performance practices are inconveniently scant. Firm evidence for whether the *Te Deum* and *Non nobis* would have been sung in Latin or English, let alone what musical settings would have been used, is lacking, although the availability of English settings like Byrd's and Tallis's would have made a vernacular performance feasible.[14] Some clues can be found in Holinshed's *Chronicles*, the source from which Shakespeare borrows the idea that the *Te Deum* would have been sung to mark key ceremonial moments, including the victory at the end of the Battle of Agincourt and the coronation of Anne Boleyn. Holinshed mentions numerous performances of the *Te Deum*, almost all of which mark triumphs of the state: victories in battle, royal weddings, and coronations. Holinshed, who criticizes "popish" beliefs when he discusses such early modern hot-button topics as Spanish military victories, does not explicitly associate the *Te Deum* with either Roman Catholic doctrine or more generally pre-Reformation practices. This treatment suggests that the *Te Deum*'s incorporation in the service of Morning Prayer made it seem fully assimilated into Protestant practice by the last quarter of the sixteenth century, even as it would also have been resonant with pre-Reformation, Catholic practice.

Accordingly, Holinshed's narration of the singing of the *Te Deum* and a psalm after Henry V's victory at Agincourt is confessionally neutral:

> The king when he saw no appearance of enimies, caused the retreit to be blowen; and gathering his armie togither, gave thanks to almightie God for so happie a victorie, causing his prelats and chapleins to sing this psalme: In exitu Israel de Aegypto, and commanded everie man to kneele downe on the ground at this verse: Non nobis Domine, non nobis, sed nomini tuo da gloriam. Which

> doone, he caused Te Deum, with certeine anthems to be soong, giving laud and praise to God, without boasting of his own force or anie humane power.[15]

This narration glosses over pre- and post-Reformation confessional differences in order to portray the king's actions as broadly pious: Holinshed depicts the king giving credit to God for the victory, without quibbling as to the specific theological content of the expression of praise. At the same time, the explicit statement that the king is not "boasting of his own force or anie humane power" reminds readers of the king's monarchical power under the guise of showing forth the king's piety. Holinshed's blending of secular kingly power with religious piety, as well as Protestant with Catholic worship, sets a precedent for Shakespeare's blurring of these seemingly opposed categories.

Shakespeare's staging of the psalm depicts the king's piety in a slightly more Protestantized form, subtly hinting at the sixteenth-century migration of English ecclesiastical power toward both the monarch and Elizabeth's Anglican church. Whereas Holinshed narrates in some detail the singing of Psalm 114 ("In exitu Israel") and the *Te Deum*, Shakespeare transforms Holinshed's narration into a succinct declaration by the king himself. After inquiring about the numbers and ranks of the dead on both sides, the king proclaims,

> KING HARRY: Do we all holy rites:
> Let there be sung *Non nobis* and *Te Deum*,
> The dead with charity enclosed in clay;
> And then to Calais, and to England then,
> Where ne'er from France arrived more-happy men. (4.8.116–20)

Henry's order for the singing of the hymn and the psalm is both more concise and more Protestantized than it is in Holinshed. As Richmond Noble notes, Shakespeare changes Holinshed's allusion to the Vulgate's and Service Book's Psalm 114 in order to make the allusion more transparent to Protestant readers, who would have been familiar with the different ordering and division of the Psalms in the vernacular Bibles of Protestant England.[16] "In exitu Israel" and "Non nobis" are one continuous psalm in the Latin Vulgate (Psalm 113), but they are numbered as Psalms 114 and 115, respectively, in the English Protestant Bibles of the late sixteenth century.[17] While Holinshed's recounting of Henry V's order that laudatory hymns be sung reflects the customs of early fifteenth-century English devotion, Shakespeare translates the king's devotion into terms more familiar to post-Reformation playgoers. This Catholic-to-Protestant translation makes both the sacred and secular dimensions of the scene legible to his audience: Shakespeare's Protestantizing is thus an act of *preserving*, rather than removing, playgoers' access to medieval Catholic kingship.

In the vernacular Bibles available to English Protestants of Shakespeare's era, Psalm 115 ("Non nobis") would have seemed to point toward the humble piety of the king and his singing army. The psalm opens, "Geve praise not unto us O God, not unto us, but unto thy name: for thy loving mercy, and for thy truethes sake."[18] This opening verse seems to point away from temporal matters, such as the claims of an English monarch on French lands, and toward eternal ones. Most playgoers would have been familiar with the entirety of the psalm, whose later verses are less suited to burial and funeral rites:

> The dead prayse not thee O Lorde: neither all they that go downe into the [place] of scilence.
> But we wyll prayse the Lord: from this tyme foorth for evermore. Prayse ye the Lorde.[19]

These lines, alluded to or possibly even sung as bodies are removed from the battlefield, detract from the portrayal (derived from Holinshed) of the king as a model of pious power. Shakespeare's King Henry's decree that the English army "do . . . all holy rites" (4.8.116) seems to share Holinshed's king's aim of "giving laud and praise to God."[20] But in Shakespeare's scene, the bodies of the dead, who "prayse not" God, as the psalm reminds us, must be subtracted from the sum total of "all" those "holy rites" that are meant simultaneously to revere the dead and to offer praise. If sung aloud, the *Te Deum* and *Non nobis* are intoned by a straggling, battle-weary army charged with burying the very bodies whose death reminds the audience that the king's power to order praise is bounded by the grave. Instead of underwriting the triumphal coronation of a monarch, this hymn and this psalm stage the limitations of the king's power. The king's official view of the victory as God-given remains in tension with the audience's view of the slain bodies that enabled the gift.

If *Henry V* blurs the boundaries between sacred and secular, Protestant and Catholic in order to render the Catholic past legible to Shakespeare's Protestant audiences, *Henry VIII* plays up the distinctions between these categories. Indeed, it theorizes them, rubbing playgoers' noses in the politico-ecclesial details of the transition from Catholic to Protestant England. As in *Henry V*, the monarch's deployment of secular power through sacred hymnody is central to the play's depiction of its sacred and secular coordinates. At first blush, the *Te Deum* in *Henry VIII* seems to depict unlimited kingly power. As a part of the new Queen Anne's coronation in act 4, scene 1, the hymn reminds audiences of the enormous religiopolitical power that Henry wielded in his pursuit of a divorce from Katherine and marriage to Anne. The grand coronation scene shows churchmen and laypeople, nobles and commoners alike participating in the ceremony that enacts the king's will. In this scene, the professional choir's performance of the *Te Deum* unites voices in the corporate singing of praise—praise directed ostensibly toward God but implicitly toward the king. The stage directions, which are unusually (and famously) copious for a Shakespearean play, are especially attentive to the aural features of the coronation scene. Before the procession enters, there is an offstage trumpet flourish and the sound of hautbois.[21] The stage directions denote, "*Choristers singing. Music*," proffering the tantalizing possibility that the *Te Deum* might have been sung onstage in early productions. The singers would have evoked the kind of choristers who were trained in a broadly humanist education that included specific training in the performance of liturgical music; some of the actors could even have been former choirboys, or current choirboys might have been used in court performances.[22] The entire procession, upon its exit, is followed by "*a great flourish of trumpets*." The effect of this scene is to prime playgoers to think about not only the visual spectacle but also the aural grandeur of state ceremonies imbued with both royal and ecclesiastical power.[23] The choristers' singing and embodied presence alike remind the audience of the many lives dedicated entirely to the performance of the king's and bishops' wills.

It is fitting, then, that this corporate triumph, with all its implications for the body politic, is celebrated by the *Te Deum*, a hymn that unites the familiarity and simplicity—not to mention the incipient Protestantism—of Morning Prayer with the long pre- and post-Reformation traditions of the pomp of state.[24] The Third Gentleman's narration of the scene increasingly links the bodily sanctity of the new queen to the hymn's aural celebration of her political triumph:

> At length her grace rose, and with modest paces
> Came to the altar, where she kneeled, and saint-like
> Cast her fair eyes to heaven, and prayed devoutly,
> Then rose again, and bowed her to the people,
> When by the Archbishop of Canterbury
> She had all the royal makings of a queen,
> As holy oil, Edward Confessor's crown,

> The rod and bird of peace, and all such emblems
> Laid nobly on her. Which performed, the choir,
> With all the choicest music of the kingdom,
> Together sung *Te Deum*. (4.1.84–94)

The political and religious strains of the scene harmonize when the Third Gentleman asks his listeners to imagine that, in the *Te Deum*, the many voices of the choir join in the "choicest" aural celebration of the triumphs of the state. This aural celebration is part of an elaborate apparatus of sanctity, which comprises "all such emblems" as are fit to the occasion of presenting the new queen's political suitability to the visual, olfactory, and auditory senses of the audience. Queen Anne is decked out in the symbols of state that signal her bodily ability to fulfill her political purpose. At the same time, these symbols are shot through with religious significance. Indeed, the hymn itself—performed on a stage where sacraments could not be represented outright—enacts the sounds of corporate devotion on a secular stage. It thus constitutes a daring reminder of the play's interwoven religiopolitical skeins. Both the visual spectacle and its aural accompaniment entwine the religious and political strands of the coronation rites until each is inseparable from the other, secular power impossible to disentangle from the sacred.

Like *Henry V*, however, the play soon undercuts its elaborately propagandistic hymnody and spectacle. In *Henry V*, the singing of the *Te Deum* and *Non nobis* is accompanied by the task of burying and performing funeral rites for the slain. In *Henry VIII*, the play calls into question the seemingly triumphal role of the *Te Deum* by juxtaposing the coronation scene with the appearances of the displaced Queen Katherine—who, audiences surely could not help but remember, once heard similarly hymnodic strains at her own coronation. Throughout the play, Katherine serves as a reminder of the pre-Reformation world that has been lost as a result of the Act of Supremacy and attendant reforms in official Church of England liturgies, theology, and devotional practices. Her presence on the stage ensures that Catholicism cannot fully give way to either Protestantism or secularity before her last scene. The character's presence literally embodies the Catholic past.

Perhaps for that reason, the scene immediately following the coronation (act 4, scene 2) draws a sharp contrast—an imaginative one, as both queens would have been played by boys—between the new queen's politically ascendant, fecund body and the old queen's cast-off, aged body. If Anne's body is processed, held on view, and venerated as a real, nearly Eucharistic presence, Katherine's is desacralized. Jay Zysk has argued that the canopy under which Anne enters during the coronation, like the singing of the *Te Deum*, "does more than focus attention on the monarch's body in a political sense . . . ; it also links royal pageantry to the eucharistic ritual that informs it."[25] Similarly, Katherine's entrance, unattended by canopy or hymnody, is divorced from Eucharistic ritual—an irony that would not have been lost on early audiences keenly aware of her role as Henry's Catholic queen. The humble privacy of Katherine's conversation with her attendants, stripped of pomp, serves as the negative image of the public splendor of Anne's coronation. Katherine theorizes her new-fallen status in the language with which she describes herself. When her usher, Griffith, asks, "How does your grace?" she replies,

> O Griffith, sick to death.
> My legs, like loaden branches, bow to th'earth,
> Willing to leave their burden. (4.2.1–3)

If there is literal "secularity" in *Henry VIII*, it is here: the queen's dying body augurs the death of an age, or *saeculum*. The end of her life is attended by the death of a former English understanding of beliefs, rites, sacraments—including marriage, the sacrament most visibly destroyed in Katherine's own life—and, indeed, the relationship of ecclesiastical to state power.

As if to mark again the manner in which the play's movement from pre- to post-Reformation England is marked by aesthetic and, especially, aural moments, Katherine requests to hear music:

> I have not long to trouble thee. Good Griffith,
> Cause the musicians play me that sad note
> I named my knell, whilst I sit meditating
> On that celestial harmony I go to.
> *Sad and solemn music.* [KATHERINE *sleeps.*] (4.2.77–80)

The tableau that follows, which is called *The Vision* in the First Folio's stage directions, depicts dancers who hold garlands aloft over Queen Katherine while the musicians play.[26] Although Katherine's words, "that sad note / I named my knell," seems to indicate music played by mortal musicians for mortal ears, the otherworldly vision associates the musicians' performance with "celestial harmony"—that is, *musica mundana*, or the "music of the spheres." The identification of the music with celestial harmony is underscored by the apparent inability of the attendants present to hear that harmony; it functions similarly in *Pericles*, in which the music of the spheres is inaudible to all but Pericles.[27]

The concept of the "music of the spheres," present in ancient Greek writings and derived in its most influential medieval form from Boethius, had been disseminated throughout later medieval and early modern music theory, and by Shakespeare's time it was prevalent—even a cliché—in Renaissance poetry and drama.[28] Boethius's *De Institutione Musica* divided music into three concentric "spheres." The first and most lowly was *musica instrumentalis*, the audible music played and sung by musicians on earth with the aid of physical instruments; it was considered relatively discordant, a poor copy of the higher spheres. This is the sphere in which the staged performance of Queen Katherine's requested "sad note / I named my knell," and indeed the sung *Te Deum*s and any other staged music, would have been located. The third and highest sphere, *musica mundana*, was cosmic music created by the orbits of the heavenly bodies. Theorists considered its harmonies the purest of those of all the spheres. *Musica mundana* was thought to be audible only to celestial beings.[29] In *The Merchant of Venice*, for example, Lorenzo's rhapsodizing on the theme of *musica mundana* emphasizes that it is unavailable to the ears of mortal listeners:

> There's not the smallest orb which thou behold'st
> But in his motion like an angel sings,
> Still quiring to the young-ey'd cherubins.
> Such harmony is in immortal souls,
> But whilst this muddy vesture of decay
> Doth grossly close it in, we cannot hear it. (5.1.59–65)

In *Henry VIII*, Queen Katherine's ability to hear the music associated with celestial harmony shows that she, as one close to death, has aural access to experiences outside the demesne of both ecclesiastical and political power. Although *musica mundana* was frequently identified with heavenly music throughout medieval and early modern English literature—as in *Henry VIII* and *The Merchant of Venice*—it was not specifically identified with the musical rites of either Church or crown. Those rites belonged to the sphere of *musica instrumentalis*. Since *musica mundana*, by contrast, could not be heard by mortal ears, it was specifically unavailable to the performance—let alone manipulation—of the religious rites that are central to the Reformation-era controversies staged in *Henry VIII*. This music, unidentified with the categories of devotion and secularity that operate in the play, is outside the bounds of the performances of state and ecclesial power that always attend the performance of the *Te Deum* in Shakespearean drama.

As a result, the pomp of the coronation music is superseded by a different, if inaudible, musical idiom. The *musica mundana* of Queen Katherine's vision announces its superiority to the music of temporal pomp that has accompanied Anne's coronation. The elder queen, fallen temporally, is responding to transcendent music, whereas the younger queen has been crowned with an ecclesiastically and politically powerful, but *temporally* located, musical rite. For the moment, the play's juxtaposed forms of music reveal the bounded limitations of both ecclesiastical and political power, which cannot extend into the realm in which the music of the spheres can be heard. At the same time, the play's staging of the vision, whose music is played in real time by embodied musicians, gives the audience access to the music that is meant to stand in for celestial harmony—that is, the music that none but the dying Queen Katherine should hear. The music of the vision, in rendering the inaudible audible, proffers fleeting sounds of a musical aesthetic beyond the reach of the competing theologies and aesthetics of the Catholic and proto-Protestant factions in the play. It is a musical aesthetic beyond the reach of the politico-ecclesial powers that battle over liturgies such as the *Te Deum* and *Non nobis*. Unavailable to those powers, it is performed only for the ears of the playgoers and the fallen queen.[30]

While the celestial harmony of the vision lets playgoers in, however momentarily, on a sempiternal aurality, the *Te Deum* points toward the transience of temporal power. Performed on the Protestant English stage, the *Te Deum* text and its musical settings gesture back in time toward medieval Catholicism, as if demonstrating how many politico-ecclesiastical regimes have been outstayed by these simple liturgical sounds. By showing the interplay of the sacred and secular elements of trans-Reformational musical liturgies, Shakespeare's *Te Deum* demonstrates how hymnody can serve as a tool for changing regimes even while it survives the vagaries of the religiopolitical state. On the battlefields and in the royal processions of Shakespeare's dramas, the hymn stages simultaneous exultation and lamentation, elevating monarchs' bodies while surrounding them with death. Shakespeare's hymnody celebrates stately power even as it presages stately downfall, reminding audiences of the finitude of each passing age.

Notes

1. Early modern English monarchs were attentive to the relationship between music and monarchy. Katherine Butler suggests, for example, that Elizabeth I and her courtiers sought to show an "affinity between musical ability and political skill," such as that adduced by the Duke of Exeter in *Henry V*:

For government, though high and low and lower,
Put into parts, doth keep in one consent,
Congreeing in a full and natural close,
Like music. (1.1.180–83)

See Katherine Butler, *Music in Elizabethan Court Politics* (Woodbridge, Suffolk, UK: Boydell Press, 2015), 28. I have quoted here from *The Norton Shakespeare*, ed. Stephen Greenblatt et al., 2nd ed. (New York: Norton, 2008). Except where indicated otherwise, all citations from *Henry V* and *All Is True* (*Henry VIII*) refer to this edition and are cited parenthetically in the text.

2. See Jay Zysk and Katherine Steele Brokaw's introduction to this volume.

3. Performances of the *Te Deum* bridged sixteenth-century confessional divides, as well as transhistorical ones. This essay discusses *Henry VIII*'s representation of its performance at the coronation of Anne Boleyn in 1533. The hymn was also performed twenty years later upon the accession of Mary I; see *The Accession, Coronation and Marriage of Mary Tudor as Related in Four Manuscripts of the Escorial*, trans. C. V. Malfatti (Barcelona: Malfatti, 1956), 20. In keeping with the transconfessional nature of such hymns, post-Reformation musical settings of the *Te Deum* show pre-Reformation influences. John Aplin argues that the *Te Deum* chant from the medieval plainsong tradition shaped the tonal design of post-Reformation *Te Deum* settings by Anglican composers in the sixteenth and seventeenth centuries; "The Survival of Plainsong in Anglican Music: Some Early English Te-Deum Settings," *Journal of the American Musicological Society* 32, no. 2 (Summer 1979): 247–75.

4. See Brian Cummings's brief discussion of the history of the liturgical text in *The Book of Common Prayer: The Texts of 1549, 1559, and 1662* (Oxford: Oxford University Press, 2011), 692–93.

5. See Alan Jacobs, *The "Book of Common Prayer": A Biography* (Princeton, N.J.: Princeton University Press), 28–34.

6. Gerald Bray, ed., *Documents of the English Reformation* (Minneapolis: Fortress Press, 1994), 67.

7. The 1559 and 1662 editions offer a choice between the *Te Deum* and another canticle, *Benedicite omnia opera Domini domino*; see Cummings, *Book of Common Prayer*, 107, 244.

8. Jacobs, "*Book of Common Prayer*," 7.

9. Cummings, *Book of Common Prayer*, 106.

10. Cummings, *Book of Common Prayer*, 692.

11. John Harley links these compositional choices to post-Reformation theological and liturgical changes: "The Te Deum seems to acknowledge both the Anglican preference for clarity and moderation, and a new need to get through a long text without undue delay" (*Thomas Tallis* [Burlington, Vt.: Ashgate Publishing, 2015], 80).

12. Craig Monson suggests that Byrd derived this style, including its foregrounding of the text, from Tallis's *Short ("Dorian") Service*; "'Throughout All Generations': Intimations of Influence in the Short Service Styles of Tallis, Byrd and Morley," in *Byrd Studies*, ed. Alan Brown and Richard Turbet (Cambridge: Cambridge University Press, 1992), 84.

13. The line between Catholic and Protestant English musical idioms is sometimes blurry: Tallis (born around 1505) began his musical career well before

Henry VIII's break with Rome, and Byrd (born around 1540) turned in the 1590s increasingly toward composing Latin musical settings for Catholic worship.

14. There is no clear stage direction indicating that the *Non nobis* and *Te Deum* must be sung, and it is possible to imagine that they would have been omitted, although such an omission would seem discordant with the practices of the music-filled Shakespearean stage. See Louis C. Elson, *Shakespeare in Music* (Boston: Page, 1900).

15. Raphael Holinshed, *Holinshed's Chronicles of England, Scotland, and Ireland*, vol. 3 (London: J. Johnson, etc., 1808), 82.

16. Richmond Noble, *Shakespeare's Biblical Knowledge and Use of the Book of Common Prayer* (New York: Macmillan, 1935), 80–81.

17. Joseph Candido analyzes the implications for *Henry V* of the psalm's contextual apparatus in the Geneva Bible; "Henry V's *Non Nobis*," *Notes and Queries* 50, no. 1 (March 2003): 42–43.

18. Psalm 115:1, from the Bishops' Bible, *The holie Bible conteynyng the olde Testament and the newe* (London: Richard Jugge, 1568).

19. Psalm 115:17–18, Bishops' Bible.

20. Holinshed, *Holinshed's Chronicles*, 82.

21. For the First Folio's extensive stage directions in this scene, see William Shakespeare and John Fletcher, *The Famous History of the Life of King Henry Eight*, in *Mr. William Shakespeares Comedies, Histories, & Tragedies, Published according to the True Originall Copies* (First Folio), London, 1623, Internet Shakespeare Editions (University of Victoria), 223–25; available at http://internetshakespeare.uvic.ca/Library/facsimile/book/Bran_F1/559/?work=H8, accessed February 16, 2016.

22. For further discussion of choristers' training in the years preceding and following the English Reformation, see Hyun-Ah Kim, *Humanism and the Reform of Sacred Music in Early Modern England: John Merbecke the Orator and The Booke of Common Praier Noted* (Aldershot, Hants, UK: Ashgate Publishing, 2008).

23. The play's aural pageantry is not limited to this moment. As Gordon McMullan has noted, although *Henry VIII* is not usually remembered as one of Shakespeare's more music-filled plays, it contains many musical moments, including the singing of "Orpheus, with His Lute" for Queen Katherine by one of her women (3.1.3–14). See William Shakespeare and John Fletcher, *King Henry VIII (All Is True)*, ed. Gordon McMullan (London: Arden Shakespeare, 2000).

24. Jay Zysk notes, "Shakespeare and Fletcher do not add the *Te Deum* as an original detail but rather retain it from Holinshed. But by no means is it an exclusively religious signifier. After all, it was used for a range of non-liturgical purposes, such the confirmation of England's victory over the French at the battle of Agincourt in *Henry V*. The use of the hymn in *Henry VIII* is different, however, for here it is contextualized by the textual description and dramatic procession of Anne's body as a real, metaphysical presence and thus operates as a metonymic reminder for the traditional devotions that were suppressed after Elizabeth I's reforms" ("Of Ceremonies and *Henry VIII*," in *Stages of Engagement: Drama and Religion in Post-Reformation England*, ed. James D. Mardock and Kathryn R. McPherson [Pittsburgh: Duquesne University Press], 251).

25. Zysk, "Of Ceremonies," 252.

26. Shakespeare and Fletcher, *Famous History*, 226.

27. *Pericles*, scene 21, ll. 209–20, in *The Norton Shakespeare*.

28. For recent discussions of the relationship of the concept of the music of the spheres to Shakespeare's work, see Katherine Steele Brokaw, *Staging Harmony: Music and Religious Change in Early English Drama* (Ithaca, N.Y.: Cornell University Press, 2016), and Joseph Ortiz, *Broken Harmony: Shakespeare and the Politics of Music* (Ithaca, N.Y.: Cornell University Press, 2011).

29. The middle sphere, *musica humana*, referred to the odd concept of an inaudible music supposedly created by the workings of humans' inner organs. As John Hollander writes, it "paralleled the cosmic music in causing 'a blending of the body's elements.'" Though supposed less dissonant than *musica instrumentalis*, it could not compare to the music of the highest sphere; *The Untuning of the Sky: Ideas of Music in English Poetry, 1500–1700* (Hamden, Conn.: Archon Books, 1993), 25.

30. For a consideration of the interpretive implications of staging putatively inaudible music by having it played by real musicians, see, on *The Tempest* and *The Winter's Tale*, Brokaw, *Staging Harmony*, 188–231.

Mirror Images: Mary and Hermione, Idolatry and Iconoclasm

Emma Maggie Solberg

Like an optical illusion, *The Winter's Tale*'s statue scene can be seen as a performance of either idolatry or iconoclasm: either as a throwback to medieval Catholic devotional practice or as an early modern reformation of that practice, interpreted in hindsight as an error.[1] After all, as James Simpson has pointed out, "Idolatrous practice is always, necessarily, in the eye of the beholder; no one ever confesses to idolatry, and there can be no reliable empirical test for it."[2] Yet the master narrative of secular progress depends on the opposition of idolatry and iconoclasm.[3] In fact, according to what Herbert Butterfield has called Whig history, the debunking of medieval miracles by early modern iconoclasts marked the shift from the premodern to the modern, from the Dark Ages of superstition to the dawning of the secular Enlightenment.[4] Reacting against this master narrative, nineteenth-century Catholic apologists and twentieth-century revisionist historians have bemoaned the loss of premodern enchantment and the onset of modern disillusionment.[5] This essentially sectarian debate between these two versions of history has shaped the reception of *The Winter's Tale*'s statue scene, often splitting its meaning into the oppositional categories of idolatry and iconoclasm, enchantment and reason.[6] When put into context with its theatrical and ritualistic antecedents (medieval Catholic ritual and drama as well as the Reformation spectacles of iconoclasm that grew out of those traditions), the statue of Hermione reveals a hermeneutics of sacred *and* secular: "both/and," as Barbara Newman would have it.[7] *The Winter's Tale*'s statue scene can be read as a ritual of both idolatry and iconoclasm, two seemingly opposite—but strangely indistinguishable—rituals.

In one sense, this scene invites a not-so-crypto-Catholic reading in which the statue of Hermione takes on the qualities of an icon of the Virgin.[8] When Leontes brings his long-lost daughter "to see the statue of our queen" (5.3.10), Perdita says (open-endedly, addressing Paulina, her father, and the audience), "Do not say 'tis superstition, that / I kneel and then implore her blessing" (5.3.43–44).[9] The figure is described as "our queen"—so close to Our Lady. Devotees kneel before it and ask for its blessing. And like a medieval statue of the Virgin, it can miraculously come to life.[10] So many medieval legends recount reports of moving images of Mary: statues that bleed, weep, smile, and descend from their pedestals to intervene in the lives of saints and sinners.[11] These legends were popular across many media, including drama, as is evident despite the paucity of extant English saint plays.[12] When performed on the stage, moving-statue miracles of the Virgin—like the statue scene of *The Winter's Tale*, which they strikingly resemble—played with the distinctions between actor and image, life and art, icon and idol.[13]

In one early theatrical Miracle of Our Lady, the Cornish *Beunans Meriasek* (The life of Saint Meriasek), a desperate supplicant kidnaps the image of the baby Jesus from a statue of the Madonna and Child (played by a statue) and holds it ransom, thereby motivating Mary in heaven (played by an actor or actress) to answer the kidnapper's prayers.[14] The simultaneity of traditional Cornish staging in a circular *plen an gwary* (round playing space, amphitheater) sets up a mirror image: the prop statue of Mary standing on one platform (representing a chapel) reflects the actor playing Mary on another platform (representing heaven).[15] As Michael Camille explains, this mirroring supports a conservatively orthodox distinction between *latria* and *idolatria*: idols animated by evil spirits appear to "come to life" and move of their own volition, while sacred icons remain respectfully "still and silent."[16]

An early miracle play about Saint Nicholas (*Le Jeu de saint Nicolas*) represents this distinction by carefully contrasting a three-dimensional and animated figure of the Saracen idol Tervagant played by a gilded actor against a two-dimensional and static image representing the saint, played by an object.[17] This play stages its final miraculous climax by means of doubling: an actor playing Nicholas descends from heaven to stand beside his appropriately unmoving image, clarifying the message that good Christian images, unlike their idolatrous others, do not encroach on the mobility that belongs to angels, saints, and the members of the Trinity.

Beunans Meriasek's statue of the Virgin knows its place: it is a lifeless sign, devoid of agency. Or so it may seem. Although *Beunans Meriasek* may at first glance seem to clarify the difference between signifier and signified (or rather between the breathing performer playing the Virgin in heaven and the wooden statue representing the image of the Virgin on her pedestal), the text also blurs those categories.[18] While the earlier *Jeu de saint Nicolas* painstakingly sets up a clear difference between a flat icon and a moving actor, the later *Beunans Meriasek* contrasts two much less-distinct categories: an actor and a life-size statue. What Kenneth Gross wrote about the statue scene in *The Winter's Tale* could also be said of *Beunans Meriasek*: "It is a testing of the idea of theater, of the conventions of dramatic unconcealment, of the ethical and epistemological burdens of fictions of recognition."[19]

This slippery distinction between statue and actor is complicated even further by the fourteenth-century French *La nonne qui laissa son abbaie* (The nun who left her abbey, from *Les miracles de Nostre Dame par personnages*), in which a statue of Our Lady moves to bar the door when a naughty nun attempts to run away with her lover.[20] The staging technique of *décor simultané* (simultaneous or multiple settings) calls for a tiered set in which a statue of the Virgin stands on a lower platform representing a chapel and an actor or actress playing the "real" Virgin stands higher up in heaven.[21] When the actor or actress playing Mary descends from heaven to perform miracles in the fallen world, he or she replaces rather than replicates the statue of Mary. The script suggests that this switch occurred in the sight of the spectators, thereby letting them in on the ensuing dramatic irony: while the nun thinks that she kneels before a statue, the audience knows that she kneels before the saint herself—or rather an actor or actress playing the part of the saint. The script requires that the actor or actress playing Mary twice stand stock-still for twenty-odd lines as the nun prays before him or her, allowing the audience ample time to enjoy the timeless pleasure of watching a person pretend to be a statue.[22] Then comes the inevitable miracle: the living statue breaks form and "displaces itself to block this door."[23] As in *The Winter's Tale*, a theatrical trick turns the otherwise unremarkable aliveness of a performer into a special effect that can "strike all that look upon with marvel" (5.3.100).

Miracles of Our Lady—like Catholic drama more broadly—no longer played on the English stage by the time *The Winter's Tale* first appeared in the Stationers' Register in the early seventeenth century.[24] Gone, but not forgotten.[25] Shakespeare could have seen civic biblical drama performed not only in Coventry before the plays were suppressed in 1579 but also in London (or Kendal or Preston) as late as 1605—not so very long before the first record of a performance of *The Winter's Tale* in 1611.[26] Many medieval theatrical conventions (like vices, cat-tearing tyrants, and the three-tiered cosmic stage) survived and thrived in the early modern commercial theater despite the cultural upheaval of the Reformation. As Kurt Schreyer has argued, "the material base" of staging practices changed surprisingly little between the sixteenth and early seventeenth century: acting companies preferred to stick with the "tried-and-true" staging technologies of their predecessors.[27]

But not all medieval theatrical traditions translated so easily onto the commercial stage. Miracles of the Virgin—the closest theatrical antecedent for *The Winter's Tale*'s statue scene—stand out in particular.[28] Hermione's statue, as both Perdita's and Paulina's disclaimers evince, takes on the risk of triggering Protestant outrage. Perdita feels the need to disavow "superstition" (5.3.43), and Paulina the dark influence of "wicked powers" (5.3.91). Protestant reformers were appalled by the rank idolatry (as it seemed to them) of venerating the image of a saint when all worship rightly belonged to God alone. As the reformer William Crashaw put it, "Such idols of indignation doth the Romish harlot advance against the sovereign majesty of God, to provoke him withal."[29] And yet despite the ascendancy of the reformist position on iconography in the early seventeenth century, Shakespeare—as Michael O'Connell writes—at least "for the moment" of the final scene of *The Winter's Tale*, "fully associates theatre with idolatry, [and] does not counter, but embraces the charge."[30]

In another sense, however, Shakespeare's statue scene seems to demystify Catholic "superstition" (5.3.43)—in that it turns out that the seeming miracle is an elaborately constructed special effect. Hermione never died (5.3.128–29), and the acclaimed statue by "that rare Italian master, Julio Romano," never existed (5.2.74). As Julia Lupton has it, "The play's rationalizing deflation of its carefully staged mystery definitively undercuts the Catholic iconography the scene so powerfully evokes, enacting the movement from the Church to its Reform."[31] Specifically, the scene reenacts the famous spectacular humiliations of Catholic images that reached their peak in 1538.[32] During that year, iconoclasts specifically targeted statues of Jesus and Mary ("those roods and these our Ladies") that were said to have miraculous powers of motion.[33] Perhaps the most famous of these miraculous images was the Rood of Boxley. According to legend, this life-size crucifix could weep, bleed, nod, beckon, and even step right off its pedestal.[34] In his *Acts and Monuments* (1583), John Foxe describes how the Rood of Boxley seemed to be able "to goggle with the eyes, to nod with his head, to hang the lip, to move and shake his jaws."[35] According to the Protestant chronicler William Lambard, the monks of Boxley Abbey demanded that spectators pay to see the show—as if they were customers at the Paris Garden or the Bell Savage.[36]

While sifting through the contents of the priory of Boxley after the dissolution of the monasteries, agents of the crown came upon this rood. According to reports sent to Thomas Cromwell, these agents found levers, wires, and engines hidden inside the statue's frame.[37] Cromwell's men brought the Rood of Boxley into the marketplace at Maidstone and exposed its internal mechanisms to the townspeople in order that they might witness "the false, crafty, and subtle handling thereof, to the dishonor of God, and illusion of the said people."[38] Cromwell then had the statue transported first to Westminster and next to London, where Bishop John Hilsey used it as a kind of theatrical and yet also antitheatrical prop in a sermon against idolatry—a rousing tirade that climaxed with Hilsey inviting the spectators to tear the image apart. As Wriothesley's *Chronicle* puts it, "The rude people and boys broke the same image in pieces, so that they left not one piece whole."[39]

According to one version of history, this event marked the end of Catholic superstition and the dawn of Protestant truth—a powerful narrative that Whig historians later hitched to the *grand récit* of secular progress.[40] In his *History of England* (1754–61), the Enlightenment philosopher David Hume retells the legend of the debunking of the Rood of Boxley without questioning the sectarian bias he inherited from Foxe, Scot, and Wriothesley.[41] It was not until the nineteenth century, thanks in no small part to the Roman Catholic Relief Act of 1829, that Englishmen started to really question this received account of the Rood of Boxley.[42] The turn began in 1842 with Augustus Pugin, the architect of the neo-Gothic Houses of Parliament, who—not soon after his conversion to Catholicism—denied that such a rood could ever have existed except in the fantasies of iconoclasts.[43] Subsequently, in the 1880s, several Catholic antiquarians, most notably Thomas Edward Bridgett, reinvestigated the matter and concluded that the received account of the matter was "bigoted and biased"—but not entirely fabricated.[44] As Bridgett wrote, "I admit the mechanism, but maintain that the existence of the mechanism gives no presumption whatever of trickery, that it had a perfectly legitimate purpose and use."[45] That purpose and use was devotional pageantry—as Bridgett put it, "childish pageantry if you like, but no imposture."[46]

Historians continue to oscillate between these two established poles. Some maintain the reformist claim that the rood constituted (to quote Philip Butterworth) "deception through mechanical means"; others counter that the image (as Leanne Groeneveld has it) "was not necessarily an object designed to trick or confuse."[47] Under these circumstances, classifying the Rood of Boxley proves difficult. Was it a commedia dell'arte marionette, a cutting-edge clockwork automaton, or merely a wild exaggeration?[48] While Catholic apologists have tended to downplay the statue's verisimilitude and dexterity, arguing instead for (in Bridgett's words) "the movement of eyes and lips, and perhaps of some joints," their antagonists have tended to describe the rood as an ingeniously constructed robot, almost indistinguishable from its human makers.[49] These dueling perspectives, these hermeneutics of the sacred or the secular, have constructed two starkly different versions of the Rood of Boxley: one, a childish toy, and the other a futuristic android (a kind of forerunner of Hal in *2001: A Space Odyssey* and the replicants in *Blade Runner*).[50]

But we need not guess. Art historians, most notably Johannes Taubert and Johannes Tripps, have catalogued hundreds of extant premodern articulable statues ("articulable" meaning able to be articulated or moved).[51] Although scholars have for some time been aware of the rumored existence of these medieval "mechanical toys" and their relevance to the case of the Rood of Boxley, this ever-increasing archive of extant artifacts has not been fully brought to bear on the debate about the rood, or the larger questions touched upon by that debate.[52] The life-size and polychromed articulable statues catalogued by Tripps and Taubert have hinges in their joints, hooks in their backs, and holes behind their eyes and mouths, mechanisms enabling them to fold their arms, turn their heads, move their mouths, and open and shut their eyes.[53] They can even bleed.[54] They wear leather skin, human hair, jewels, and clothes—necessarily, for modesty's sake, since they also have genitals.[55] Evidence reveals that these objects were used in late medieval liturgical celebrations: they were crucified, entombed in sepulchers, and then raised into heaven—or rather to the rafters.[56] Furthermore, they bear no small resemblance to the puppets implied by the stage directions in early playscripts.

For centuries, historians had only the polemic of reformers (and secondhand reports of exotic customs far away) to consult when trying to imagine the Rood of Boxley in action.[57] In the absence of tangible evidence, apologists could offer reassurances that medieval articulable statues must have been quite unremarkable. Nothing to see here. Nonetheless, contrary to these reassurances, coming face-to-face with the real thing does not put the old debate to rest. The sight of these remarkable artifacts elicits a reaction—a frisson, even a bit of a shock.[58] When Johannes Tripps showed a series of images of articulable statues from his archival research at the Forty-Seventh International Congress on Medieval Studies at Kalamazoo, the audience (demographic: professional medievalists) sometimes gasped.[59]

These gasps bring us to the crux of the matter. How did medieval Catholic spectators respond to articulable images? According to early modern iconoclasts like William Crashaw, "the common people" had been "delude[d]" into mistaking "lying wonders" for "true miracles."[60] Polemicists offer a clear motivation for this deception: filthy lucre. As Lambard has it, the monks of Boxley—the "false Romish foxes," in his words—got rich off of their "imposture, fraud, juggling, and legerdemain," theatrical lies imposed upon spectators as gospel truths.[61] Wriothesley's chronicle emphasizes this point, specifying that the iconoclasts who debunked the Rood of Boxley felt the need to reveal to the crowd that the "image was made of paper and clouts" and timber.[62] In other words, the iconoclasts assumed that the credulous masses expected to see something else entirely: presumably the skin and bones of a living Christ.

But is this what the people expected to see? Were they surprised to discover that the rood was a machine and not a man? Catholic apologists have responded with a resounding no. They offer counterevidence in support of this denial: even antipapist records written by iconoclasts sometimes seem to slip up by admitting that the mechanics inside the rood were no secret, and that not all the spectators of iconoclasm reacted according to plan—some (infuriatingly, from the iconoclasts' perspective) continued to pray to images that had been broken and burned right before their eyes.[63] But, of course, iconoclasts have a ready answer for this rebuttal too. They blamed the blindness of popery—a blindness so profound that papists did not suspect fraud even after seeing with their own eyes the exposure of "the wires that made [the image's] eyes goggle."[64] But there is another way of interpreting this evidence. What if the spectators' awareness of the mechanics of ritualistic miracles did not forestall their sense of religious wonder?

It seems clear that iconoclasts oversimplified the audience response of the Catholic pilgrims who visited the Rood of Boxley. These spectators were not simply deceived by Romish foxes and then enlightened by good Protestant shepherds. However, accepting this revision of history hardly resolves the question of how these pilgrims managed to see both the mechanism and the miracle at once. For Bridgett, credulity explained everything. He understood the cult of the rood as a "childish" (i.e., harmless) eccentricity—the spiritual milk craved by simple people at an earlier stage of spiritual development. And while Bridgett merely tolerated this childish credulity, more recently Charles Taylor has mourned the loss of medieval "enchantment," a phrase that he borrows from Max Weber and Friedrich Schiller.[65] Both Bridgett and Taylor assume (and, in different ways, admire) the strength and purity of medieval faith: the capacity to believe even in a puppet with its wires showing. Both characterize pre-Reformation faith as innocent and magical—thereby, unfortunately, reinscribing the condescension of the iconoclasts by applauding the same simplicity or blindness that was once condemned.

Steven Justice, on the other hand, offers us another way.[66] Warning against believing too credulously in the modern myth of monolithic medieval faith, Justice interprets medieval miracles as affronts against "common sense and even common sensibility" designed to activate critical thinking rather than blind faith. For Justice, this confrontation "provokes faith to work," even at the risk of nurturing "deep skepticism."[67] Rather than finding medieval belief in miracles simplistic—whether tragically and blindly simplistic (as Foxe would have it) or innocently and magically simplistic (as Bridgett would have it), Justice finds this faith intricate and formidable, finally resetting the terms set by iconoclasts in the sixteenth century. Justice's approach also has the benefit of acknowledging and allowing for the Rood of Boxley's remarkability, which apologists have tended to downplay—its capacity to shock, awe, confuse, and disturb.[68]

Playing fair, the Rood of Boxley has embarrassed its critics and apologists alike—then as now. Medieval clerks and early modern iconoclasts shared a mutual distrust of objects of this sort.[69] Indeed, medieval clerks spilled much more ink excoriating and policing such things than they ever did in celebration of their virtues.[70] So many extraordinary medieval devotional images (such as the Rood of Boxley, triple-headed Trinities, shrine Madonnas, and obscene pilgrimage badges) exist unsupported by extensive or substantive explanation or justification, leaving us to classify them under the vague and insufficient rubrics of "popular devotion," "lay spirituality," and "folk belief."[71] Medieval enthusiasm for articulable devotional images left little trace behind other than the artifacts themselves, which cannot answer our questions. The history of their reception demonstrates that we moderns find these images unsettling. In our terms, they are Gothic, by which we mean strange, creepy, queer.[72] Catholic apologists may take this affective response as an insult, which is indeed how iconoclasts intended it—in that iconoclastic polemic attempted to turn Catholicism itself into an insult. However, attempting to circumnavigate this bias by rebranding the rood (and medieval Catholicism more broadly) according to modern norms of decorum only repeats the recurring pattern of iconoclastic erasure.

For better answers to the questions raised by the Rood of Boxley, I suggest that we look to the texts of early English drama, a genre that extensively overlaps with religious ritual. The use of mechanical miracles characterizes this art form to the extent that Middle English records tend to refer to religious theater with the striking phrase "miracle plays"—which means, in a sense, fake miracles.[73] The late medieval antitheatrical diatribe "A Tretise of miraclis pleyinge" focuses much of its anger on this concept of "pley and bourde [game and joke]" miracles, accusing theater of attempting to "tak[e] awey oure bileue [take away our belief]."[74] To a certain extent, I take the "Tretise" at its word: the overlapping categories of medieval drama and ritual do indeed seek to challenge the audience's faith. These spectacles seem designed not only to preach to the choir but also to provoke shock and confusion with their startling theatrical paradoxes.[75]

Take, for example, the gory Croxton *Play of the Sacrament*, in which a posse of anti-Judaic stereotypes torment a Eucharist wafer in order to test the claims of Catholic doctrine. Can "a cake" (as they call the host) really be the "flessh and blode" of Jesus Christ (200–204)?[76] What we would call empiricist discourse is explicitly used: the Jews want to "putt yt in a preve [put it to the proof]" (208). According to scholastic theology, transubstantiation cannot be proved with hard evidence: the flesh and blood of Jesus in the transubstantiated wafer is a substance inaccessible to human discernment.[77] Late medieval Christians struggled with this difficult doctrine, as demonstrated by both the backlash of heretical Lollard mockeries of transubstantiation and the explosion of reports of miraculous exceptions to the rule: stories of the wafer turning into bleeding flesh in the mouths of stunned worshippers, making the numinous impossibly and yet also actually accessible to the senses.[78] *The Play of the Sacrament*'s Jews give voice to this urgent desire for hard proof, for which they are either severely punished or amply rewarded, depending on your reading—the text allows for both.[79]

The Croxton *Play of the Sacrament* sets itself a difficult task with high stakes: proving the veracity of a controversial new doctrine. All it can offer by way of miraculous proof, though, is theatrical trickery.[80] Only a crescendo of pyrotechnic special effects proves the truth of transubstantiation: a limb pops off, a bleeding cauldron explodes, and—in the climax—a bleeding "image" (as the stage directions call it) of the baby Jesus ascends from the gory wreckage to chastise his tormentors. Happily for our purposes, a merchant named Philippe de Vigneulles recorded his impressions of a similar play, which he witnessed in Metz in 1513. Philippe's account dwells on the impressive "devices and secrets" (*engien et secret*) that made blood squirt out of the Eucharist wafer—"just as if it were a child who pissed," as he puts it—and transformed a cracker into a small floating infant Christ.[81] While at first blush the Croxton miracle might seem only to demonize doubt by casting villains (combination heretics and anti-Judaic stereotypes) as skeptics, upon closer consideration the play also seems designed to unravel this neat conclusion. After all, the play starts some serious trouble by mocking and testing the new and difficult doctrine of transubstantiation—and then attempts resolution only by means of ostentatiously fake miraculous proof that undermines the logic of that doctrine.

Miracle plays exaggerate and celebrate the *camp* inherent in sacramental theatrics: "the love of the exaggerated, the 'off,' of things-being-what-they-are-not."[82] As Augustine wrote, theatrical signs are *mirabile* (marvelous, miraculous): "in some way true precisely because they are in some way false."[83] Miracle plays express this camp sensibility in no small part by deliberately confusing images and actors (as in the cases of *La nonne qui laissa son abbaie* and *Beunans Meriasek*). Actors wore beards, wigs, and masks that rendered their faces immobile, like the faces of painted icons.[84] Playscripts often leave principal actors onstage without lines for extended periods (the most famous example being Jesus in the York Crucifixion), allowing the audience time to fully take in the tableau vivant of actor as image.[85] Furthermore, actors playing the role of images share the stage with images designed to look like actors—mechanized puppets (like Croxton's Christ-child puppet), polychromed statues (like *Beunans Meriasek*'s statue of the Madonna), and stunt-double dummies (like Judas hanging from the tree).[86] Even more strikingly, actors—like their polychromed wooden doppelgangers—wore leather-skin suits to represent nudity.[87] The famous York Mercers' indenture of 1433 costumes Jesus in a "Sirke Wounded"; Adam and Eve wear "whytt lether" bodysuits in Eden, as do the resurrected dead on Doomsday.[88] Rather than representing the flesh of Adam, Eve, and Jesus with their own skin, performers covered the surfaces of their bodies with rawhide, just as iconographers covered the naked wood of articulable statues.[89] This confusion of wood and flesh challenges spectators to distinguish life from art. It makes one wonder. Is that statue breathing? Is that flesh or wood? Which of the faces of that double-faced mask is looking back at me?[90]

Thanks to the work of revisionist historians like T. E. Bridgett and Eamon Duffy, we now know to distrust claims that assume the foolishness of medieval spectators. However, too often, I think, attempts to correct this old error go too far in the other direction and end up confining medieval religiosity within the limits of modern propriety, which results in a distorted and often sentimentalized perspective on the past. Put in context with either a decorous revisionist or polemical reformist version of history, the statue scene in *The Winter's Tale* reads as an iconoclastic break with precedent. But when removed from these limiting sectarian contexts, the scene becomes—as Julia Lupton has argued—still another iteration of an ancient and continuous Christian tradition of "typological renovation and iconoclastic destruction."[91]

The statue scene reenacts two seemingly opposite Christian rituals at once, thus revealing their almost indistinguishable similarity: one, the staging of a miracle, and two, the breaking of an image. Neither of these strangely similar rituals inherently or essentially means what we might expect. Iconoclasm seems sacrilegious—even irreligious or secular (in the sense of "nonreligious") in our contemporary context. I have a specific illustrative example of this in mind: in 2008, a professor of biology at the University of Minnesota, Morris desecrated a Eucharist wafer, following the guidelines of anti-Judaic woodcuts that he found on Wikipedia, in defense of science and protest against religiosity.[92] And yet (as Lupton points out), iconoclasm is an ancient devotional practice that, strangely, desecrates what is *un*holy (like the Golden Calf) in order to consecrate what is sacred (like the Ten Commandments)—thus, in a strange sense, staging a miracle.[93] The visible destruction of the onstage idol creates the impression of the triumph of an invisible god. As in a miracle play, what you see functions as a sign of what you do not see: stagecraft signifies the supernatural, play signifies miracle.

Iconoclasm's theatricality even animates the very idol that it purportedly debunks.[94] The narrative of the first book of Samuel gives agency to the idol of Dagon rather than to the invisible force that destroys it (i.e., Jehovah)—the text mocks Dagon for "falling on his face," as if he were a stumbling toddler (1 Samuel 5:3–4).[95] This joke is typical of iconoclastic discourse, which likes to ironically pretend that idols can move in order to stress that they cannot budge an inch—or, in a variation on this theme, not only to *pretend* to claim that idols can move but also to actually claim that they do. The power of Satan can animate dead stocks, especially in their final moments—a twist that makes their destruction even more spectacularly dramatic.[96] Iconoclasts describe idols stealing food from the poor, speaking false prophecies, and dying in agony.[97] Thus, iconoclasm seeks to maintain that an idol is a lifeless block obviously incapable of movement *and* that it is a demonic puppet indistinguishable from the real thing—as Gross puts it, "a thing at once dead and uncannily alive."[98]

Beyond these complications, the breaking of an icon can also in itself function as a kind of devotional practice classified as "ritual humiliation" by the historian Patrick Geary. Geary describes ritual humiliation as the abuse of relics and sacred images for the purposes of punishing local saints "in order to force them to carry out their duties."[99] In other words, images are broken in the practice of ritual humiliation not to extinguish but rather to motivate their power and agency. Although Pope Gregory X forbade this custom in 1274 at the Second Council of Lyons, ritual humiliation lived on in late medieval English sermons, art, and hagiography, and especially religious theater—for example, in *Beunans Meriasek* and the Croxton *Play of the Sacrament*.[100] Early English playscripts call for actors to stab Eucharist wafers and kidnap the baby Jesus from the arms of the Virgin Mary, abuses that incur miraculous special effects and moral edification—instruction and delight rather than wrath or punishment.[101] The practice of ritual humiliation blurs the line between devotion and desecration; it is in many ways indistinguishable from iconoclasm and yet has opposite intentions.

Even more confusingly, ritual humiliation and iconoclasm both resemble the ritual of martyrdom: when early modern iconoclasts destroyed Catholic images, their abuse functioned—for some spectators—as the persecution, and thus ennoblement, of an innocent victim. When English Protestant soldiers maimed a statue of the Virgin Mary in Cádiz in 1596, their violence gave her new value in the eyes of her Catholic devotees, who renamed her *La Vulnerata*—the Wounded One.[102] Counterintuitively, the furious intensity of iconoclasm can endow its victims with efficacious potency.

Iconoclastic spectacles, then, can do more than secularize or desecrate: they can stage the invisible power of God and the visible power of Satan, petition supernatural intervention, and martyr and canonize their smashed victims. Likewise, theatrical miracles—like the articulation of the Rood of Boxley or the movement of the "statue" of Mary in *Beunans Meriasek*—can challenge faith as well as reward credulity. These two rituals, iconoclasm and miracle playing, seem diametrically opposed: the one breaks sacred images to demonstrate their lifelessness while the other articulates them to demonstrate their agency and mobility. And yet in practice, iconoclasm and miracle playing can be so hard to tell apart. Thus, the ambiguities of *The Winter's Tale*'s statue scene adapts this rich and complex tradition of theatrical spectacle in order to stage both superstition and faith, both Catholicism and its reformation, both the secular and the sacred.

Notes

1. Thanks to Katie Brokaw, John Parker, Gretchen York, and Jay Zysk for their invaluable feedback on various drafts of this essay. For background on the Reformation controversy over images, see Margaret Aston, *England's Iconoclasts: Laws Against Images*, vols. 1, 2 (Oxford: Clarendon Press, 1988–89); Huston Diehl, *Staging Reform, Reforming the Stage: Protestantism and Popular Theater in Early Modern England* (Ithaca, N.Y.: Cornell University Press, 1997); Joseph Leo Koerner, *The Reformation of the Image* (Chicago: University of Chicago Press, 2003); and James Simpson, *Under the Hammer: Iconoclasm in the Anglo-American Tradition* (Oxford: Oxford University Press, 2011). For discussions of *The Winter's Tale* in this context, see Julia Reinhard Lupton, *Afterlives of the Saints: Hagiography, Typology, and Renaissance Literature* (Stanford, Calif.: Stanford University Press, 1996); Michael O'Connell, *The Idolatrous Eye: Iconoclasm and Theater in Early Modern England* (Oxford: Oxford University Press, 2000); and Marion O'Connor, "'Imagine Me, Gentle Spectators': Iconomachy and *The Winter's Tale*," in *A Companion to Shakespeare's Works, Volume 4: The Poems, Problem Comedies, Late Plays*, ed. by Richard Dutton and Jean E. Howard (Oxford: Blackwell Publishing, 2003), 365–88.

2. Simpson, *Under the Hammer*, 13.

3. For more on the secular progress metanarrative, see Jules Michelet, *History of France*, trans. by G. H. Smith (New York: Appleton, 1967); Jacob Burckhardt, *The Civilization of the Renaissance in Italy*, trans. by S. G. C. Middlemore (London: Penguin Classics, 1990); Max Weber, *The Protestant Ethic and the Spirit of Capitalism*, trans. Talcott Parsons (New York: Routledge Classics, 2001); Marcel Gauchet, *The Disenchantment of the World: A Political History of Religion*, trans. Oscar Burge (Princeton, N.J.: Princeton University Press, 1999); Charles Taylor, *A Secular Age* (Cambridge, Mass.: Harvard University Press, 2007); and Janet R. Jakobsen and Ann Pellegrini, eds., *Secularisms* (Durham, N.C.: Duke University Press, 2008).

4. Herbert Butterfield, *The Whig Interpretation of History* (New York: Norton, 1965).

5. For more on revisionist history, see Eamon Duffy, *The Stripping of the Altars: Traditional Religion in England, c. 1400–c. 1580*, 2nd ed. (New Haven, Conn.: Yale University Press, 2005); Christopher Haigh, *English Reformations: Religion, Politics and Society under the Tudors* (Oxford: Clarendon Press, 1993); and Peter Marshall, *Reformation England, 1480–1642*, 2nd ed. (New York: Bloomsbury, 2012).

6. For more on the turn to religion in Shakespeare studies, see *Shakespeare and Religion: Early Modern and Postmodern Perspectives*, ed. Ken Jackson and Arthur F. Marotti (Notre Dame, Ind.: University of Notre Dame Press, 2011); *Religion and Drama in Early Modern England: The Performance of Religion on the Renaissance Stage*, ed. Jane Hwang Degenhardt and Elizabeth Williamson (Burlington, Vt.: Ashgate Publishing, 2011); David Scott Kastan, *A Will to Believe: Shakespeare and Religion* (Oxford: Oxford University Press, 2014); Julia Reinhard Lupton, "Religion and the Religious Turn," in *A Handbook of English Renaissance Literary Studies*, ed. John Lee (Hoboken, N.J.: Wiley, 2017), 70–85.

7. Barbara Newman, *Medieval Crossover: Reading the Secular against the Sacred* (Notre Dame, Ind.: University of Notre Dame Press, 2013), 7.

8. While I focus on the statue scene in the context of Marian devotion, its resonances with Christ's resurrection, transubstantiation, Purgatorial hauntings, hagiography, and the legend of King Herod (as well as with Reformation debates about miracles and repentance more broadly) have also been explored; see Mario DiGangi, "Hermione's Statue," in *The Winter's Tale: Texts and Contexts* (New York: Bedford/St. Martin's, 2008), 362–65, and Elizabeth Williamson, *The Materiality of Religion in Early Modern English Drama* (Burlington, Vt.: Ashgate Publishing, 2009), 62–68. For Marian readings, see Ruth Vanita, "Mariological Memory in *The Winter's Tale* and *Henry VIII*," *Studies in English Literature, 1500–1900* 40, no. 2 (2000): 311–37; John Parker, Review of *The Dream of the Moving Statue*, by Kenneth Gross, *Shakespeare Studies* 36 (2008): 270.

9. All quotes from *The Winter's Tale* are taken from DiGangi, *The Winter's Tale*.

10. Michael Camille, *The Gothic Idol: Ideology and Image-Making in Medieval Art* (Cambridge: Cambridge University Press, 1989), 220–41.

11. Gautier de Coinci, *Les miracles de Nostre Dame*, ed. Frédéric Koenig, 4 vols. (Geneva: Droz, 1966–70); *Songs of Holy Mary of Alfonso X, The Wise: A Translation of the "Cantigas de Santa Maria,"* trans. Kathleen Kulp-Hill (Tempe: Arizona Center for Medieval and Renaissance Studies, 2000); Adrienne Boyarin, *Miracles of the Virgin in Medieval England: Law and Jewishness in Marian Legends* (Cambridge: Brewer, 2010).

12. For more on hagiographic drama, see Clifford Davidson, ed., *The Saint Play in Medieval Europe* (Kalamazoo: Western Michigan University Press, 1986). Extant early English plays about miracles of the Virgin include the Durham Prologue, *The Pride of Life*, and possibly also *Dux Moraud*; see Darryl Grantley, *English Dramatic Interludes, 1300–1580: A Reference Guide* (Cambridge: Cambridge University Press, 2004).

13. For more on this, see Alice Dailey, "Easter Scenes from an Unholy Tomb: Christian Parody in *The Widow's Tears*," in *Marian Moments in Early Modern British Drama*, ed. Regina Buccola and Lisa Hopkins (Burlington, Vt.: Ashgate Publishing, 2007), 127–40, and Phebe Jensen, *Religion and Revelry in*

Shakespeare's Festive World (Cambridge: Cambridge University Press, 2015), 194–233.

14. *Beunans Meriasek*, ed. and trans. Whitley Stokes (London: Trübner, 1872). On the gender of performers in medieval drama, see James Stokes, "Women and Performance in Medieval and Early Modern Suffolk," *Early Theatre* 15, no. 1 (2012): 27–43.

15. *Beunans Meriasek*, 208–10. See also Philip Butterworth, *Staging Conventions in Medieval English Theatre* (Cambridge: Cambridge University Press, 2014), 38, 42; Brian O. Murdoch, "The Cornish Medieval Drama," in *The Cambridge Companion to Medieval English Theatre*, ed. Richard Beadle (Cambridge: Cambridge University Press, 2001), 214–15.

16. Camille, *The Gothic Idol*, 129–35, 233.

17. See *Le Jeu de saint-Nicolas de Jehan Bodel*, ed. and trans. Albert Henry (1962; repr., Geneva: Droz, 1981).

18. For more on the complexities of the relationship between the Virgin Mary and images of the Virgin Mary, see Elina Gertsman, *Worlds Within: Opening the Medieval Shrine Madonna* (University Park: Penn State University Press, 2015), 102–13.

19. Kenneth Gross, *The Dream of the Moving Statue* (Ithaca, N.Y.: Cornell University Press, 1992), 104.

20. *Two Miracles: La Nonne qui laissa son abbaie; Saint Valentin*, ed. Nigel Wilkins (Edinburgh: Scottish Academic Press, 1972); *The Nun Who Left Her Abbey: A Fourteenth-Century French Miracle Play*, trans. Nigel Wilkins (Lancaster, UK: Medieval English Theatre Texts in Translation, 1987).

21. Wilkins, *The Nun Who Left*, 26–27; Wilkins, *Two Miracles*, 6–7. See also Donald Maddox and Sara Sturm-Maddox, introduction to *Parisian Confraternity Drama of the Fourteenth Century: The "Miracles de Nostre Dame par personnages"* (Turnhout, Belg.: Brepols, 2008), 2–4.

22. See Gross, *Dream*, 3–6.

23. This is Wilkins's translation in *The Nun Who Left*, 28; in French, the lines read as follows: *Vostre image s'est venu mettre / si droit au travers de cest huis / que nullement passer ne puis* (29).

24. Though the tradition lived on via adaptation; for more on early modern adaptations of medieval Marian theatrical traditions, see Buccola and Hopkins, *Marian Moments*. For two influential and conflicting accounts of the transition from medieval to early modern drama, see H. C. Gardiner, *Mysteries' End: An Investigation of the Last Days of the Medieval Religious Stage* (New Haven, Conn.: Yale University Press, 1946), and Bing D. Bills, "The 'Suppression Theory' and the English Corpus Christi Play: A Re-examination," *Theatre Journal* 32, no. 2 (May 1980): 157–68. For a more recent overview, see James Simpson, *Reform and Cultural Revolution*, The Oxford English Literary History, vol. 2:1350–1547 (Oxford: Oxford University Press, 2002), 528–39.

25. On the influence of medieval English drama on Shakespeare, see E. K. Chambers, *The Mediaeval Stage*, 2 vols. (Oxford: Clarendon Press, 1903); Emrys Jones, *The Origins of Shakespeare* (Oxford: Clarendon Press, 1977); Michael O'Connell, "Vital Cultural Practices: Shakespeare and the Mysteries," *Journal of Medieval and Early Modern Studies* 29, no. 1 (Winter 1999): 149–68; Curtis Perry and John Watkins, eds., *Shakespeare and the Middle Ages* (Oxford: Oxford University Press, 2009); Sarah Beckwith, *Shakespeare and the Grammar*

of Forgiveness (Ithaca, N.Y.: Cornell University Press, 2011); Helen Cooper, *Shakespeare and the Medieval World* (London: Arden Shakespeare, 2012); Heather Hirschfeld, *The End of Satisfaction: Drama and Repentance in the Age of Shakespeare* (Ithaca, N.Y.: Cornell University Press, 2014); Kurt A. Schreyer, *Shakespeare's Medieval Craft: Remnants of the Mysteries on the London Stage* (Ithaca, N.Y.: Cornell University Press, 2014); Ruth Morse, Helen Cooper, and Peter Holland, eds., *Medieval Shakespeare: Pasts and Presents* (Cambridge: Cambridge University Press, 2015); and Jay Zysk, *Shadow and Substance: Eucharistic Controversy and English Drama across the Reformation Divide* (Notre Dame, Ind.: University of Notre Dame Press, 2017).

26. Beatrice Groves, *Texts and Traditions: Religion in Shakespeare 1592–1604* (Oxford: Clarendon Press, 2007), 33–39.

27. Schreyer, *Shakespeare's Medieval Craft*, 118.

28. Martin Stevens, "The Missing Parts of the Towneley Cycle," *Speculum* 45, no. 2 (April 1970): 258–63.

29. William Crashaw, *The Iesuites Gospel* (London, 1549), Early English Books Online, 29.

30. O'Connell, *The Idolatrous Eye*, 141. See also Lupton, *Afterlives of the Saints*, 216, and Phebe Jensen, "Singing Psalms to Horn-Pipes: Festivity, Iconoclasm, and Catholicism in *The Winter's Tale*," *Shakespeare Quarterly* 55, no. 3 (2004): 282.

31. Lupton, *Afterlives of the Saints*, 216.

32. See Helen Parish, *Monks, Miracles, and Magic: Reformation Representations of the Medieval Church* (New York: Routledge, 2005), 81; Ronald C. Finucane, *Miracles and Pilgrims: Popular Beliefs in Medieval England* (New York: Palgrave Macmillan, 1995), 204–12; O'Connor, "'Imagine Me: Gentle Spectators,'" 366–67; and Aston, *England's Iconoclasts*, 225–29.

33. William Thomas [1524–54], *The Pilgrim: A Dialogue on the Life and Actions of King Henry the Eighth* (London: Parker, Son, and Bourn, 1861), 37–38.

34. Peter Marshall, "The Rood of Boxley, the Blood of Hailes and the Defence of the Henrician Church," *Journal of Ecclesiastical History*, 46, no. 4 (October 1995): 689–96.

35. John Foxe, *The Unabridged Acts and Monuments Online*, 1583 ed. (Sheffield: HRI Online Publications, 2011), 1188.

36. William Lambard, *A Perambulation of Kent: Containing the Description, History, and Customs of That Shire* (London, 1576), Early English Books Online, 187.

37. Marshall, "Rood of Boxley," 691–92; C. John Sommerville, *The Secularization of Early Modern England: From Religious Culture to Religious Faith* (Oxford: Oxford University Press, 1992), 24.

38. Marshall, "Rood of Boxley," 691–92.

39. Marshall, "Rood of Boxley," 691–92.

40. Butterfield, *Whig Interpretation*, 34–63.

41. David Hume, *The History of England* (London: T. Cadell, 1778), 1:649.

42. See Eamon Duffy, "A. G. Dickens and Late Medieval Church," *Historical Research* 77, no. 195 (February 2004): 98–110.

43. Augustus W. N. Pugin, *The Present State of Ecclesiastical Architecture in England* (London: Dolman, 1843), 139–40.

44. T. E. Bridgett, "The Rood of Boxley; or, How a Lie Grows," *Dublin Review*, 3rd ser., 19, no. 1 (January 1888): 2; see also J. Brownbill, "Boxley Abbey and the Rood of Grace," *The Antiquary* 7 (April 1883): 162–65, 210–13.

45. Bridgett, "The Rood of Boxley," 6. For more on Bridgett, see Cyril Rider, *The Life of Thomas Edward Bridgett* (London: Burns and Oates, 1906).

46. Bridgett, "The Rood of Boxley," 7.

47. Philip Butterworth, *Magic on the Early English Stage* (Cambridge: Cambridge University Press, 2005), 123–24; Leanne Groeneveld, "A Theatrical Miracle: The Boxley Rood of Grace as Puppet," *Early Theatre* 10, no. 2 (January 2007): 43.

48. For more on the rood as an automaton, see Kara Reilly, *Automata and Mimesis on the Stage of Theatre History* (New York: Palgrave Macmillan, 2011), 19–23; Wendy Beth Hyman, ed., *The Automaton in English Renaissance Literature* (Burlington, Vt.: Ashgate Publishing, 2013), 97–98. See also Elly R. Truitt, *Medieval Robots: Mechanism, Magic, Nature, and Art* (Philadelphia: University of Pennsylvania Press, 2015).

49. Bridgett documents how Whig accounts embellished the story over the centuries ("The Rood of Boxley," 4–6); see also Finucane, *Miracles and Pilgrims*, 691.

50. Truitt, *Medieval Robots*, 2–3.

51. Johannes and Gesine Taubert, "Mittelalterliche Kruzifixe mit schwenkbaren Armen," *Zeitschrift des deutschen Vereins für Kunstwissenschaft* 22 (1969): 79–121; Johannes Tripps, *Das handelnde Bildwerk in der Gotik* (Berlin: Mann, 2000). See also David Freedberg, *The Power of Images: Studies in the History and Theory of Response* (Chicago: University of Chicago Press, 1989), 286–91; Giovanna Sapori and Bruno Toscano, *La deposizione lignea in Europa: L'immagine, il culto, la forma* (Perugia: Electa, 2004); John T. Paoletti, "Wooden Sculpture in Italy as Sacral Presence," *Artibus et Historiae* 13, no. 26 (1992): 85–100; Amy Knight Powell, *Depositions: Scenes from the Late Medieval Church and the Modern Museum* (New York: Zone Books, 2012), 81–94; Kamil Kopania, *Animated Sculptures of the Crucified Christ in the Religious Culture of the Latin Middle Ages* (Warsaw: Wydawnictwo Neriton, 2010).

52. Finucane, *Miracles and Pilgrims*, 210.

53. See Paoletti, "Wooden Sculpture," 86, and Powell, *Depositions*, 83–84.

54. See Paoletti, "Wooden Sculpture," 97.

55. The most striking extant examples are perhaps Oswald Bierstorfer aus Memmingen's fifteenth-century rood (Powell, *Depositions*, 84–85; Tripps, *Das handelnde Bildwerk*, 49, 166) and *El Santo Cristo de Burgos*: this remarkable fifteenth-century statue has joints in its neck, arms, fingers, and legs; it wears a human-hair wig and leather skin. See Maria José Martínez, "El Santo Cristo de Burgos y los Cristos dolorosos articulados," *Boletín del Seminario de Estudios de Arte y Arqueología* 69–70 (2003–4): 207–46.

56. See Powell, *Depositions*, 84.

57. Bridgett, for example, cites hearsay about articulable statues in "Bavaria and the Tyrol" ("The Rood of Boxley," 7).

58. Simpson, *Under the Hammer*, 48–49, 119.

59. Johannes Tripps, "The Mechanical Presentations of Marian Statues in the Late Gothic Period," trans. Patricia Smith (lecture given at the Forty-Seventh International Congress on Medieval Studies, Western Michigan University,

Kalamazoo, May 11, 2012); available at http://archiv.ub.uni-heidelberg.de/artdok/2106/1/Tripps_The_mechanical_presentations_of_Marian_Statues_2012.pdf.

60. Crashaw, *The Iesuites Gospel*, 18.

61. Lambard, *A Perambulation of Kent*, 182.

62. *Letters and Papers, Foreign and Domestic, of the Reign of Henry VIII*, ed. J. S. Brewer, J. Gairdner, and R. H. Brodie (London: Longman, 1862–1910), 8:1, 130–31.

63. See C. E. Moreton, "The Walsingham Conspiracy of 1537," *Bulletin of the Institute of Historical Research* 63, no. 150 (February 1990): 39; Dominic Janes and Gary Waller, *Walsingham in Literature and Culture from the Middle Ages to Modernity* (Burlington, Vt.: Ashgate Publishing, 2010), 14.

64. Reginald Scot, *The Discovery of Witchcraft* (London, 1584), Early English Books Online, 138.

65. Taylor, *A Secular Age*, 80–88, 553.

66. Steven Justice, "Did the Middle Ages Believe in Their Miracles?" *Representations* 103, no. 1 (Summer 2008): 1–29; Steven Justice, "Eucharistic Miracle and Eucharistic Doubt," *Journal of Medieval and Early Modern Studies* 42, no. 2 (Spring 2012): 307–32.

67. Justice, "Eucharistic Miracle," 21.

68. Pugin, for one, denied that the rood could move at all, while Bridgett tried to maintain that its verisimilitude was as unremarkable as that of a wax figure in Madame Tussauds (as if the wax figures in Madame Tussauds are unremarkable). See Bridgett, "The Rood of Boxley," 6; see also Duffy, *Stripping of the Altars*, 403, Finucane, *Miracles and Pilgrims*, 208 and Camille, *The Gothic Idol*, 220–39.

69. See Camille, *The Gothic Idol*, 197–241.

70. See, for example, Émile Mâle, *Religious Art in France of the Thirteenth Century*, trans. Dora Nussey (New York: Dutton, 1913), 48–49.

71. See W. R. Jones, "Lollards and Images: The Defense of Religious Art in Later Medieval England," *Journal of the History of Ideas* 34, no. 1 (January 1973): 27–50; Nicholas Watson, "'Et que est huius ydoli materia? Tuipse': Idols and Images in Walter Hilton," in *Images, Idolatry, and Iconoclasm in Late Medieval England: Textuality and the Visual Image*, ed. Jeremy Dimmick, James Simpson, and Nicolette Zeeman (Oxford: Oxford University Press, 2002), 95–111. For more on triple-headed Trinities, see Robert Mills, "Jesus as Monster," in *The Monstrous Middle Ages*, ed. Bettina Bildhauer and Robert Mills (Toronto: University of Toronto Press, 2003), 28–54; for more on shrine Madonnas, see Gertsman, *Worlds Within*; for more on obscene pilgrimage badges, see Jos Koldeweij, "'Shameless and Naked Images': Obscene Badges as Parodies of Popular Devotion," in *Art and Architecture of Late Medieval Pilgrimage in Northern Europe and the British Isles*, ed. Sarah Blick and Rita Tekippe (Leiden: Brill, 2004), 493–512.

72. For more on the association of medieval Catholicism with horror and deviance, see Susan M. Griffin, *Anti-Catholicism and Nineteenth-Century Fiction* (Cambridge: Cambridge University Press, 2004); Patrick R. O'Malley, *Catholicism, Sexual Deviance, and Victorian Gothic Culture* (Cambridge: Cambridge University Press, 2006); Colleen McDannell, "Catholic Horror," in *Catholics in the Movies* (Oxford: Oxford University Press, 2008), 197–226.

73. See Chambers, *The Mediaeval Stage*, 2:103; Karl Young, *The Drama of the Medieval Church*, 2 vols. (Oxford: Oxford University Press, 1951), 2:408.

74. "A Tretise of miraclis pleyinge," *Selections from English Wycliffite Writings*, ed. Anne Hudson (Toronto: University of Toronto Press, 1997), 22, 35.

75. See also Erin E. Kelly, "Doubt and Religious Drama Across Sixteenth-Century England, or Did the Middle Ages Believe in Their Plays?," in *The Chester Cycle in Context, 1555–1575: Religion, Drama, and the Impact of Change*, ed. Jessica Dell, David Klausner, and Helen Ostovich (Burlington, Vt.: Ashgate Publishing, 2012), 47–63.

76. All quotes from *The Croxton Play of the Sacrament* come from the TEAMS edition ed. John T. Sebastian (Kalamazoo, Mich.: Medieval Institute Publications, 2012).

77. For more on the theology of the Eucharist in the late Middle Ages, see Ian Christopher Levy, "The Eucharist in the Fourteenth and Fifteenth Centuries," in *The Oxford Handbook of Sacramental Theology*, ed. Hans Boersma and Matthew Levering (Oxford: Oxford University Press, 2015), 235–48, and Zysk, *Shadow and Substance*.

78. On the Lollard response, see Ann Hudson, "The Mouse in the Pyx: Popular Heresy and the Eucharist," *Trivium* 26 (1991): 40–53; Patrick Hornbeck, *What Is a Lollard? Dissent and Disbelief in Late Medieval England* (Oxford: Oxford University Press, 2010). On Eucharistic countermiracles, see Benedicta Ward, *Miracles and the Medieval Mind: Theory, Record, and Event, 1000–1215* (Philadelphia: University of Pennsylvania Press, 1987), 15; Miri Rubin, *Corpus Christi: The Eucharist in Late Medieval Culture* (Cambridge: Cambridge University Press, 1991); and Justice, "Eucharistic Miracle."

79. See, for example, the readings of Cecilia Cutts, "The Croxton Play: An Anti-Lollard Piece," *Modern Language Quarterly* 5, no. 1 (March 1944): 45–60, and Tamara Atkin, *The Drama of Reform: Theology and Theatricality, 1461–1553* (Turnhout, Belg.: Brepols, 2013), as opposed to the reading of John Parker, *The Aesthetics of Antichrist* (Ithaca, N.Y.: Cornell University Press, 2007), 125–35.

80. Sarah Beckwith, "Ritual, Church, Theater: Medieval Dramas of the Sacramental Body," in *Culture and History, 1350–1600: Essays on English Communities, Identities and Writing*, ed. David Aers (Detroit: Wayne State University Press, 1992), 68.

81. See *Gedenkbuch des Metzer Bürgers Philippe von Vigneulles*, ed. Heinrich Michelant (Amsterdam: Rodopi, 1968), 244. See also Darryll Grantley, "Producing Miracles," in *Aspects of Early English Drama*, ed. Paula Neuss (Cambridge: Brewer, 1983), 78–91.

82. Susan Sontag, "Notes on 'Camp,'" in *Susan Sontag: Essays of the 1960s and 70s*, ed. David Rieff (New York: Library of America, 2013), 262. For more on the campiness of Catholicism, see also Mark D. Jordan, *The Silence of Sodom: Homosexuality in Modern Catholicism* (Chicago: University of Chicago Press, 2000), 184–85, 279n8. For more on the theatricality of the sacraments, see Augustine, *De Civitate Dei* X.5, ed. Emanuel Hoffmann, Corpus Scriptorum Ecclesiasticorum Latinorum 40, 2 vols. (Vienna, 1899), 1:452; Augustine, *Epistola* 98.9, ed. Al Goldbacher, Corpus Scriptorum Ecclesiasticorum Latinorum 34, 2 vols. (Vienna, 1898), 530–31; and Atkin, *The Drama of Reform*, 1–4.

83. Augustine, *Soliloquies: Augustine's Inner Dialogue*, trans. by Kim Paffenroth (New York: New City Press, 2000), 2.10, p. 74; for the Latin text, see *Saint Augustine: Soliloquies and Immorality of the Soul*, trans. Gerard Watson (Warminster, UK: Aris and Phillips, 1990), 2.18, p. 94. See also Donnalee Dox, *The Idea*

of the Theater in Latin Christian Thought (Ann Arbor: University of Michigan Press, 2004), 38–40.

84. Butterworth, *Staging Conventions*, 113–20; Schreyer, *Shakespeare's Medieval Craft*, 112. See also Meg Twycross and Sarah Carpenter, *Masks and Masking in Medieval and Early Tudor England* (London: Routledge, 2016).

85. See Jill Stevenson, *Performance, Cognitive Theory, and Devotional Culture: Sensual Piety in Late Medieval York* (New York: Palgrave Macmillan, 2010), 120–25.

86. Butterworth, *Staging Conventions*, 151.

87. I would like to thank Gretchen York for her feedback on this matter. See Gretchen York, "Losing Eden: Theater and the Fall from Medieval Drama to Milton" (Ph.D. diss., University of Virginia, 2017), 21–71.

88. See Alexandra F. Johnston and Margaret Rogerson, eds., *Records of Early English Drama: York*, 2 vols. (Toronto: University of Toronto Press, 1979), 1:55; Clifford Davidson, ed., *Material Culture and Medieval Drama* (Kalamazoo, Mich.: Medieval Institute Publications, 1999), 112–13; Schreyer, *Shakespeare's Medieval Craft*, 121.

89. For more on the correspondence between wood and flesh, see Elina Gertsman, "Image and Performance: An Art Historian at the Crossroads," in "Opportunities in Medieval and Renaissance Drama," ed. Mario Longtin and Jill Stevenson, special issue, *Research on Medieval and Renaissance Drama* 51 (2012): 53.

90. See Johnston and Rogerson, *Records*, 1:55–56.

91. Lupton, *Afterlives of the Saints*, 218.

92. See P. Z. Meyers, "The Great Desecration," *Pharyngula* (ScienceBlogs), posted July 24, 2008.

93. Lupton, *Afterlives of the Saints*, 216–18. See also David Lawton, *Blasphemy* (Philadelphia: University of Pennsylvania Press, 1993), 35.

94. Gross, *Dream*, 45.

95. See also Isaiah 19:1 and John Parker, "Valhalla Is Burning: Theory, the Middle Ages, and Secularization," *PMLA* 130, no. 3 (May 2015): 787–98.

96. Simpson, *Under the Hammer*, 82.

97. Parish, *Monks, Miracles, and Magic*, 46–47; Simpson, *Under the Hammer*, 54–59.

98. Gross, *Dream*, 50.

99. Patrick Geary, *Furta Sacra: Thefts of Relics in the Central Middle Ages* (Princeton, N.J.: Princeton University Press, 1978), 135. I specifically refer to the subcategory of ritual humiliation that Geary calls humiliation as coercion (134); see "Humiliation of Saints," 123–40. See also Lester Little, *Benedictine Maledictions: Liturgical Cursing in Romanesque France* (Ithaca, N.Y.: Cornell University Press, 1996), 26–30, 83–85, 133.

100. See Powell, *Depositions*, 93, and Parish, *Monks, Miracles, and Magic*, 76.

101. Parker, *Aesthetics of Antichrist*, 125–35; Justice, "Eucharistic Miracle," 307–32.

102. Anne J. Cruz, "Vindicating the *Vulnerata*: Cádiz and the Circulation of Religious Imagery as Weapons of War," in *Material and Symbolic Circulation between Spain and England, 1554–1604* (Burlington, Vt.: Ashgate Publishing, 2008), 39–60.

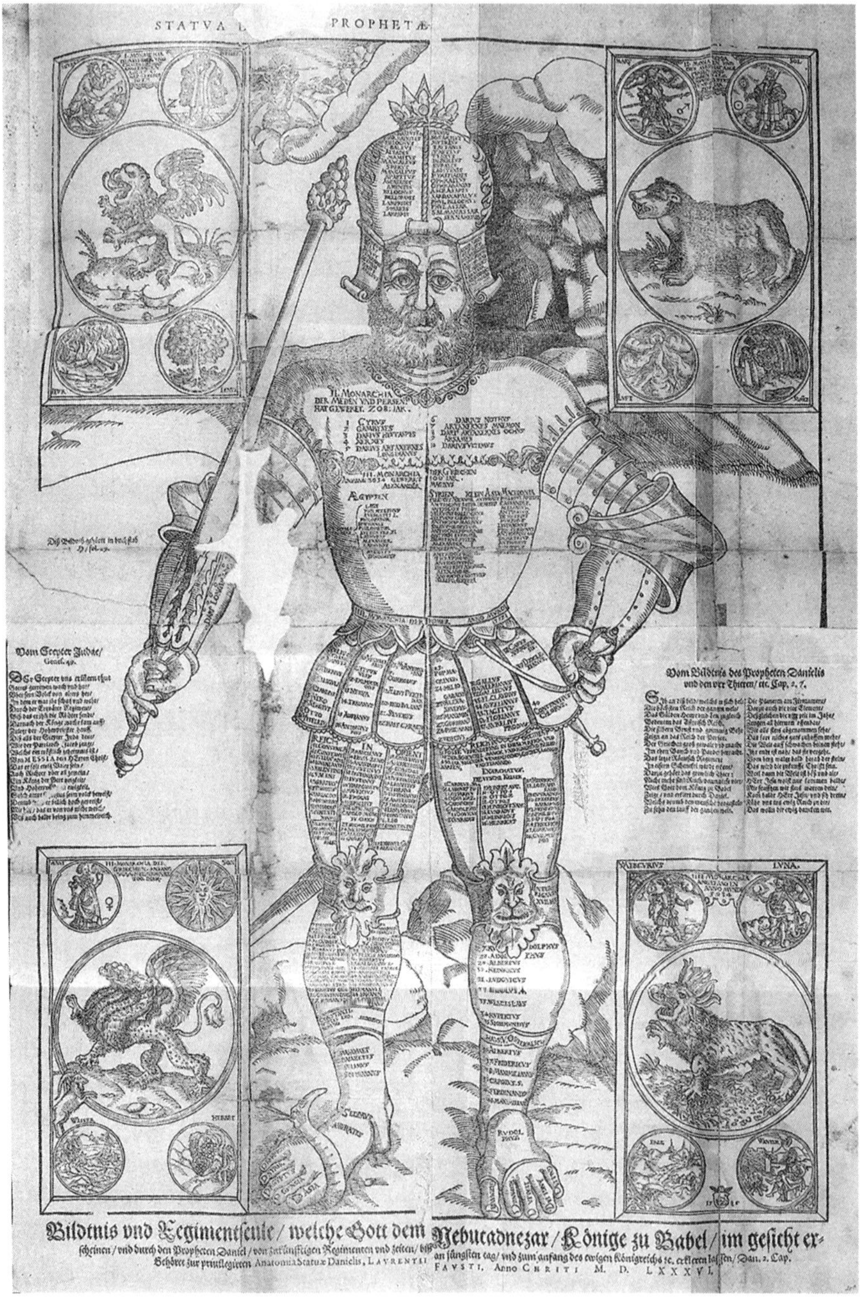

Figure 1. *Statua Danielis Prophetae*, from Lorenz Faust, *Anatomia Statuae Danielis* (1585); engraver unknown. By permission of the British Library.

Afterword

Margreta de Grazia and Brian Cummings

This striking woodcut (figure 1) might serve as a strong endorsement of this volume's commitment to what the editors in their introduction term the hermeneutics of the sacred and the secular.[1] On the span of a page, it illustrates all world history as the fulfillment of a prophecy. Its source is the biblical summoning of the prophet Daniel to interpret the vexingly enigmatic dream of Nebuchadnezzar, King of Babylon (Daniel 2:32–35). In the dream, a statue—with a head of gold, shoulders of silver, belly of brass, and legs and feet of iron and clay—is smashed to smithereens by a stone that expands to a massive world-consuming mountain. According to Daniel's divinely inspired interpretation, the four parts of the statue's anatomy represented the four great world empires: Nebuchadnezzar's own kingdom of Babylon was the first, to be superseded by three as yet unidentified empires; the fourth would end in universal destruction after which "the God of heaven [shall] set up a kingdom which shall never be destroyed" (2:44). About a millennium after Daniel, Jerome in his commentary on Daniel, looking back on what Daniel had foreseen, would identify the other three monarchies: Babylon had fallen to Medes-Persia, Medes-Persia to Greece, and Greece to Rome. That the fourth empire, Jerome's Rome, had fallen to the Goths and Vandals and the apocalypse still had not come in no way invalidated the prophecy. By the mechanism of *translatio imperii*, Rome's dominion would continue as the Holy Roman Empire passed westward from one kingdom to another.

In the 1586 woodcut, the statue of Nebuchadnezzar's dream appears as a colossal emperor, retrofitted with modern armor, a truncheon, and a sword. The image is itself gigantic: on the foldout on which it was printed, it is more than three times as large as its reproduction here.[2] The raw materials of the statue's four body parts in Nebuchadnezzar's dream have been fashioned into four pieces of armor, each imprinted with the name of one of the four great empires: a helmet for Nebuchadnezzar's Babylon, shoulder plates for Persia, a cuirass or breastplate for Greece, and a skirt

Figure 2. Detail of *Reich in Occident*, *Statua Danielis Prophetae*.

of tassets hanging from the waist for Rome. The armor, like empire itself, continues beyond the hem of Rome's skirt to cover two sturdy legs in chausses, or chain-mail leggings, and they, too, are labeled. The eastern leg, or *Reich in Orient*, consists of several sequences of Byzantine rulers until it cracks at its clay ankle with the fall of Constantinople, followed by a run of Ottoman sultans. The western leg, or *Reich in Occident*, registers the fall of Rome, but imperial succession continues in unbroken numbered sequence from the Franks (Charlemagne, the first Holy Roman Emperor) to the Ottonians, from the Ottonians to the Houses of Luxembourg and Hohenstaufen and finally the Habsburgs. As long as the Roman Empire endured, Daniel's prophecy that the world would end would remain unfulfilled. In this respect, world empire was the *katechon* to the prophesied *eschaton*: its transfer from one kingdom to another indefinitely postponed the imminent end of the world.[3]

In the woodcut, the end is nigh.[4] Time is running out, as is space on the colossus's suit of armor. The catalogue of empires that have come and gone is so long that it covers the colossus's carapace from head to foot, leaving no room for future monarchies—unless it be on the blank surface of the *Reich in Occident*'s toenails (figure 2). Only the eight block letters

Figure 3. *Salvator Mundi*, detail, *Statua Danielis Prophetae.*

of Germania on the big toe have been spaced to extend over the toenail (the eight letters of Catholic Hispania fall short of the cuticle). Published in the Lutheran stronghold of Leipzig, the woodcut gives pride of place to Germania: it will be the first to experience the long-awaited *eschaton*.[5]

Intimations of that *eschaton* hover in the background. The world-annihilating rock threatens in the shape of the boulders behind the head and legs of the colossus. Overhead and breaking through the historical plane of the page, the airborne *Salvator Mundi* is on his way, riding high on the convenantal rainbow, with the world he will save at his feet (figure 3). As Jerome notes in his commentary on Daniel, Christ is himself the rock who will destroy the kingdoms of this world to usher in the everlasting kingdom of the next: "A rock (namely, the Lord and Savior) . . . the strongest power at the end of the ages, will crush all realms and will rule forever."[6] At each of the four corners of the page are the fabulous beasts

Figure 4. Title page engraving for Thomas Hobbes's *Leviathan* (London: Andrew Cooke, 1651) by Abraham Bosse, 240 x 155 mm. By permission of the British Museum.

that "came up from the sea" in Daniel's own apocalyptic vision (Daniel 7:3–7), one for each empire, prefiguring the apocalyptic beasts of Revelation, restrained in the woodcut by their quadrilateral cages.

Two generations after the apocalyptic 1586 woodcut, another remarkable image appears to encapsulate the relationship between secular and sacred. The engraved frontispiece to Thomas Hobbes's *Leviathan* (figure 4) has been called the most famous visual image in the history of political philosophy.[7] Dominating the engraving, almost although not quite escaping from its frame, stands another colossus, this time showing the sovereign ruler, wearing an imperial crown. In each hand, he holds a symbol of, respectively, state and church: an open sword in his right and a bishop's crozier in his left. Either is angled toward the other, so that in principle the lines formed by each will meet, not far above the sovereign's head.[8]

To some readers, the image from *Leviathan* heralds the dawn of the secular age, and the passage of time between 1586 and 1651 represents a decisive shift in the hermeneutics of sacred and secular. However, such a reading ignores the landscape in the engraving just below the monarch's body. Here is a pastoral scene, encompassing both a city and countryside. The vista reaches out toward the sea, visible in the distance on the viewer's left, beneath the sword hand. There are rivers, including rather a broad one; even the highest hills show signs of habitation, and (we note), wherever there is habitation, there is almost always some kind of church or chapel with a steeple. This feature is also highly prominent in the walled city that dominates in the foreground. The city contains houses, streets, public squares, a fortress, and also an extremely tall church. This has a double elevation, a nave with its west front and a minimal transept, and a larger apse, with the crossing surmounted (slightly oddly) by twin towers, topped by needlelike steeples.

To interpret the place of the church within the image, however, we have to return to the figure of the sovereign. The leviathan body, on closer inspection, is a clever artistic illusion. For it consists of innumerable individual bodies. These figures, whether standing or kneeling, look up toward the sovereign, with their backs to the viewer. The technique used by the engraver, Abraham Bosse, is similar to that of anamorphosis, in which an image can be viewed in two quite different ways, according to the perspective of the viewer.[9] The artistic illusion suggests, but never states, two kinds of reading: either that sovereignty is made up of, and derives its power from, all the individual bodies of its subjects, or that these small bodies owe their very being to the overwhelming constitutive whole of the sovereign power.

This double view of the contract between sovereign and people is matched by the engraving's double view of the nature of power, both ecclesiastical and temporal. For far from suppressing religion, Hobbes devotes about half of the whole of *Leviathan* to the sovereign's obligation to manage spiritual as well as temporal affairs. Indeed, the spiritual is the cause of considerable social conflict, which no sovereign can afford to ignore. It could be said, indeed, that the terms "sacred and secular," like "temporal and spiritual," can be understood only in relation to each other: each makes sense only in dynamic tension with the other.

If a previous age has wished to see Shakespeare as part of the shift from religious to secular, this volume of essays is concerned with their creative juxtaposition. The two graphic colossi of 1586 and 1651, the one illustrating world history and the other contract theory, mark not the end of an age so much as a period of intense scrutiny and self-reflection. In an era of almost continuous religious war, the politics of religion is at the heart of both. At the same time there are differences, not least in the representation of time itself. If the *katechon* is imminent in the one, in the other eschatology appears of no immediate concern—the future lies in the hands of the sovereign.[10] While time is running out for the emperor in 1586, the sovereign in 1651 has all the time in the world. The future, like the open horizon of the image, stretches out without limit.

To the readers of this volume, the imperial colossus and the giant sovereign might bring another larger-than-life figure to mind: the ghost of King Hamlet, armed cap-a-pie, grizzle bearded, truncheon in hand. King Hamlet's very armor bears witness to his imperial ambitions. Having fought Poland to the east and subjugated England to the west, Denmark is still engaged in territorial skirmishing with Norway.[11] So, too, the authority of kingship is at issue, though it is hardly as absolute as in the *Leviathan* engraving. Regicide drives the plot. It is represented again and again: narrated in the ghost's account of his poisoning, recited and enacted by the players at court, threatened by Laertes's armed assault, and finally accomplished by Hamlet. But in the *Leviathan*'s title page, is regicide even imaginable? Who among those unarmed puny subjects could possibly rise up against him? And yet it took a regicide in order for the book to be written and published.

Along with empire and kingship, the *eschaton* hovers over the worldly events of the play. The soul's final destination is a matter of urgent concern, and not only for King Hamlet's purgatorial ghost: Hamlet notoriously would damn Claudius's soul, as Laertes would that of Hamlet and, even more shockingly, that of the priest. In the graveyard, Ophelia's soul lies precariously in the balance: crown and church clash over whether she should be buried in consecrated ground. At Hamlet's death, Horatio consigns his soul to the ministry of angels, yet the play's final business is the transfer of rule from one kingdom to another.

In proposing a hermeneutic of the sacred and secular, the essays in this volume go far toward resetting the relation of religion and secularity in Shakespeare's plays. No longer can criticism readily assume the periodizing and secularizing narrative by which the Reformation, for better or worse, released history into modern secularity. Early modernity, if we are still to observe period designations, involves less the supersession of one term by the other than their vexed and variable coexistence. In the woodcut, world history is a fulfillment of prophecy; in the engraving, sovereignty assumes the aspect of divine omnipotence and omnipresence. The sacred and secular are not mutually exclusive but mutually constitutive. In the two images, their copresence is writ large: indeed their imaginative daring and conceptual power depend on it. We have chosen to round off this collection with them for the strong impression they leave of the difficulty if not impossibility of severing the sacred and profane. For were these images to be approached as one or the other, they would cease to be comprehensible or even affecting. We cannot say the same of Shakespeare's plays, for readings predicated on their divide have been legion over the generations. At the very least, however, after the intervention of *Sacred and Secular Transactions in the Age of Shakespeare*, the division will appear less clear-cut.

Notes

1. *Anatomia Statuæ Danielis: Kurtze und eigentliche erklerung der grossen Bildnis des Propheten Danielis* (Leipzig: Johann Steinman, 1586).

2. *Statua Danielis Prophetae*, folded woodcut illustration, 73 x 48.6 cm, in *Anatomia Statuæ Danielis*, 28.

3. Reinhart Koselleck, *Futures Past: On the Semantics of Historical Time*, trans. Keith Tribe (Cambridge, Mass.: MIT Press, 1979), 6–7.

4. That the foot of the *Reich in Orient* has stepped on a hissing asp with Turkish turban and caricatured features fulfills another condition of end-time: the quelling of the infidel Ottomans. For the latter, see Koselleck, *Futures Past*, 12.

5. According to Daniel Rosenberg and Anthony Grafton, the face of the colossus is a portrait of Augustus I, the Lutheran elector of Saxony, an electorate of the Holy Roman Empire; *Cartographies of Time: A History of the Timeline* (New York: Princeton Architectural Press, 2010), 56.

6. Saint Jerome, *Jerome's Commentary on Daniel*, trans. Gleason L. Archer Jr. (Eugene, Ore.: Wipf and Stock, 2009), 32.

7. Noel Malcolm, ed., *The Clarendon Edition of the Works of Thomas Hobbes, Volume 3: Leviathan; Editorial Introduction* (Oxford: Oxford University Press, 2012), 128.

8. Anthony Griffiths, *The Print in Stuart Britain, 1603–1689* (London: British Museum, 1998), 165.

9. Noel Malcolm, "The Title Page of Leviathan, Seen in a Curious Perspective," in *Aspects of Hobbes* (Oxford: Oxford University Press, 2002), 200–229

10. J. G. A. Pocock, "Time, History and Eschatology in the Thought of Thomas Hobbes," in *Politics, Language and Time: Essays on Political Thought and History* (Chicago: University of Chicago Press, 1989), 148–201.

11. William Shakespeare, *The Tragedy of Hamlet, Prince of Denmark*, in *The Norton Shakespeare*, ed. Stephen Greenblatt et al., 3rd ed. (New York: Norton, 2016), 1.1.59–62, 3.6.57.

CONTRIBUTORS

Sarah Beckwith is the Katherine Everett Gilbert Professor of English and Theater Studies at Duke University. She is a coeditor of the *Journal of Medieval and Early Modern Studies*, a founding editor of the ReFormations series at the University of Notre Dame Press, and the author of *Signifying God: Social Relation and Symbolic Act in the York Corpus Christi Play* and *Shakespeare and the Grammar of Forgiveness*. She is currently completing a work on Shakespeare's late tragedies and ethics.

Katherine Steele Brokaw is an associate professor and the chair of Literatures, Languages, and Cultures at the University of California, Merced. She is the author of *Staging Harmony: Music and Religious Change in Early English Drama* as well as several articles on Shakespeare and early modern drama and the editor of the forthcoming Arden Performance Edition of *Macbeth*. She is also the cofounder of Shakespeare in Yosemite.

Kent Cartwright is a professor of English at the University of Maryland, College Park. He is the author of books and essays on Shakespeare and on Tudor drama. Most recently, he has edited *The Comedy of Errors* for the Bloomsbury Arden Shakespeare Third Series. He is currently working on a monograph on Shakespeare's comedies.

Brian Cummings is Anniversary Professor at the University of York in the Department of English and Related Literature. His books include *Mortal Thoughts: Religion, Secularity, and Identity in Shakespeare and Early Modern Culture* and *The Book of Common Prayer: A Very Short Introduction*. He is a Fellow of the British Academy and a Fellow of the Society of Antiquaries.

Rachael Deagman teaches medieval and early modern literature at the University of Colorado Boulder. Her current book project investigates literature, architectural history, and religion in a study of community building in medieval and early modern drama. She has published an article on forgiveness in *Piers Plowman* in the *Journal of Medieval and Early Modern Studies*.

Margreta de Grazia is Emerita Sheli Z. and Burt X. Rosenberg Chair in the Humanities at the University of Pennsylvania. She is the author of *Shakespeare Verbatim* and *"Hamlet" without Hamlet* and coeditor of *Subject and Object in Renaissance Culture*, *The Cambridge Companion to Shakespeare*, and *The New Cambridge Companion to Shakespeare*. Her *Four Shakespearean Period Pieces* is forthcoming from University of Chicago Press.

Tobias Döring is a professor of English literature at the Ludwig-Maximilians-Universität München and past president of the German Shakespeare Society. He has published on both early modern and postcolonial literature and theory. Recent publications include *Thomas Mann and Shakespeare: Something Rich and Strange* (with Ewan Fernie), *Edward Said's Translocations: Essays in Secular Criticism* (edited with Mark Stein), and *Critical and Cultural Transformations: Shakespeare's "The Tempest"—1611 to the Present* (with Virginia Mason Vaughan).

Helga Duncan is an associate professor in the Department of English at Stonehill College, where she teaches courses on Shakespeare and early modern literature and culture. Her essays on Shakespeare have appeared in *Comparative Drama*, *Early Theatre*, and the *Journal of Medieval and Early Modern Studies*. She is currently completing a monograph that examines early modern perceptions of sacred space in Spenser, Marlowe, Shakespeare, and Behn.

Angela Heetderks earned her Ph.D. in English language and literature at the University of Michigan in 2014. Her research focuses on medieval and early modern English literature; disability studies; and intersections between music, religion, and literature.

Robert Hornback is a professor and chair of the English and Comparative Literature program at Oglethorpe University, Atlanta, where he teaches literature courses of the ancient world to the Renaissance. He has published widely on Renaissance fools, stage clowns, early blackface, religious satire and comedy, and the influences of classical literature. He is the author of *The English Clown Tradition from the Middle Ages to Shakespeare* and *Racism and Early Blackface Comic Traditions: From the Old World to the New*. He is presently at work on his third book, *Clowning in the Age of Print*.

Jeanne H. McCarthy is an associate professor of English at Georgia Gwinnett College. She has published extensively on the influence of the children's performance tradition, most recently in *The Children's Troupes and the Transformation of English Theater, 1509–1608: Pedagogue, Playwrights, Playbooks, and Play-Boys*.

Jennifer R. Rust is an associate professor in the Department of English at Saint Louis University. She is the cotranslator with David Pan of Carl Schmitt's *Hamlet or Hecuba* and author of *The Body in Mystery: The Political Theology of the* Corpus Mysticum *in the Literature of Reformation England*.

Emma Maggie Solberg is an assistant professor of medieval literature and culture at Bowdoin College. Her scholarly work is concerned with representations of the Virgin Mary in early English drama. She is the author of the monograph *Virgin Whore*.

William N. West is an associate professor of English, classics, and comparative literary studies at Northwestern University, where he also edits the scholarly journal *Renaissance Drama*. His books include *Theatres and Encyclopedias in Early*

Modern Europe and *As If: Essays in "As You Like It."* He is the author of recent articles on theater and speculation; Spenser and performance; Renaissance fantasies of Euclidean geometry and Victorian fantasies of the Renaissance; and Aby Warburg's attention to detail. His current work focuses on understanding and confusion in the Elizabethan playhouses.

Jay Zysk is an assistant professor of English at UMass Dartmouth. He specializes in English drama of the thirteenth through seventeenth centuries. He is the author of *Shadow and Substance: Eucharistic Controversy and English Drama across the Reformation Divide* as well as articles on early English drama and Shakespeare, Marlowe, and Middleton and several essays in edited collections.